# THE KOGAN PAGE GUIDE TO

# EFFECTIVE MANAGEMENT

## ROGER BENNETT

**KOGAN PAGE**

First published in 1994

Kogan Page Limited
120 Pentonville Road
London N1 9JN

© Roger Bennett, 1994

---

**British Library Cataloguing in Publication Data**

A CIP record for this book is available from the British Library.

ISBN 0 7494 1134 1

---

Typeset by Saxon Graphics Ltd, Derby
Printed in England by Clays Ltd, St Ives plc

WITHDRAWN

7

A

THE KOGAN PAGE GUIDE TO

# EFFECTIVE
# MANAGEMENT

# CONTENTS

# CONTENTS

# PREFACE

Managers today are confronted with a bewildering array of statutory obligations, codes of practice, government guidelines, and new administrative tasks, methods and techniques. As a manager you have to appraise colleagues, make presentations, implement health and safety regulations, deal with employee grievances, and apply equal opportunities rules (many of them legally binding) when hiring, firing or promoting workers.

My aim in writing this book is to bring together within a single cover the essential information that a busy manager needs in order to perform effectively when dealing with people, budgets and organisation systems. It is intended for use by anyone who is responsible for others and who must control and direct their activities. I hope the text will be especially valuable for recently appointed managers with little experience of the issues discussed. Far too often, newly appointed managers are 'thrown in at the deep end' and left to sink or swim with minimal help or advice concerning their statutory obligations, the management of interpersonal relationships, or other crucial aspects of their non-technical work.

The text has three parts: people management, organisation, and management communications. Nearly all managers must supervise colleagues' activities, so the development of interpersonal skills is relevant for all kinds of managerial work. Hence there is material on interviewing, appraisal, handling grievances, personal efficiency and assertiveness; on how to lead and motivate, and on how to take high-quality decisions. Individuals fresh to management need to refine their communication abilities (including the capacity to listen and counsel sensitively) and to develop the arts of advocacy, negotiation and written and oral presentation. Material on all these topics is included in the text.

My thanks are due to Rosalind Bailey who word processed the manuscript, and to Kogan Page Ltd for the efficient processing of the book.

Roger Bennett

# Part 1

# GETTING ORGANISED

# 1

# PERSONAL ORGANISATION

## INTRODUCTION

Effective managers are busy people and, in consequence, are commonly short of time. Efficient personal organisation, therefore, is essential in order to keep abreast of daily work while creating enough time to consider more general and strategic issues. Thus you need to:

- identify ways in which you can improve the management of your own time and the time of the people who work for you;

- draw up personal timetables and plan your working day;

- delegate work in a sensible manner;

- use electronic mail, electronic diaries, etc to maximum effect.

## MANAGING TIME

In management, time is a *resource* to be allocated in the best way, like any other scarce commodity. Each unit of a manager's time has several possible alternative uses. Time spent in a committee meeting, for example, could instead be devoted to a (possibly more productive) one-to-one counselling session with a colleague. The time used to write a letter may be better used discussing an important order with a customer, or perhaps in dealing with a workplace quality control problem. Choices are necessary: busy managers cannot do everything they would like, so *decisions* are required regarding the distribution of time among various duties.

## Selecting priorities

You should rank activities in order of importance, and consciously adjust the time devoted to each job — a few extra minutes spent reading a report might be worth two or three hours in a meeting. Choosing priorities may not be easy, so you need to organise your personal timetable systematically with a view to maximising the creative output of each working day.

Routine administration, tactical decision taking and day-to-day control involve duties that are scattered and prone to frequent interruption. Yet interruptions waste a great deal of time. Often interruptions arise from unwanted communications — letters, telephone calls, memoranda, etc — that disrupt more creative work. So select some part of your working day (between 2 and 3 in the afternoon, for instance, by which time all the day's mail will have arrived) for communication duties, and stick to this rigidly. If a piece of routine correspondence cannot be completed by the end of this allotted period, leave it until the following day when it will receive first priority. Where possible, handle each item of correspondence only once; much time is wasted through duplicated activity resulting from repeated consideration of the same item.

## Planning the day

Much time can be saved by grouping together similar tasks. Write all your letters and memoranda at the same time, and make your telephone calls one after another. Plan your calls — have all the necessary information, files, etc on your desk before picking up the telephone so that you will not have to ring again after looking up missing information. Jot down a list of all the points you want to make during the conversation, and write your notes on each call on separate pieces of paper. Most modern telephones have at least 10 memories for commonly dialled numbers, so record these in a clearly visible position.

If you deal with outside visitors, see them all during a prearranged period. Try to see people by appointment, and keep discussions within appointed times. Casual callers should be discouraged (within reason — you do not want to appear remote and inaccessible) or reserve a predetermined period for casual calls.

Each category of task has its own 'set-up time' just like a production line — although in managerial work the 'tooling up' operation might be as much concerned with switching into an appropriate frame of mind as with technical considerations.

# PERSONAL ORGANISATION

## *Structuring the workload*

Establish a schedule and follow it rigidly. Certain activities may be temporarily put off, others cannot be avoided and might demand use of resources that have to be withdrawn from other activities. Since further urgent problems may follow immediately after the resolution of the one to hand, there is a tendency for the busy manager to postpone indefinitely the proper consideration of less pressing matters. In consequence, a large backlog of petty administration accumulates and this, itself, ultimately becomes a major problem. You should avoid this situation arising by deliberately reserving a limited period each day exclusively for routine work. The best time for this is when you are tired, since then the relief of doing mundane duties helps you to relax following the completion of more demanding activities.

If you are normally fresh and energetic during the first part of the morning, do your difficult work then — if conversely you are a person who 'warms up' as the day goes by, then do mundane work in the mornings and reserve the demanding tasks for later. A common mistake is to use intellectually productive hours for work that is interesting but which does not require the exercise of discretion or other intense mental effort. Suppose, for example, that you are most creative between 9.00 and 11.00 am. You open your mail at 9.15 am and immediately become immersed in petty administration. Your brain 'locks in' to the minor issues raised by the correspondence and you spend all morning dealing with these matters. By the time you come to consider more substantial problems you are too tired to attend to them properly so they are put aside and never fully resolved! The answer, in this case, is to have a strict rule *never* to deal with correspondence before (say) 4.00 pm. I suggest also that you read reports at the end of the day. Then you can plan your response to them for the following day and not become immediately immersed in unplanned activities resulting from their recommendations.

## *Interruptions*

You must learn to deal with interruptions — to switch your attention from one thing to another and then back again — quickly and without loss of momentum to your work. Set aside some part of the day, even if only half an hour, when you will not allow yourself to be interrupted for any reason whatsoever, and use this period for intellectually demanding tasks. The balance of your working day should be under *your* control, and you should adjust the balance whenever the time spent on a particular activity becomes excessive.

## Routine duties

Take care not to attend inessential meetings, and leave a meeting early if the remaining items on the agenda do not concern you. Meetings can be enjoyable, and by attending you remain in touch with your colleagues, but they often waste time. The same applies to routine work which, although agreeable, could be done by a secretary. You should not personally undertake too much simple work; equally, you ought not to assume total responsibility for all difficult tasks — specialists can be consulted, committees established, or outsiders engaged. Not only is difficult work potentially stressful, but it also takes longer to complete if a single person tries to do things that should be handled by a team.

Much routine work is undertaken unnecessarily because its purpose has never been clearly defined. Look carefully at your job description to determine what your duties actually should involve (although note how the isolation of particular responsibilities becomes difficult in integrated, computerised management control systems). A useful timesaver is to insist that all problems referred to you by members of the department should be accompanied by a recommended solution, and that every report submitted should begin with a summary.

## Monitoring progress

Overexertion, resulting perhaps in stress and other illnesses, can be caused by attempting to achieve creative goals while simultaneously trying to keep on top of current communication and other routine duties. You need therefore to allocate your time systematically by setting goals, assigning priorities, and identifying and eliminating time-wasting activities. Often future workloads can be forecast — at least in outline. Prepare a schedule of anticipated activities built around the most critical future tasks, and keep a diary to record how closely you adhere to the programme. Predict and list all jobs needing attention, attach priorities and estimate the time required for each activity. The actual time you spend on various tasks should then be monitored, recorded and subsequently compared against the forecast schedule.

## ORGANISATIONAL TECHNIQUES

Many technical devices are available today to help you to save time. The diary is the basic tool of time management, representing at once a means for planning activities and a record of the time available for various tasks. Electronic diaries and other information technology based innovations greatly improve the manager's capacity to schedule activities efficiently. An electronic diary — operated via a desktop computer (or a word processor with a computing facility) — records in its permanent memory all your appointments for as long ahead as you wish (several years if you so desire). You enter as much detail as you can about each appointment, so that recall of appointments on to a visual display screen can be presented under any one of several headings: name of appointee, date, time of day, nature of appointment, etc. This enables you to analyse the *structure* of your activities, since you can ask the diary to list all your appointments relating to a particular type of work, category of person seen at each appointment, etc, and thus identify the areas that absorb most of your time.

### Network diaries

Electronic diaries may be 'networked' within a firm, between various subsidiaries of the same organisation, or (increasingly) between different independent organisations. Networking means the linking together of computers and their peripherals (especially printers) so that information can be transmitted instantly from screen to screen, from printer to printer, or from one person's screen to someone else's printer. 'Local' networks are confined to a single organisation. 'Global' networks — operated through telecommunication systems — may span the entire world. Long-distance links are usually made via satellite; lesser distances through normal telephone lines using a modem that converts (modulates) computer output into an audible signal for transmission down a telephone line to another modem which translates the signal for input into the receiving computer.

Networked electronic diaries thus enable the appointments of several people to be synchronised. Suppose you are the head of an accounts department and want to arrange a meeting with three colleagues in the production, personnel and marketing departments of the same firm. You type an instruction to this effect into your own electronic diary, which then activates the networked system into searching the electronic diaries of your three colleagues to establish a mutually convenient time for the meeting. Your colleagues are notified of your request for their presence at the meeting on the screens of their own VDUs when they next 'log in' to receive their electronic mail (see below).

Needless to say, networked electronic diary systems create their own problems, such as:

- managers making appointments over the telephone or in other conversations and forgetting to register them in their diaries;

- failure to log in to the system first thing every morning to determine the day's appointments;

- not giving sufficient notice of days off or short holidays, and failing to report absences due to sickness.

If someone within the system puts you down for a meeting that you do not want to attend you must cancel the entry in your own diary, whereupon the cancellation is automatically transmitted to the diary of the initiator. Should you wish to attend but not on the day and time specified, you simply type in a message to this effect and the system searches not only your own diary but also those of other intended participants in order to find a new, mutually convenient, alternative date and time.

## Electronic mail

Great improvements in personal organisation and efficiency are possible through the use of electronic communications with other people and organisations via desktop computers. To go 'on line' you type an appropriate command on your terminal keyboard and your modem then automatically dials the number you want and connects you to the recipient's system. Thereafter, anything you type into your machine is sent down the telephone line to the other computer. In a commercial electronic mail (Email for short) system each user has a personal 'mailbox', which is a separate file on a computer disk 'dedicated' to that individual — a password and code number are required for access to the file. Incoming messages are temporarily held in the mailbox until the recipient has accessed and read them, so that recipients need not be present when messages are transmitted. A complete set of messages may be sent at times previously specified by the sender (say at 12.00 and 3.00 pm each day), and the same message can be sent simultaneously to several hundred users. When accessing your mailbox you choose either to 'scan' stored documents, in which case a list of the document headings appears on your VDU, or you read each item in full. Then you may delete messages, hold them for later action, copy them on to another disk, or forward them (perhaps with added comments) to other users. The sender automatically receives an acknowledgement of safe receipt of the message.

### Advantages of electronic communication

Email is an excellent time saver and extremely cost effective. It removes the need to print hard-copy messages before transmission, and cuts the cost of postage, envelopes, etc. Various companies provide Email services. Firms rent an account with the 'host' company and are allocated a block of account numbers which are then assigned to named employees. Most systems operate at normal telephone charge rates, and it takes only a few minutes to send even long messages. Communication is instant (unlike the post or internal memoranda) and, in contrast to the telephone, the other person need not be there at the time of transmission. The main problem is that you can only communicate with other people on the same commercial system.

Larger Email systems (such as those offered by British Telecom) provide access to a number of public databases, including for example the entire UK railway timetable, UK statutes and information about towns and cities.

### Voice messagers

A voice messager is a form of answering machine that not only enables callers to leave messages, but also allows callers to record and transmit an identical message simultaneously to anyone possessing a 'mailbox' within the system. A single call can be transmitted to several different people at the same time and recipients do not need to be in when the message is sent. This avoids having to ring (or write to) several people with the same information. And of course, by recording your message for later transmission you escape being drawn into irrelevant conversations (however enjoyable) with the people you contact.

Radiopaging is an alternative to a cordless phone. You carry a 'pager' (receiver) in your pocket which bleeps when your telephone extension is called or when you are needed elsewhere. Then you go to the nearest telephone to contact the originator of the message. Modern pagers emit different alert tones according to the urgency of the message, and they may enable the paging system operator to communicate directly with the carrier. Sophisticated pagers can store incoming messages in a memory for recall whenever the carrier wishes (for example, you would not want your pager to bleep during an important meeting, so you would store notifications of receipt of messages until afterwards).

# KEEPING RECORDS

Records are necessary for three purposes: to store data for future reference, as a basis for rational decision taking, and to maintain documentary evidence of communications. Keep your records simple, easy to maintain, and strictly relevant to your requirements. Prepare an inventory of all your information needs and list all the data you have to transmit to others. The inventory will probably include details of cost, output and other performance indicators; staff records (appraisal reports, job descriptions, references, training programmes, etc); health and safety records (including the dates of inspections of fire and other equipment); minutes of important meetings, plus copies of essential letters and memoranda. Records are used for planning, and to enable you to justify past decisions.

## Forms

Often records consist of forms or are compiled from data extracted from forms. If you have to design forms, make them simple, comprehensive, and quick and easy to complete. The fewer the number of forms used in the department the better, so try to integrate forms — or redraft them so they can be used for several purposes. Avoid the temptation to design special forms to gather information that is only infrequently needed — once a form is incorporated into the information-gathering system it might stay there regardless of how often it is used.

In some circumstances all the forms within a department (indeed within an entire organisation) can be standardised, with common layouts and uniform dimensions to facilitate handling and storage. Instructions on how forms are to be filled in should be clear and precise. Forms should be big enough to contain all the information they are intended to gather, and strong enough to withstand frequent transit and long retention periods. The data written down on a form should be easily read and extracted.

## Form structure

A form's structure should depend on the purpose for which it is intended. One regular complaint about form layout from those who have to use them is that insufficient space is provided for answers. Other complaints concern ambiguity about the data required, inadequate margins, and insufficient delineation between sections.

The best way to design a new form is to ask yourself a series of questions. Why is the form necessary in the first place, what objective does it seek to achieve, and what would happen if the form was not produced? Who is to fill in the form (the answer to this question will determine its complexity and style of presentation) and under what conditions will the form be completed? A lengthy questionnaire for completion at home needs to have a different format to one that will be filled in hurriedly on the factory floor.

Periodically, all the forms currently in use should be assembled in order to eliminate any which have ceased to serve their original purpose. Some forms can be abolished entirely, others combined. The data being gathered might no longer be needed, or may be available elsewhere. The fewer forms there are the less has to be spent on paper, printing and filing cabinets. Too often, forms are distributed far too widely. Copies are sent to people and departments that have no interest in their contents. Apart from wasting time and paper, excessive distribution can mean that forms are out of stock during periods of heavy demand.

## Disposal of records

Record keeping is boring, and is thus frequently overlooked or delegated to subordinates. Yet good records are essential for effective executive management. Have a clear-out once every six months; out-of-date records are not worth maintaining. Note, however, that any document relating to a contract should be kept for at least six years (after which it ceases to be legally actionable), and anything to do with job evaluation or equal opportunities (job applications, for example) for at least one year, after which time it is reasonable to suppose that no complaint will be registered (if it is it will not be considered by an Industrial Tribunal).

## WORKING WITH A SECRETARY

Perhaps the most effective way for a manager to manage time efficiently is to have a sound and well planned working relationship with a secretary. Depending on the nature of your work and the organisation of secretarial duties within the firm, you might either have your own secretary working entirely within the company, or you might share a secretary with other managers in other departments. Whichever is the case, your secretary is your communication link with the rest of the firm and the outside business world — and your working habits have to alter once you acquire a secretary. Two problems commonly arise: inappropriate structuring of secretaries' workloads; and unwillingness to recognise the value of secretaries' contributions to the boss/secretary team. Some managers with personal secretaries see them as appendages to themselves rather than as important employees in their own right.

### Need for two-way communication

Your secretary takes over much of your correspondence and effectively represents you to the outside world. In doing so, the secretary creates your 'public image' — an image which might be difficult to live up to and which possibly contradicts your own view of yourself. It is thus essential that you and your secretary communicate well with each other and have a common understanding of how you will present your joint efforts to outsiders.

Together you must agree, perhaps tacitly, on the degree of formality of your relationship, and on who will ultimately determine the style and layout of letters, reports and memoranda, bearing in mind that secretaries are invariably better qualified in these respects. Most importantly, you must agree about the way records are to be kept and the diary controlled within the office, and about the aspects of work where the secretary is to be free to make independent decisions. Who, for example, will choose filing systems and other clerical procedures, determine the locations of desks, chairs and cabinets, and so on?

### Working as a team

Secretaries should perform those tasks they can do best, which today could involve acting as an information technology specialist — perhaps possessing a higher level of IT knowledge than the boss! Some managers resent this situation. It may not be easy to accept that the person who types letters, does the filing, etc, is also capable of operating sophisticated business software which many managers cannot understand — but without which they cannot work effectively. And bosses themselves now need to possess rudimentary keyboard and software skills; otherwise they are not able to function (e.g. by accessing computer-stored data) when their secretaries are away.

More than ever before, boss and secretary need to work together as a team, which requires both to be able to make and take criticism without causing or perceiving offence. You must take your secretary into your confidence and provide all the information necessary to do the job effectively. It is easy to criticise a secretary's actions while conveniently forgetting that you have not kept your secretary up to date with all the information available on the various projects with which you are involved. If you believe that a secretarial task should be completed in a certain way, then say so before it is finished. Standards should be established from the outset — on both sides. If, for example, you are pedantic about the style of layout and typing accuracy of letters leaving the office, it is unfair for you to imply that anything less than a high (predetermined) standard is acceptable, only to complain that work has not been completed according to specified standards when it is finished and presented for signature.

*Use common sense*

With the advent of word processing there is a tendency for bosses to redraft work several times, on the assumption that little effort is involved in retyping. This is a false assumption: files have to be found, programs loaded and points in the text requiring amendment located. Further time is then absorbed in finishing the edit and printing the revised version. Yet in fact, the boss's feeling in retrospect that a different wording might have improved the style of a document may have been little more than a passing fancy.

Always think twice before asking for work to be repeated. Poor typing is a reasonable complaint, as is transcription that significantly alters the meaning of the text — but insistence that transcription must be word for word as dictated is unreasonable and unnecessary. It implies that the secretary does not have the ability to transcribe notes properly and/or is not competent to decide when a slight change in wording will improve the style of a document.

People interpret tasks differently, and as long as the end product is completed to a satisfactory standard within a reasonable time it is irrelevant — and extremely annoying — for either boss or secretary constantly to give opinions on the other's working methods. This does not mean that a secretary (or a boss) should never be criticised or that working methods should not be discussed, only that such conversations should be planned and conducted dispassionately. The best time to do this is normally during periods set aside for dictation or for organising future work.

## Selecting a secretary

Too often, firms appoint overqualified secretaries to jobs that require only elementary office skills. Bosses frequently imagine there is a special prestige attached to employing a highly qualified person as a secretary — perhaps insisting that the secretary be a graduate and/or have high shorthand/typing speeds or speak several languages. Managers are attracted by high qualifications in candidates for secretarial posts, but fail to realise how bored a secretary possessing these qualifications will feel when asked to perform unskilled clerical tasks.

If highly qualified people are used as receptionist/coffee makers with little prospect of applying their knowledge, they will quickly look for better jobs. Secretaries should not be appointed, therefore, until the nature of the work they will be expected to complete has been thoroughly examined, and you should be realistic when recruiting secretarial staff. Ask yourself how you would react in a similar situation. Most bosses would not willingly remain long in positions bearing little relation to their job descriptions or which offered negligible opportunities for interesting work. When recruiting a secretary, seriously consider the precise role you want the secretary to play, and the skill levels and knowledge actually needed to perform that role effectively. The aim should be to utilise the strengths of the secretary as well as the strengths of the boss, and to establish rapport and good communications between the two.

## Organising the secretary's workload

You and your secretary must 'negotiate' the secretary's workload. Managers commonly fail to realise that in allocating work to a secretary they are, in effect, structuring their secretary's working life. Bosses typically have many work contacts and work interests beyond the boss/ secretary relationship, yet very often secretaries are entirely dependent on their bosses for work. A boss who, for example, gives a secretary large amounts of copy typing may not appreciate the consequences of hour after hour spent in front of a word processor or the tedium that long uninterrupted periods spent on humdrum work can create.

Serious problems occur when bosses become so reliant on good secretaries that they are reluctant to recommend them for promotion. By doing the job well the secretary becomes indispensable and so can only advance by leaving the organisation! This prospect can frustrate and distress the secretary to such an extent that current performance suffers. It is obviously reasonable that well qualified secretaries should have career aspirations, and view each job as a means of enhancing their experience. Thus you should never interfere with your secretary's promotion prospects — doing so will simply encourage the secretary to resign.

## Working for several bosses

An important consequence of the introduction of information technology is that today many secretaries work for several bosses. There are obvious advantages to this situation: secretaries are given a greater variety of work, are fully employed, accumulate wider experience and are more likely to use advanced secretarial and other qualifications. The system also overcomes the not uncommon problem of secretaries sometimes being hired for their looks and the prestige they bring to a boss rather than for their actual contribution — incompetent secretaries cannot survive long when they have to work for many bosses.

Against the system is the difficulty of coordinating the secretary's work, and the conflicts of loyalty to various bosses that the situation creates. A one-to-one relationship enables a sort of unwritten boss/secretary contract to exist, so that (for example) you might tolerate the secretary's occasional absence or frequent lateness — in return for the secretary's willingness to work overtime whenever required. Secretary and boss might take turns to make the tea (bosses should remember that secretaries' time can be just as valuable as theirs at crucial moments); and clear and precise criteria for defining the decisions the boss should take from those which can be taken by the secretary can be mutually agreed — it is unfair to expect a secretary to take important decisions that should be taken by the boss, even if the boss happens to be out when crucial decisions are necessary.

Secretaries should always be present when the division of their work is debated. And it is essential that when there are several bosses the various bosses delegate to the one secretary some interesting as well as routine work. Patterns of authority and accountability within the team must be defined exactly — secretaries sometimes resent being directly supervised by even a single boss, and find the experience of being given work by several bosses intolerable, especially when they can exercise no discretion about how much of each manager's workload to assume. Rules are needed to ensure that conflicting instructions are not issued, and the bosses must jointly realise that secretaries are entitled to job satisfaction. Tasks need to be varied, and secretarial jobs 'enriched' (by increasing the importance of decisions taken) and enlarged (through extending the range of the secretary's activities).

# DELEGATION

Delegation — the assignment of duties to other people, accompanied by the devolution of authority necessary to implement decisions — is essential for efficient administration, because managers do not have the time or specialist knowledge to take all important decisions. Care is necessary in the choice of duties for delegation, and managers must ensure that employees selected to receive delegated work are competent to complete it successfully. The recipients of delegated authority must be given all necessary resources, information and executive authority. Systematic delegation is crucial for management development programmes. Work of increasing difficulty can be delegated, gradually improving an employee's capacity to act independently.

*Why delegate?*

Delegation within a department means that a greatly increased volume of work can be completed. It enables tasks to be allocated to those best able to undertake them and helps managers to save time. Further benefits are that:

- it can be used to create yardsticks against which individual performance can be assessed;

- it facilitates the planning and scheduling of work;

- performance-related pay can be implemented more easily;

- employees become more involved with and committed to their work;

- individuals are presented with the opportunity to rise to challenging duties and have their contributions recognised.

Apportionment of tasks among department members is something that many inexperienced managers find extremely difficult. Either they will not delegate, with the consequence that they become overloaded with work, or they delegate too much or to inappropriate people. And there is perhaps a natural tendency for successful managers to avoid delegating work to colleagues. A manager is successful precisely because he or she is good at completing difficult duties, exercises initiative and becomes personally involved in all aspects of important tasks. Effective transition from doing work yourself to getting a larger volume of work completed through other people requires, nevertheless, that you learn how to delegate. Note moreover how:

- your own bosses will assess your competence as a manager in large part against your ability to delegate;

- once you have learned the skills of effective delegation you will carry them with you throughout your working life.

Excuses for *not* delegating abound: lack of confidence in colleagues' abilities, overestimation of your personal value, or a feeling that you should be seen personally undertaking certain duties. Recognise that you are not necessarily the best person to perform every task associated with your job. If you have no confidence in your colleagues' abilities to complete delegated work satisfactorily, ask yourself why they are working in the department in the first place. Such a situation represents failures in the firm's recruitment, training and staff development systems; shortcomings that need to be remedied by the speedy implementation of training programmes and/or the redeployment of employees. Recognise also that higher-level management is all about doing things through others, and that combined effort is necessary to attain wider organisational goals. Therefore you should take as much pride in seeing a colleague complete a difficult task successfully as if you had done it yourself.

A not uncommon, although entirely inappropriate, reason for not delegating is that a manager may fear that colleagues will acquire skills that enable them to threaten the manager's job. Indeed, some managers even go so far as to delegate duties knowing that the tasks involved are impossible — simply to discredit the people receiving the work. This policy will backfire in the long run, as it is sure to lead to stress and overwork for the manager concerned and the eventual collapse of the system.

## Consequences of not delegating

Failure to delegate is a prime reason for being constantly short of time (as well as demotivating subordinates through not involving them in higher-level duties) and you will, eventually, lose effective control of the situation simply through being inundated with work. You will become bogged down in detail, your staff will not initiate activity in your absence and will be unable to cope with crises when you are not there. Routine work will take a long time to complete, while major tasks will not be given proper attention. Further problems resulting from failure to delegate include:

- poor communication between managers and the people who work for them;
- staff with insufficient training and experience to take on higher-level duties;
- boredom among staff who are not given challenging assignments;
- managers not knowing what is actually going on within their departments;
- haphazard work flows with deadlines frequently being missed;
- uneven workloads within the department, with some employees having much more to do than others;
- employees being unsure of what to do and the standards expected of them.

## What to delegate

Delegate whenever your personal workload becomes excessive; when confronted by technical problems of a highly specialist nature; or whenever you believe that colleagues will be better motivated, feel a greater sense of participation, or will learn something useful from performing the delegated tasks. Be prepared to give up to colleagues some of the work you find particularly enjoyable — your staff will appreciate this and the loyalty it creates will more than pay you back in the longer term. Ask yourself the following questions when considering whether to delegate particular duties:

- Can the task be delegated?
- Should it be delegated?

- Is there a person in the department capable of handling it?

- If not, should someone be trained?

- Will a particular person benefit from doing this work? How will the experience fit in with his or her career development?

## How to delegate

For delegation to work, discernible chains of command are needed, so that everyone knows to whom they are responsible, the work they are expected to do, and the standards that are required. To delegate effectively you need:

- a comprehensive knowledge of the nature of the department's work and of the requirements of particular jobs within it;

- a sound working relationship with colleagues;

- good interpersonal skills;

- knowledge of the skills and experience of each person in the department, in order to know to whom you should delegate;

- awareness of the levels of motivation of various department members.

It is especially important to establish priorities, to sort out the critically important from the less important tasks, and hence to delegate in a systematic manner.

Review briefly the particular strengths and weaknesses of each of your colleagues. List the skills and experience needed to perform each of the tasks you intend delegating, and relate these to the attributes of various members of your team. Note that it is not always appropriate to delegate a task to the best qualified person, since you may wish to introduce a less experienced employee to new and different types of work. Further rules for delegating are that:

- each employee should know precisely what is expected of them;

- targets involved in delegated work should be thoroughly discussed with the people to whom tasks are delegated;

- all data relating to delegated work must be provided;

- delegated work should be coordinated, but without giving employees too detailed a set of instructions concerning how they should accomplish goals. The expected results should be described together with required performance standards. Everyone with an interest in the outcomes of the work must be informed of who is responsible for its completion.

## Routine duties

Apart from saving your time, delegation can help you to avoid stress — provided of course you do not need to worry about your colleagues' abilities to cope with the delegated work — and this itself will increase your efficiency. Work that has a high communication content (letter writing, first drafts of reports, telephone calls, routine meetings, etc) might be your prime target for delegation, since you then avoid many of the frequent interruptions (ringing telephones, memoranda to be answered, dealing with suppliers and/or customers, and so on) associated with routine communications. Bear in mind, however, that if you delegate too much repetitive administrative work to one person you could make his or her job intolerable. Try to plan your delegation as an integral part of a training and staff development scheme, not simply as a way of ridding yourself of distasteful duties.

Work that is particularly suitable for delegation includes fact-finding assignments, preparation of rough drafts for reports, tasks for which certain colleagues have a particular aptitude, investigation of the feasibility of possible solutions to problems, or straightforward analysis of routine information. Make crystal clear the objectives of the people who work for you, and progressively increase the level of difficulty of the work delegated to them. Insist that people present you only with brief, condensed accounts of their normal day-to-day activities, but tell them always to come and see you whenever they find a recently delegated task too difficult to handle alone.

It is important to realise that some routine work is useful, in small measures, for relieving the stresses imposed by creative exertion. Heavy concentration that cannot be sustained for long periods is needed for important management work. Easier tasks, undertaken intermittently, can break up your day — your workload becomes more varied and your personal efficiency may increase. What point is there in delegating all your mundane duties if in consequence you spend long periods of complete inactivity when the inspiration for creativity has gone?

## The problems involved

Several difficulties can arise when delegating work, including the following:

(a) Employees may come to perceive you as aloof and inaccessible — a figurehead who 'passes the buck' but who then declines to assume responsibility for the failure of projects which, from the outset, had no hope of succeeding.

(b) Work could be delegated that is outside the normal and proper chain of command. An example is when a senior manager delegates to a supervisor responsibility for dismissing casual or part-time labour, even though the senior manager (although he or she may not know this) has no legal authority to dismiss.

(c) Colleagues may feel you are disinterested in the work you delegate and, by implication, in them.

(d) If employees do all the work but are not involved in taking final decisions based on their efforts their morale might fall, especially if they believe the final decisions are wrong.

(e) Frequent staff changes cause confusion over who is responsible for delegated work. A manager who leaves the firm may have delegated a task to a particular person who might not inform the manager's incoming replacement that this is so. The work may then remain unfinished or not be satisfactorily completed. Always keep a record of the tasks you delegate.

Employees should never be made to feel that work is delegated to them only when you are confronted with difficult problems that you are not personally competent to handle, so always tell people why you want them to perform the delegated tasks.

## Back your colleagues' decisions

Delegation is an excellent means for developing the talents of the people who work for you, especially in areas which require the exercise of discretion. However, colleagues will inevitably make mistakes as increasing amounts of authority and responsibility are delegated — many skills are learnt largely through experience, and errors of judgement will certainly occur. These mistakes should be regarded as normal consequences of the delegation process. Always be ready to back up the decisions of the people who work for you, even if you do not whole-heartedly agree with their actions.

Do not monitor your colleagues continuously as they complete delegated work. Constant checking stifles initiative and generates insecure feelings among junior staff. Delegation is difficult, moreover, where boss and employee do not share common perspectives about how problems should be dealt with. You ought not to specify in too much detail how you expect delegated work to be completed, since you need to develop your colleagues' independence and ability to assume personal responsibility for decisions. But take care to indicate the form of the problem-solving activity you consider most appropriate for achieving the objectives you set.

Problems resulting from delegation might be resolved through regular meetings for management by objectives, through the availability of grievance procedures (preferably, in this context, a company 'ombudsperson' to whom an employee may complain if he or she feels that too much or too difficult work is being delegated), or some other forum (a departmental committee perhaps) for discussing how and which work is to be delegated. Try as far as possible to break down the work you delegate into logically divided packages rather than random *ad hoc* tasks, each unit having a discernible purpose, objective and timetable for completion.

## PLANNING A CAREER

An important long-term aspect of personal organisation for younger managers is looking ahead and consciously planning their careers. If you are in the fortunate position of working in an organisation and/or occupation that offers the prospect of a career, then you need to do the following:

- analyse ruthlessly and comprehensively your personal strengths and weaknesses;

- identify the career alternatives open to you;

- determine the departments, divisions and specific positions within an organisation that offer the best means for gaining useful experience, and look for other organisations that might provide suitable career opportunities;

- establish career priorities and intermediate career goals;

- regularly monitor your achievements to date and carefully examine the reasons for shortcomings.

It is particularly important to observe closely the behaviour, attitudes and approaches of people who have already succeeded in your chosen line of work. Why did they succeed? What distinguishes them from other equally well qualified individuals? Have they risen to the top through nepotism, conformism, aggression, 'doing their own thing', creativity, or what? Important lessons can be learnt from such observations. Quite a lot of academic research has been undertaken into these matters and, while the results have been mixed, it does seem that on the whole the people with successful careers are those who think for themselves, are not afraid to make independent decisions, but who remain strictly within the culture and expectations of their employing organisations and do not move too far out of line.

# 2

# ORGANISING THE DEPARTMENT

## INTRODUCTION

To 'organise' a department is to arrange its workload in a precise and logical manner through breaking work down into manageable units which are then allocated to the sections and individuals best suited to undertake them. The departmental organisational structure needs to determine a division of labour for the completion of tasks; an authority and responsibility structure; who is to be in charge of specific functions; and systems for communication, coordination and control.

## THE MODERN APPROACH

Modern thinking on organisation systems is that there is no unique organisational structure that is always applicable to every situation. Rather, choices are necessary and organisations need to be designed to suit the requirements of specific sets of circumstances. It is always the case, however, that patterns of authority, responsibility and accountability have to be fashioned and employees made aware of their duties. Individuals should know whose instructions they should follow and in what circumstances. Unfortunately, the demarcation between departmental and personal responsibilities is sometimes confused, with employees receiving conflicting instructions from different bosses. To clarify matters most firms prepare a formal document that defines precisely the roles of various employees. Typically (although not always) the situation is illustrated in an 'organisation chart'.

## Organisation charts

Nearly every manager will see (perhaps draft) an organisation chart at some time in their careers; yet few pause to question whether organisation charts are genuinely useful and, if so, how they ought to be constructed. For the uninitiated, an example of a simple organisation chart is given in Figure 2.1.

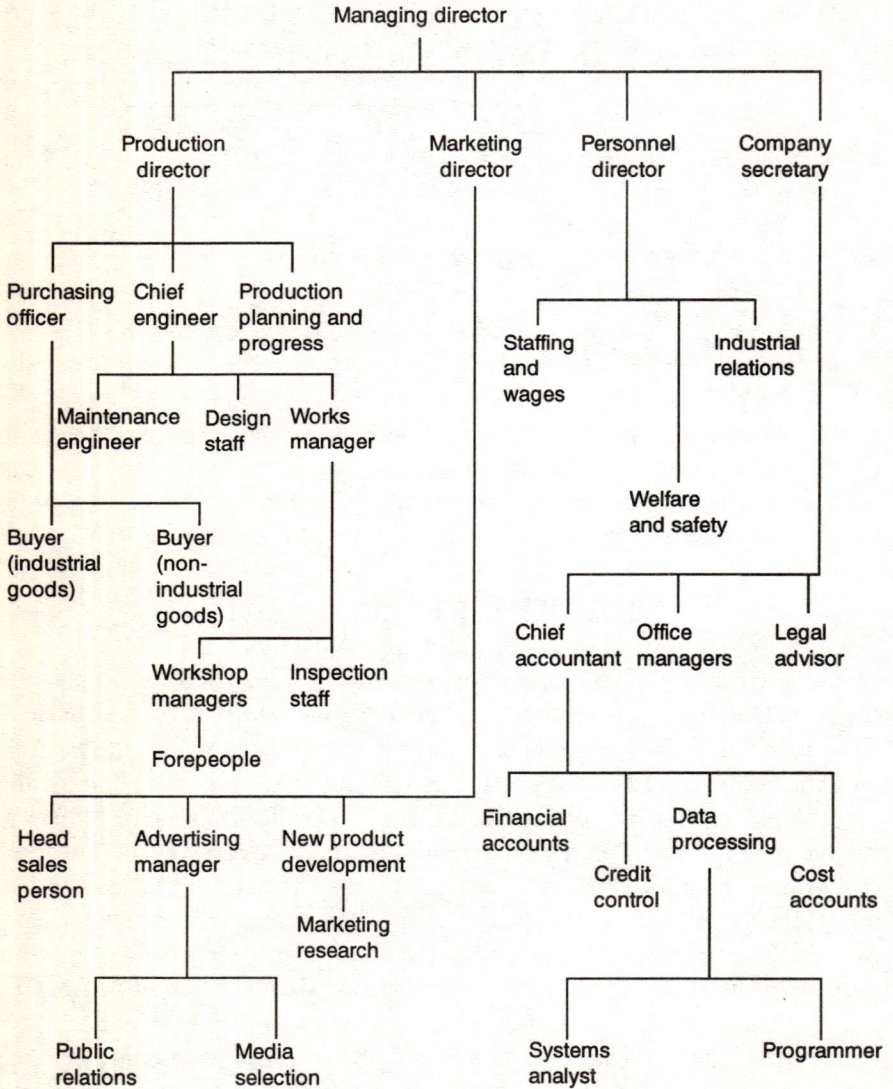

**Figure 2.1** *An organisation chart*

The aim of an organisation chart is to clarify individual responsibilities and to define the system of accountability within the organisation. Associated with each position in the diagram is a job specification stating the duties and responsibilities of that particular post. Horizontal as well as vertical linkages can be included to highlight areas of mutual concern and joint responsibility (although the resulting diagrams might be complicated and difficult to understand). A major benefit of preparing an organisation chart is that it forces management to specify the pattern of accountability within the firm. Also new employees — who will be given a copy of the organisation chart on appointment — will be in no doubt about their roles and responsibilities.

## Problems with organisation charts

One criticism of organisation charts is that they encourage inflexible approaches to spheres of responsibility, the scope of individual duties, interdepartmental relations, and so on — structural inconsistencies not shown in an organisation chart lie behind many organisational problems. Charts, moreover, illustrate nothing more than a desired organisational structure at a specific moment in time. They do not reveal emotional conflicts, personal favouritism, or differences in senior management's perceptions of the calibre of various employees. Only formal relationships are highlighted. On paper, a certain person might have just one boss, but in practice that individual might actually report to several different superiors depending on the particular aspect of the job. Business environments continually change, and organisations need to be able to respond quickly and effectively to new external situations.

Organisation charts can quickly become out of date, and if so, the effort spent on their preparation is wasted. Moreover, relationships within an organisation are typically far more complex than they appear in a diagram. Note also that actual behaviour is frequently influenced by informal channels of communication. Indeed, informal channels can be faster and more efficient than the official system (rigid adherence to bureaucratic formal procedures can inhibit initiative and effective decision taking).

## Line and staff

Despite these problems, there can be few businesses of any size that do not have an organisation chart. They can be prepared quickly and — in general terms at least — are easy to understand. Organisation charts are good for showing line and staff relationships within the firm. The line structure identifies points of contact between managers and the people for whom they are directly responsible. Each position in the system shows the individuals or functions controlled by its occupant and to whom that person is responsible. Vertical communication in this sort of system is supposed to proceed only through the line system; if a manager cannot handle a problem it is referred upwards to that person's immediate boss. Equally, work may only be delegated to the subordinates of a specific position.

The 'staff' organisation is advisory to the line system. It consists of specialists who give counsel to line executives but who do not themselves take important decisions. Line managers ask staff advisers for assistance, yet are not obliged to accept their advice. Lawyers, researchers, industrial relations specialists and technical experts are likely to occupy 'staff' positions. Sometimes staff and line organisations are mixed together, the result being that staff managers are empowered to implement their own decisions within certain predetermined areas. For example, a personnel officer may be authorised to select media to carry job advertisements, but not to choose applicants for certain positions.

Conventional 'line and staff' systems have a number of characteristics, as follows:

- There is an unambiguous chain of command and clearly defined areas of responsibility.

- Non-executive specialists are relegated to subsidiary roles.

- The system will typically rely on the contributions of a few key personnel. The resignation or sudden illness of an important line manager can cause an entire administrative system to collapse. Line managers avoid becoming immersed in detailed analysis of technical issues, but tend to concentrate power into a few pairs of hands. The small number of line managers available to take executive decisions finds itself the centre of authority, receiving advice from an army of specialist counsellors. This type of organisation can succeed, provided line executives possess sufficient ability and stamina to cope with the heavy demands made on them.

## Spans of control

Organisation charts can also be used to illustrate a manager's 'span of control', ie the number of people he or she controls. 'Wide' spans involve (say) 15 or 20 employees, narrow spans contain just two or three. Most authorities suggest that a span of any more than six or seven people represents too wide a span of control because of the resultant complicated relationships and competing demands on the controlling manager's time. Four factors are relevant to the choice of a span of control: organisational diversity, complexity of work, the calibre of the manager, and the qualities of the employees reporting to that person.

Organisational diversity affects the efficiency of internal communication. If face-to-face contacts between a manager and the people he or she controls are impossible, communication depends on telephone calls, letters, memoranda and similar indirect means. Interruptions in information flows and other communication breakdowns cause loss of effective control, especially if people and departments are geographically separate. Complex work means that managers need time to assess the reports and suggestions of subordinates, and they ought not to be overburdened with minor problems arising from lower levels. A narrow span of control is appropriate in this case.

Some managers are better able to handle large numbers of employees than others, depending on their training, experience and personal qualities. The degree of authority given to the manager is also relevant here. Similarly, well-trained, enthusiastic and competent workers need less control and supervision than others, so that wide spans of control may then be applied.

Narrow spans of control recognise that an individual's capacity to supervise others is limited, and that it is better to deal with a small number of people properly than to have contact with many employees but only in casual ways. However, wide spans also offer advantages — they force managers to delegate (so that colleagues acquire experience of higher-level work), employees may experience a higher degree of job satisfaction, and the cost of supervision is low. On the other hand, coordination of colleagues' activities may be poor. Communication between employees with the same boss could be inadequate and lead to much duplication of effort.

## Tall and flat organisations

Narrow spans of control create several levels of authority within an organisation. This has advantages and disadvantages. The benefits are as follows:

- managers may devote their full attention to the demands of the people for whom they are responsible;
- employees are presented with a career ladder and so can expect regular promotion through the system;

- there is less need to coordinate the activities of large numbers of employees than in a flat structure;

- it facilitates the specialisation of functions and the creation of logically determined work units.

Flat structures, on the other hand, lead to a larger number of employees acquiring experience of higher-level duties, can improve face-to-face communication, and give people more discretion over how they achieve their objectives. Managers and lower-ranking workers meet directly without having to communicate through intermediaries. Information will therefore not be lost or misinterpreted as it passes up and down the organisation.

# WHAT IS A DEPARTMENT?

A 'department' is a set of activities under a particular manager's control. Departments may be defined by product, market, function, or in personal terms.

## Organising by product

Product departmentation means creating departments, each of which deals with a single product or service. Department staff control all activities associated with the item, including purchase of raw materials, administration of processing, and the sale and distribution of the final product. Senior departmental managers acquire a wide range of general managerial skills. They become experts in the problems associated with their own product. This specialised knowledge might be essential if the firm produces technically complicated goods. One advantage of product departmentation is that coordination between relevant functions and stages of production is easily achieved. Performance appraisal is relatively straightforward in product department systems, since profit and cost centres are easily defined. Managers' performance can be measured against the costs, revenues and output levels of a product.

## Organising by market

Market departmentation occurs when departments are constructed around geographical regions or particular customer types (regional sales offices, or a separate department to deal with wholesale customers, for example). It may be cheaper to locate a department near to customers; local factors may then be taken into account when deciding policy. Similarly, market departmentation could relate to customer size (eg special facilities for large buyers), or to various distribution channels, export or home markets, etc. Problems of coordination may ensue, and some loss of central control will be experienced. As with product departmentation, this method necessarily involves the duplication of activities.

## Functional departments

To avoid overlapping responsibilities, many firms establish departments to cover specific functional areas — production, accounts, transport, administration, and so on. The major functional departments contain sections, so that an advertising department, for example, might be subdivided into sections for media selection, sales promotions, package design and other promotional activities. The responsibilities of functional departments follow logically and naturally from the work of the organisation, and will be parallel to occupational distinctions. Everyone concerned with selling will be in the marketing department, all who are involved in manufacture will be in production, and so on. Functional departmentation is easy to understand but may encourage narrow and introspective attitudes. Departments with wider responsibilities might provide staff with challenging environments that stimulate effort and initiative.

Another problem here is that functional specialists, production managers for instance, often develop patterns of thought and behaviour related more to their specialisms than to the wellbeing of the organisation as a whole. It is therefore essential that staff within a single functional department are regularly exposed to, and preferably involved with, the work of other departments.

## Organising around people

In small family businesses and partnerships it is common for departments to be created around specific people. As new functional needs arise they are allocated according to the interests of the family members. Eventually each department controls a variety of unrelated activities. A partner in a small firm might, for example, be interested in finance and advertising. Thus all things concerned with these functions will be dealt with in that partner's department. This may be manageable in a small business where there is good coordination, but gets out of hand as the firm acquires more and more employees and undertakes an increasing number of functions.

| Function | FINANCE | | | PERSONNEL | | |
|---|---|---|---|---|---|---|
| | Costing section | Data processing | Credit control ...etc | Recruitment section | Industrial relations | Wages and salaries ...etc |
| **MARKETING** | | | | | | |
| Sales | | | | | | ✓ |
| Distribution | | | ✓ | | | |
| Packaging | ✓ | ✓ | ✓ | | | |
| New product development | ✓ | | | | | |
| (plus other marketing functions advertising, research, etc) | | | | | | |
| **PRODUCTION** | | | | | | |
| Design | ✓ | ✓ | | | | |
| Labour deployment | ✓ | | | ✓ | ✓ | |
| Efficiency | ✓ | | | ✓ | ✓ | |
| Production control | ✓ | | | | | |
| Purchasing | | ✓ | | | | ✓ |
| Stock control | | ✓ | | | | |
| etc | | | | | | |
| **PERSONNEL** | | | | | | |
| etc | | | | | | |

**Figure 2.2** *A team based organisation structure*

40

# TEAM BASED ORGANISATION SYSTEMS

It is possible to organise a firm or large department around project teams which cut across sectional boundaries. The aim is to tie up specific functional requirements to the skills available within the firm, creating 'project teams' across departmental boundaries. The idea is illustrated in Figure 2.2 which shows how various sections of major departments contribute to particular functions — which may be defined as narrowly as the firm requires. We see that the credit control section has interests in the selling and distribution functions; that the personnel department representative responsible for industrial relations should have a say in determining policy for (among other things) work study (efficiency) exercises, and so on. Committees can now be assembled to oversee the administration of any area of the firm's business. Of course, a real-life system would be far more extensive and detailed than the above. It would name individual people within departments and identify their areas of activity. Subsystems can be created for departments and sections.

## When to use team based organisation

This type of organisation offers a practical and coherent device for analysing the make-up of an enterprise. Personal and departmental contributions to the organisation are systematically classified, and crucial activities that absorb large amounts of effort and resources are highlighted. The method is commonly used where several departments performing related duties are grouped together into divisions. In this way, interdepartmental communications are enhanced and duplication of effort avoided. Note that this kind of structure does not show authority systems, which makes it especially suitable for joint activities that involve colleagues of equal grade.

Each team will need a leader/facilitator responsible for publicising its aims; securing agreement on the tasks that must be completed and on policies and accountability; and obtaining resources from external sources. Project work involves much coordination and planning, leading therefore to many meetings and much committee work. The latter fact could, of course, lead to bureaucracy and slow decision making, and all the other problems (high operating costs, discussion of trivial issues, etc) that 'management by committee' involves.

## Problems with team based organisations

Managers who operate the system need to be flexible both in the duties they undertake and their involvement with other sections. Authority is shared, and confusion about who precisely is responsible for which function may ensue. Project leaders are entirely responsible for their projects, although heads of department remain and have authority over their own departments. In consequence, team members might receive conflicting instructions from heads of department and project team leaders; so it is important to establish at the outset who, ultimately, each individual should obey — and whether employees are to regard themselves first and foremost as members of a department or as members of a particular project team. Usually departments take precedence since projects last only for limited periods, and individuals will normally be assigned to a number of projects at the same time.

Further problems with the system are as follows:

(a) duplication of effort;

(b) possibly fewer discrete promotion opportunities than in conventional, more hierarchical systems;

(c) the need to appraise teams rather than individuals, so that unsatisfactory employees may be difficult to identify;

(d) unofficial links between members of various project teams may emerge which subvert teams' abilities to achieve their objectives;

(e) staff need to be trained in the methods of team management and the cost of such training could be substantial;

(f) team members may be unclear about the precise nature of their roles in the team and in the organisation.

Nevertheless, team based organisation offers exciting opportunities for the practical application of participatory approaches to management and the rapid development of decision-taking skills. Junior staff are given scope to contribute to managerial work; there is interdepartmental crossfertilisation of ideas and interdisciplinary transmission of managerial expertise. Also, separation and compartmentalisation of management functions is avoided: each element in the structure has to be dovetailed into the organisation as a whole and in so doing senior management is compelled to ensure that all the elements interlock.

## Managing a project team

Your role as leader of a project team is to coordinate rather than direct, so you should aim to facilitate the generation of new ideas and create a climate in which members' natural enthusiasm will develop. Team members are sometimes unclear about the precise nature of their roles, especially if they have no experience of project work. They look for hierarchies within groups, and might even create new and unnecessary status differentials where hierarchies do not already exist.

With project based systems, however, responsibility for decision taking is shared, and fast and efficient project completion — not occupational status — is the primary criterion for determining the allocation of work. Two problems can emerge: the development of charismatic leaders within teams who, although popular as individuals, are not as technically competent as other members; and the reluctance of some members to perform low-status tasks. Yet if all members are to contribute to important decision making and the development of new ideas, they should all contribute to the completion of both innovative development and routine work. Imagine the paradoxical situation of having a six-person team designing a new ignition system for a motor car, meeting two or three times a week, pooling ideas, reporting on individual assignments, brainstorming, etc — but then assigning all mundane and boring duties (filing, petty correspondence, minor secretarial work) to just two or three members. Suppose moreover that the members performing low-status tasks come up with the best innovative ideas. How then can the high-status members reconcile their avoidance of routine work (justified by superior occupational rank) while occupying secondary roles in important development matters? Resentments and interpersonal conflicts — fundamentally incompatible with the ethos and efficiency of a well run project team — will arise.

## CONTROL

Control involves setting targets (see Chapter 6), monitoring what actually happens within your organisation and comparing this with the targets set, and taking whatever action is necessary to remedy any shortfalls (or amending targets in appropriate ways). Effective control relies on the availability of accurate and comprehensive information about the organisation's work. So, the first step in devising a control mechanism is to establish what information needs to be collected for control purposes, by whom it should be gathered, and when. Note how much time and money might be spent on compiling control data. It is essential therefore for each item of information collected to have a clearly identifiable and valuable use, and that:

(a) current activities are reported accurately;

(b) any inadequacies in historical records are taken into account;

(c) faults in information-retrieval systems are sorted out.

## *Exception reporting versus continuous monitoring of operations*

You can choose between continuously gathering information from the people in your department, and adopting an 'arm's length' approach. The latter involves the people who work for you submitting only brief, condensed reports on normal operations, but extensive reports on deviations from past average performance or targets set by higher management. Once established, standards should be monitored through picking out significant deviations from predetermined norms. Exceptionally good or bad results are analysed in depth, but reasonable deviations from standard performance are not questioned. Therefore routine matters are dealt with at lower levels, leaving higher-level managers free to devote their time to unusual problems and policy issues.

This approach has been popular because of the enormous volume of information generated within firms, and the physical impossibility of continuously monitoring actual activities. So data can be collected continuously but analysed periodically (weekly, monthly, quarterly, annually). By specifying tolerable deviations from target performance and intervening only if the limits of tolerable deviation are exceeded, managers can avoid becoming immersed in trivial issues and instead reserve time and effort for more demanding problems.

## *Problems with exception reporting*

There are, however, several difficulties associated with this approach. First, there are time lags between the moment a problem arises, the moment it is noticed, and the time remedial action is implemented. Manufacturing cost data, for example, may be collated and analysed once a month; if a particular production line develops a fault and begins to generate unacceptably high expenses at the start of the month, the situation will not be recognised until the month's end. Then there is a further delay before a report goes to higher management, followed by another lag until corrective action is taken, and during these delays high extra costs are being incurred. The second major problem is that since 'acceptable' deviations from target performance are tolerated without investigation, it is possible for a particular activity to be perpetually above or below standard by a relatively small amount without the fact ever being reported. Hence minor defects continue and overall performance is constantly lower than could be the case.

Equally, the cause of consistently superior performance just below the upper reporting boundary will not be examined; there is no mechanism for isolating the factors contributing to high achievement and applying these factors elsewhere.

## New possibilities

Continuous monitoring of a large business's activities is today much easier than it was in the past because of the availability of increasingly powerful desktop computer systems. Information on costs, outputs, revenues and other relevant variables can be immediately analysed at the moment of collection, and existing summaries can be updated at once. Trends in costs and outputs can be picked up, hour by hour, as they occur. Managers in control of a computerised system can requisition information at will and order its presentation in any one of a variety of alternative forms. Problems are highlighted instantly — they will be observed on the appropriate manager's visual display unit (VDU) whenever he or she types into the system a command to update information on current activities. Production lines which begin to produce defects, labour and material costs which start to get out of hand, increasing overheads, falling sales, etc can be identified as they happen so that remedial action can be applied at once.

## Non-computerised systems

In a non-computerised system, monitoring may be undertaken in several ways. You must accept that the time and cost of collecting useful information require you to be highly selective in the data you collate. First, decide which targets you most want to monitor, and assess the cost of control (collecting figures, meetings, discussions with colleagues, etc). Ask yourself what would happen if you did not bother monitoring specific activities. What questions will the information collected answer, and are those questions really worthwhile? Then you must decide how to gather the information — whether to do it yourself or delegate the task to someone else. In the latter case you must issue clear and precise instructions about how, when and where the data is to be collected, and you need to ensure that the person to whom you entrust the responsibility is reliable and competent at these tasks.

# HOW TO ORGANISE YOUR DEPARTMENT

The people who work for you need to know exactly what is expected of them, and how their activities fit into the work of the firm. List your department's objectives, and describe briefly the activities necessary to achieve them. Make a note of all the constraints that might prevent the successful completion of these activities, and how they might be overcome. Ask yourself how much sectional specialisation is possible, and whether specialisation will improve or worsen employees' morale. If specialisation is appropriate, examine how you can best integrate the efforts of various colleagues towards the achievement of common departmental goals. How will you ensure that the right job is done at the right time and in the right way? Is extra training needed to enable staff to work effectively within your intended organisational framework?

## Allocating work

In structuring the tasks that employees perform you are in fact structuring the content of their working days, so ensure that certain people are not left with insufferably repetitious and boring workloads. Divide work evenly and fairly, ensuring that everyone has at least some non-routine and challenging duties to perform. Next, draft outline job specifications for each position and include in each description a statement of the aims of the job. Check that jobs do not overlap and are congruent with departmental aims. Now draft an organisation chart, and assess whether each position within the structure possesses sufficient authority and resources for effective operation. Look for possible co-ordination problems, conflicts of interest and potential clashes of personality among employees. Determine spans of control, who will be responsible to whom, and tell the people involved about the proposed structure, inviting their comments.

Once established, the structure will determine the departmental 'chain of command'. It is unwise for a senior person to bypass a level of authority when issuing instructions, since the staff they are instructing might then receive conflicting orders from their immediate bosses, who themselves may bitterly resent their authority being (as they see it) undermined.

Aim always to clarify personal roles, objectives and relations with other positions. And be realistic about your expectations of the volume of work that each person can reasonably be expected to perform.

The next thing to consider is how easily colleagues can communicate laterally in order to solve problems without having to refer them to a higher level. Specify the types of problem you expect people to sort out themselves and those you expect to be passed upwards, and tell each person who to consult for advice on various issues.

## Managing the work flow

Analyse the intended work flow, determining the stages through which each work unit must pass and the levels of authority at which decisions relating to it must be taken. Identify points of contact with other departments for various jobs. Each work unit begins as someone's input and ends as an output from that person, so make sure that outputs and inputs coincide as work changes hands. Examine the implications of the proposed work flow for the layout of the department, and analyse its role in the work of the firm as a whole. Does it, for example, supply work to a single recipient, or to several? Is the department capable of completing all its formal duties using its own resources, or is external assistance required? If the latter, then how are external relations to be regulated?

## Parallel organisation: friend or enemy?

Large organisations consist of a number of smaller groups, each possessing its own organisational system. In particular, informal organisational structures arise which operate in parallel with the official system, each possessing coherent internal communication channels, group norms, perceptions and methods for allocating duties. Informal organisations are important because they sometimes develop goals and work routines contrary to the interests of the formal system. They often result from poor management/worker communication within the firm, for example:

(a) staff not knowing the organisation's true objectives;

(b) absence of procedures for interdepartmental consultation and/or joint departmental decision taking;

(c) a single favoured department dominating others, even to the extent that other departments feel they need its permission to undertake certain actions;

(d) conflicts between individual and organisational objectives, including the pursuit of personal rather than company goals;

(e) higher management casually overruling the decisions of lower-level executives. If senior managers do not back their juniors then the latter will conceal some of their activities and a hidden authority system may develop.

It is essential that you prevent informal systems from usurping the official structure. Can you identify individuals or small groups who, although believing that their actions are fully compatible with the organisation's formal aims, in fact steer the firm away from its proper objectives?

## Personal relationships

You need to analyse patterns of relationships within the department, and their importance to the achievement of formal departmental goals. Large groups contain subunits, some of which are permanent and officially recognised, others transitory and arising purely to satisfy a passing need. Yet the personal relationships created within temporary conditions, their supportive nature and obvious relevance to practical and immediate problems, may cause them to persist long after the original problems have been solved.

In reality, organisational 'politics' can override patterns of relationships suggested by the firm's organisation chart. Groups form to improve the relative power of sectional interests, staff and departments compete with each other informally for the attention of higher management, cliques, networks and alliances emerge — formal structures are undermined by unofficial organisational manoeuvres.

## Total quality management (TQM)

The modern approach to maintaining the quality of a firm's or department's output is to attempt to integrate practical techniques for controlling quality (inspection, statistical quality control, etc) with the overall strategies and tactics of the organisation. In particular, TQM aims to create within the firm a culture that is conducive to the continuous improvement of quality. It focuses on the totality of the system rather than its individual parts, seeking to identify the causes of failure rather than the simple fact that failures have occurred. Great emphasis is placed on teamwork, leadership, motivation of employees, the bonding of workers to the employing firm, and the direct involvement of operators in solving technical and/or equipment problems. Successful implementation of TQM requires managements to trust their workers' abilities to deal with quality problems; to train employees to undertake a multiplicity of tasks; and to provide workers with terms and conditions of employment (including long-term security of employment) designed to encourage their commitment to the firm.

Some companies have found it useful to identify within their workforces a number of 'quality champions' whose services can be used to facilitate the introduction of TQM methods. Quality champions are individuals who are known, liked and respected by fellow employees and as such will be highly influential in persuading workers that ... is a good thing. These people are far more likely to be believed than official management communications on quality matters. Once identified, quality champions are given the information and resources necessary to help effect change. They might be invited to participate in planning the implementation of systems and in solving problems as they arise.

# 3

# WORKING WITHIN A BUDGET

## INTRODUCTION

Budgeting is without doubt the commonest and most popular technique for controlling expenditure within businesses. It provides a basis for appraising individual and departmental performances, and forces managers to think hard about their resource needs. Budgets impose financial discipline; spendthrift departments can be identified and penalised, for example by reducing their allocations in the next financial year.

### Functions of budgets

Budgets compare actual costs and achievements with planned costs and achievements. Upper spending limits (or minimum performance standards — sales or production levels, for instance) are specified for each of a number of functions (purchase of supplies, secretarial assistance, office equipment, etc) over a predetermined period (usually 12 months). Often budget resource allocations are made by a 'budget committee' consisting of representatives of all major departments. The amounts given to departments are then distributed by further committees within departments.

Frequently budget committees issue both short-term budgets, which cannot be altered, and long-term budgets which can be varied as situations change. Two factors normally determine the period a budget is to cover: the accuracy of currently available information on expected costs, and the degree of environmental uncertainty facing the business (if the environment is highly unstable the firm will not want to make long-range budgetary plans).

*51*

The meetings, discussions, joint decision making and general coordination of activities necessitated by budget planning encourage cooperation among departments, and the quantitative targets that budgets imply offer a basis for the establishment of departmental and individual objectives.

Budgetary control is an administratively convenient means for authorising discretionary expenditure, and provides tangible objectives which can act as a motivator for employees.

## Fixed and flexible budgets

Budgets may be fixed or flexible. Fixed budgets assume a constant level of activity and resource cost. Flexible budgets relate amounts allocated to appropriate performance indicators. Production budgets, for example, are frequently determined by the volume of sales achieved — it is assumed that increasing sales will require additional resources to sustain and continue expansion.

Another approach to flexible budgeting is the simultaneous specification of not one but several different budgets for the same department or activity. The budget actually applied will depend on the particular circumstances prevailing at the moment of implementation. Here the firm recognises the impossibility of foreseeing all future circumstances and so makes allowances for several contingencies.

Allocations of fixed budgets may relate to operations (expected costs are aggregated under various departmental headings and the totals allotted as departmental budgets), or to responsibilities — individuals specify how much they think they will require to attain certain objectives, resources are distributed, and the individuals concerned then assume personal responsibility for administering the amounts received.

## ZERO BASE BUDGETING

The 'zero based' approach to budget allocation attempts to solve the problem of managers deliberately overspending in order to increase future allocations. There is no presumption whatsoever that the amount given in this budgetary period will be repeated. Indeed, each departmental budget is initially set at zero, assuming thereby that no funds will be made available at all. Heads of department must argue for new allocations at the start of each period. Managers are forced to review periodically their plans and working methods, and are thus encouraged to identify high-cost activities. The obvious drawback to zero base budgeting is the enormous amount of time managers must devote to periodic assessments of costs and functions, and to repeated presentation of budget demands.

# PROBLEMS OF BUDGETING

Despite its widespread use, budgetary control has many problems, including the following:

(a) Cost consciousness, essential for effective budgeting, can go too far — causing managers to cut costs by unreasonable amounts. Managers who keep well within their budgets earn the approval of seniors. Hence some managers regard cutting costs as more important than implementing the measures necessary to improve performance. Businesses need investment; failure to inject capital obviously cuts costs, but the business might suffer in the longer run.

(b) To be meaningful, a budget should be broken down into constituent parts, but too much detail in a budget will increase the probability that not all of its components will be achieved, since budgets, after all, are forecasts of future spending needs. The more specific the predictions, the greater the likelihood they will be wrong. Moreover, preparation of detailed budgets is time consuming and expensive.

(c) Some budgets are overspent, others underspent, so that a mechanism is necessary for transferring unused balances to areas which require extra funds. Since this is the case, why bother establishing detailed budgets?

(d) Budgets can hide inefficiencies. Once a budget has been allocated the manager in charge may seek to spend the entire amount even though, objectively, not all the funds are needed. Naturally managers tend to use fully all resources at their command. Wasteful expenditure might occur simply to exhaust outstanding balances.

(e) It is difficult to distinguish between a budget which has been exceeded because of genuine additional spending needs and one exceeded through administrative incompetence. Indeed, unscrupulous individuals may deliberately overspend in order to have their allocations increased in the next period. Usually budgets are determined following 'bids' registered by heads of departments in meetings of budget committees. The firm's resources are limited, so not all bids can be met. Heads of departments/sections realise this and put in exaggerated bids, anticipating cuts that will leave the amounts actually allocated roughly equal to their requirements. Budgetary control becomes haphazard in such circumstances.

## RULES FOR SETTING BUDGETS

If you have to allocate budgets to people or sections within your department, always ensure that:

- the sums involved are reasonable;

- individuals and sections are clear about who is responsible for keeping within budgetary targets;

- information for budgetary control is understood by everyone who has to use it;

- the system is regularly monitored;

- staff are given some rudimentary training in budgetary control procedures;

- targets can be altered to meet changing conditions;

- you give the system your full support.

## INSTALLING A BUDGET SYSTEM

Budgets result from plans which themselves rely on forecasts. Estimates are prepared of the various costs of the activities needed to achieve targets embodied in the firm's corporate plan, and budgeted expenditures thus determined for the next accounting period.

The commonest budgeting period is the financial year. Annual budgets will be given to appropriate cost centres (departments, for example) which then break them down into budgets for shorter periods (usually months and quarters) and perhaps into budgets for narrowly defined functions — advertising or equipment maintenance, for instance. The term 'budget' is also applied to certain expectations of outcomes, so we speak of the firm's 'sales budget' when describing planned sales revenues.

Some firms use comparisons of actual and budgeted monthly expenditure to compile 'continuous' budgets, whereby the monthly budget for a calendar month one year ahead is based on last month's experience. For example, if February's budget is overspent this year then on 28 February a new and higher budget is set for February next year. This saves the time, cost and inconvenience associated with annual budget meetings, negotiations, forecasting systems, etc.

## Limiting factors

The sales budget is often the first to be established because sales revenues ultimately determine how much the firm can spend. It is not necessarily the case that the sales budget is prepared first, although this practice is very common because sales revenues typically represent the 'principal limiting factor' (sometimes called the principal budget factor) which constrains the firm's activities and thus the extent of its spending. However, the limiting factor could just as well be a shortage of labour (in which case a labour utilisation budget will be the first drafted), or a scarcity of raw materials, or restricted machine capacity. In the latter instances the materials or plant utilisation budgets will be the first constructed.

## TYPES OF BUDGET

Firms define their own particular budget categorisations according to circumstances. The main types are briefly described below.

### The sales budget

The sales budget shows anticipated revenues from the sale of target numbers of units of output at certain prices, allowing for the effects of bulk order discounts and/or special promotions (money-off coupons, etc); and the associated costs of selling output. The budget will be broken down into sales by product, and will indicate precisely when various revenues are expected.

All projections of sales income are speculative and subject to considerable error because so many external variables are involved: behaviour of competitors, the effects of advertising, consumer incomes and preferences, and several other factors. However, estimates of monthly output requirements are essential for monitoring and controlling production — supplies must be available when and where required, labour has to be hired, machinery acquired, raw materials purchased, etc. Marketing and distribution costs depend substantially, although not entirely, on sales volume. Salespeople's commissions, travelling expenses and possibly advertising vary with sales volume; while the rent of the sales office, basic salaries of marketing staff and the capital cost of salespeople's cars are largely fixed.

### The production budget

Production budgets specify the expected costs of creating the output specified in the sales forecast. They need to allow for the costs of overtime working (perhaps through a separate labour utilisation budget), for warehousing and other inventory costs, and for raw materials and finished component purchases. Usually separate sub-budgets are established for the acquisition of significant inputs. For example, a raw materials budget might be established to plan the purchase and delivery of raw materials and to ensure that storage facilities are available when they arrive. Likewise, a labour utilisation budget could be drafted to itemise the costs of employing and deploying labour. This should include training costs, recruitment expenses and overtime costs, and should estimate (normally from past experience) the probable amount of time that will be lost through employee sickness and other sources of absenteeism. Plant utilisation budgets state when and in what circumstances plant and equipment are to be operated, plus their anticipated operating costs (although the capital costs of new equipment are usually dealt with separately in a 'capital expenditure budget' — see below). Maintenance costs may be included here, or placed in a separate overhead budget.

### The capital expenditure budget

The capital expenditure budget defines the new physical resources needed to achieve the firm's production objectives. Some resource acquisitions will benefit the organisation for several years, so capital budgets are usually broken down into subunits for major and minor projects. Major projects are those which will affect the business over a long period, even though they may be paid for in single lump sums. Only a proportion of the capital costs of such assets is set against a particular year's capital budget.

### The cash budget

The purposes of cash budgeting are to avoid cash flow deficits while fully utilising cash inflows. Every anticipated receipt and payment must be stated, including allowances for credit sales and bad debts, and for the effects of discounts offered for prompt payment. Missing an important cash flow item can spell disaster for a business — many a profitable firm has collapsed because of sudden and unanticipated cash flow deficits. The expected receipts and payments must be listed strictly according to the month in which they are likely to occur, regardless of contract dates and details.

### Overhead budgets

Overhead budgets may be drafted in categories for production, marketing and administrative overheads. Research and development could reasonably be classified as an overhead and thus included here. Further subdivision is possible into classes for controllable overheads (stationery, cleaning materials, and so on) and those which are fixed: rent and insurance, for example.

Additional budgets may be prepared for administrative costs such as general management, legal services, audit fees, etc; and for whichever particular functions (personnel, packaging, distribution, special production processes) are relevant to the firm.

All budgets which are measured in monetary units are drawn together into a master budget which shows all anticipated sales revenues and operating expenses.

## BUDGET REPORTS

Differences between, say, monthly actual and budget figures must be quickly identified and reported to the managers who are in a position to implement corrective action. It is important that information is transmitted to the people who are empowered to take significant decisions, otherwise much of the effort expended in preparing the budget is wasted.

Reports should be clear, precise and easily understood by recipients. They must highlight problems and, wherever possible, indicate the measures necessary for their solution. Simple, straightforward reports are the best. Thus:

- figures should be directly comparable, so that like is compared to like and similar quantities are analysed;

- reporting procedures should be reviewed periodically to ensure there is no duplication of information;

- information overload must be avoided;

- all units and time periods should be clearly stated;

- guidelines regarding appropriate remedial action should be available so that a large divergence of actual from budget performance will automatically trigger relevant follow-up action.

## COST CONTROL

Costs are divided into two categories: direct costs and overheads. Direct costs are the costs of materials, labour and other direct expenses. Overheads are costs that are not attributable to specific products. They relate to the creation of the environment in which production takes place. Examples are maintenance of buildings, rent of premises, lighting and heating, secretarial and administrative services, costs of cleaning and so on. Unlike most direct costs, overheads usually do not vary with respect to the volume of production, although in practice the categorisation of particular costs as 'fixed' or 'variable' can be difficult. Rent is clearly fixed, electricity used to power a machine is variable, but electricity used for lighting the premises which is switched on for longer periods during busy spells is partially fixed and partially variable. The sum of direct costs for materials, labour and other expenses is sometimes called the 'prime' cost of a product. So final production cost comprises prime cost plus overheads.

## Allocation of overheads

There are problems associated with the allocation of overheads to individual items, since firms typically supply several products. Fixed costs must therefore be split among the various products according to predetermined criteria.

### Cost centres

Many firms define 'cost centres' to which all the costs of producing particular goods (or services) may be apportioned. Cost centres can be departments, sections of departments, processes or production lines. All direct costs are easily attributable to appropriate cost centres. Overheads, however, are not. Deciding how to allocate overheads is difficult, and varying the criteria used can dramatically alter the estimated costs (and hence price) of an individual product.

Cost centres are said to 'absorb' the overheads allocated to them. Some overheads are easier to apportion proportionately than others. Rent and rates, for example, can be allocated to departmental cost centres in relation to the cubic footage of the space they occupy. Heating, lighting and cleaning may be similarly apportioned, or through the numbers of radiators, lightbulbs, or units of cleaning materials used in each section. The costs of running a works canteen can be allocated proportionate to the numbers of employees in each department, as can training costs and the costs of administering pension schemes and PAYE.

However, some service functions serve not only production cost centres but also other service activities, thus contributing to the latter's operating costs. The canteen, for instance, requires light and heating while the workers who administer these services themselves need to be fed! Complex allocation systems may ensue, with the result that the final apportionment of overheads to products creates product prices which do not truly reflect actual production costs. Many firms consequently adopt simplistic but administratively convenient rules of thumb for allocating overheads. For example, they might classify overheads under a handful of major headings which are then absorbed by products according to a single criterion, such as a straight predetermined percentage of some other cost. Typical overhead categories are:

- *production overheads*, consisting of factory rent, heating, maintenance of equipment, supervisors' and factory office workers' wages, inspection costs, etc;

- *marketing overheads*, eg advertising costs, salespeople's remunerations and expenses, marketing research and sales promotion costs, public relations;

- *administrative overheads* such as stationery, managers' salaries, office expenses, insurance, costs of company cars, maintenance of buildings, and so on.

These overhead classes might be absorbed into products by adding some predetermined percentage of the direct cost which is most important to each product. Thus if direct wages are the dominant direct cost in the production of a certain item, then overheads are absorbed into that product by adding a percentage of the value of the wage cost to account for overheads. Different percentages can be used for different categories of overhead.

To illustrate, suppose the direct labour cost of producing an item is £1000 and the firm decides to add 50 per cent for production overheads, 20 per cent for marketing overheads, and 10 per cent for administration. We then have:

| | |
|---|---:|
| direct labour | £1000 |
| production overhead | 500 |
| marketing overhead | 200 |
| administrative overhead | 100 |
| | 1800 |

Add this to the product's direct material cost and we have the total production cost of the item.

In choosing these percentages the firm must ensure that the total value of the three classes of overhead is fully recovered by absorption into products. If materials cost is the dominant direct cost, then overheads could be expressed as percentages of this rather than the cost of direct labour. Note how a change in the percentages applied alters (somewhat arbitrarily) the estimated final production cost — and hence the selling price — of the product.

Alternatively, overheads might be allocated in proportion to the number of labour hours used in manufacturing various items, or to machine hours, or to some other variable. The advantages of using direct labour cost are that it (usually) reflects the time taken to produce the item, and the number of employees associated with the item's production and hence their need for support services. However, the method does not account for differences in wage rates among workers employed to produce different products or for the distortions created by overtime working.

If overheads are significantly related to material costs then material inputs might conveniently serve as the basis for overhead absorption. Unfortunately, material input prices might fluctuate according to market forces while overheads remain constant, resulting in frequent over- or underallocation of overheads. And high material input prices do not mean that much time or equipment are required to produce the product.

*Standard costing*

Standard costing applies the work study concept of 'standard' performance to the estimation of production costs. Predetermined expected values for material usage, labour time, machine expenses, etc are aggregated and subsequently compared with the actual cost of making a certain product. Differences between expected and realised costs are called 'variances'; they highlight deviations of actual performance from prior assessments of how long an item should take to produce, how much raw material it should require, and the value of the overheads it should (theoretically) absorb. Careful analysis of variances will reveal sources of inefficiency.

## CONDUCTING A MANAGEMENT AUDIT

Periodically (say once every 18 months) you should audit the operational efficiency of your department. A typical audit will examine such things as:

- whether organisation charts and job specifications are up to date;
- communication within the department;

- whether organisational and departmental objectives are understood by all department members;

- possible duplication of activities;

- operational efficiency within sections;

- office layout.

A large amount of a department's work will involve paper, and the more unnecessary paperwork that can be abolished the better. So, you should seek to eliminate redundant procedures, combine documents to reduce the number of documents transmitted, and shorten the transit time for documents in circulation.

Write out a list of all the clerical activities your department undertakes (issuing invoices, credit control, placing orders with suppliers, etc), and then ask the following questions in respect of each operation:

1.  What is being done and how?

2.  What is the purpose of the activity; is it connected with any other operation, and if so, how?

3.  Who performs the operation, and what special skills, training and experience are needed for its execution? Must a certain person (eg yourself) perform the operation or can anyone do it?

4.  Where does the activity take place? Does it have to take place there, and if so, why?

5.  When are operations performed? Is starting one activity dependent on completing another? What will happen if the operation is not completed on schedule?

6.  How are operations completed? What equipment and other resources are necessary? Might alternative methods be used?

7.  What are the costs, including overheads, of individual operations?

Answers to these questions can be used to reduce costs, redeploy staff, reorganise procedures and smooth out work flows. You may well find that you can combine operations and/or avoid delays by rerouting documents. The exercise should result in better coordination of activities, faster and simpler procedures, fewer clerical errors and tighter management control.

# 4

# PLANNING AND DECISION MAKING

Planning and decision making are the very essence of management, and whether you succeed or fail as a manager will depend in large part on your abilities to plan ahead and take high-quality decisions. Planning means deciding now what to do in the future given certain predicted or intended conditions. It is troublesome and expensive: troublesome because it requires forecasts of the future; expensive because it absorbs large amounts of time. Nevertheless, planning is invariably worthwhile. It forces you to prepare for unforeseen eventualities, to clarify your objectives, to develop criteria for monitoring performance, and to think ahead systematically. Moreover, the planning process itself might:

- identify opportunities for greater efficiency;

- reveal duplications of effort, bottlenecks in work flows and foreseeable pitfalls;

- indicate fresh initiatives that the firm might undertake in order to influence future events;

- assist in integrating activities.

Planning enables you to take decisions unhurriedly, using the maximum amount of information and considering all available options. This avoids making decisions in crisis situations which prevent you from studying all the relevant factors in depth. There are three basic approaches to tactical planning: 'top-down' planning, which means that senior management plans and establishes targets for all levels of authority within the firm; 'bottom-up' planning, whereby each department prepares an estimate of what it believes it can achieve and submits this to higher management for approval; and a third (and common) method whereby senior management imposes general objectives, leaving individual departments to devise plans for attaining them.

In practice, top-down planning is more common than bottom-up planning. The major point in its favour is the inexperience of junior managers in policy making. Another drawback to bottom-up procedures is that employees might not be familiar with the work of other departments. Their judgements may therefore be shortsighted, and might conflict with the needs of other aspects of the organisation. Good quality feedback is essential for the success of a plan. Unless there is a mechanism for relating plans to actual performance, much of the effort that goes into their formulation is wasted.

The first stage in a planning process is the specification of objectives, ie statements of what you want to do (as opposed to 'policies', which state how objectives are to be achieved). The more concrete your objectives the easier the choice of the policies required. Higher-level targets are subdivided into specific objectives (preferably expressed in quantitative terms) to be achieved within predetermined periods. Departments and employees might contribute to the setting of their own targets through a system of management by objectives.

## PLANS AND FORECASTS

Forecasts might be needed before targets can be set. A forecast is a prediction of future events, in contrast to a 'plan' which is a predetermined response to anticipated future events. Forecasting is an essential prerequisite to effective planning but, in management, accurate forecasts are notoriously difficult to achieve. Environmental change can occur quickly — production techniques become obsolete, employment and other laws alter, new agreements are negotiated with unions. Usually the shorter the forecast period the more accurate its predictions.

Long-term forecasts are subject to greater uncertainty, so larger margins of error must be allowed. So many firms prepare both short-term and long-term forecasts, the former in detail, the latter in outline only. It is not worth spending enormous amounts of money on long-range predictions of highly uncertain events. The accuracy of predictions should be monitored by comparing them with events as they occur, and sources of error (inadequate or incorrect data, faulty forecasting techniques, poor judgements by forecasters, etc) identified to find out whether forecasts are on average persistently overestimating or underestimating actual performance.

## THE DEPARTMENTAL PLAN

When preparing a departmental plan, analyse systematically the strengths and weaknesses of yourself, the department, and your colleagues. Does the department possess all the skills, equipment and human and other resources needed to attain its targets? Specify your objectives as precisely as you can and list all the activities necessary to achieve them. Evaluate the consequences of various courses of action and choose the best. Then prepare a list of all the instructions you need to issue to employees to secure implementation of the plan, and establish criteria (preferably quantitative) for monitoring progress.

Plans should be as detailed as expenditure constraints allow, but should not extend too far into the future since accurate prediction of the distant future is impossible. All alternative courses of action should be considered, not just some of them, and the side effects and implications of the actions envisaged should be examined. Instructions to individuals and departments must be incorporated into the body of the plan. What is the point of preparing an expensive and detailed plan if no one assumes responsibility for its implementation? As the plan is executed its effectiveness in achieving stated objectives must be monitored, and this will be facilitated if the plan is concise and easy to understand.

## NETWORK PLANNING METHODS

Network planning methods are common devices for planning a business's activities. A 'network' in this context is a schematic description of all the activities involved in a project and all the interconnecting links between events. Its purpose is to determine how quickly the project can be completed and to assist in scheduling, coordinating and controlling work. Network methods are already common in some industries (notably construction) and — because of the widespread availability of standard software packages that run on small desktop computers and which produce networks quickly, cheaply and without a great deal of effort on the user's part — are increasingly popular elsewhere.

The 'critical path' of a network is the sequence of key activities that cannot be held up without postponing the completion date of the entire project. Other activities have 'float' time associated with their duration. Float is the extra time that can be taken over an activity, in addition to its expected duration, without affecting the completion time of the project as a whole. Critical path analysis (CPA) has long been recognised as a valuable management technique, but only recently has the price of CPA software fallen to the degree where network planning methods can easily be used at the departmental level. The value of network planning is perhaps best illustrated by considering a large construction project such as building a house. Scores of activities are involved: a survey, soil testing, ordering supplies, hiring labour, laying foundations, inspection of work, etc. Many of these tasks will interact, some need to be completed before others can begin, while some may be undertaken at any time. The builder must calculate the expected duration of each task, and sort tasks into the order in which they have to be completed. It is then possible to work out which activities can be performed alongside others, and which must be finished before others can begin. The critical path is the shortest time between the first activity and the last, given that some activities can be completed while others are in progress. So crucially important activities are highlighted, and you can see how the project can be speeded up through reallocating labour and other resources from some tasks to others, and how strikes, holidays, staff illnesses, non-delivery of supplies, etc might affect the project's estimated completion date.

## Preparing a network

To prepare a network you need to list in as much detail as is appropriate all the operations that must be completed within the project, and specify the interrelations between them — particularly which parts of the project must be completed before others can begin. When building a house, for example, a firm needs to lay the foundations before building the walls, and must fit a roof before installing the electrics. However, other internal fittings can be installed during the period the electrics are being installed, and the firm might be getting on with other internal work (decorating, for instance) at the same time. Next, you estimate the time required to complete each operation, assess the materials, labour and other resources required at each stage, predict costs, and place orders for resources to arrive as they are needed.

The information is loaded into a network analysis software package (of which numerous varieties are available) which, in a few seconds, will determine the complete plan and be ready to print out detailed instructions on when each activity should start and finish, and will check the logic of the scheme (ie it will look for inconsistencies in the order you have stipulated for the various activities). Possible problems are highlighted so that you can redefine the order of activities until they make sense. Then you can ask the program 'what if' questions, involving assorted alterations in your presuppositions about resources, activity times and so on. The critical path is produced for each set of eventualities and you select the best.

## Resource reports

A series of reports will be generated by the software showing activity schedules, resource requirements and cash flow forecasts. If desired, reports can be printed out as bar charts or pie charts as well as in conventional tables. Among the reports available are listings of the earliest and latest times that particular operations can be started, and of activities (with dates) specifically relevant to the work of a certain department — all the activities involving electrical work, for example, or all the jobs associated with a certain phase of the project. Resource reports can be requisitioned showing requirements if all activities occur as early as possible, or as late as possible. In this way you can identify peak periods for resource needs and, if necessary, adjust the network to reschedule these demands.

This type of exercise is extremely useful for analysing complicated projects involving a great deal of coordination over a lengthy period. They help you to predict resource bottlenecks and other difficulties, and generally assist in clarifying your thoughts. You can forecast the workloads of subordinates, determine priorities and preplan tasks. Such benefits feed through into better budgetary control, detailed analysis of resource needs, greater consideration of the feasibility of targets, identification of interrelations between activities and personnel, and hence improved coordination. Other advantages are the abilities to compare actual and predicted costs as projects develop, to recognise opportunities for reallocating resources and effort in order to expedite project completion, and to isolate sources of delay and exceptional cost.

# CORPORATE PLANNING

Corporate planning focuses on strategic issues, although some tactical aspects of management are necessarily involved. A good corporate plan will facilitate the coordination of activities, assist in the allocation of resources, and increase the organisation's ability to cope with change. So corporate planning concerns the total resources and intended activities of the firm. Above all, it is about the management of change — new methods, materials, skills, processes and techniques; and consideration of the effects of change lies at the heart of the corporate planning process. Corporate plans cover all aspects of the firm's operations:

personnel, finance, production, organisation, marketing, management and control.

A corporate plan offers guidelines against which the performance of the organisation may be assessed. It is analogous to a route map showing the direction in which the organisation should proceed. Corporate plans rarely extend to more than four or five years ahead, because of the great uncertainty of long-term predictions; few organisations would claim to possess information systems capable of looking more than five years into the future. The plan will describe the activities and resources needed for intended future operations, identifying possible new markets, applications of new technology, and the likelihood of environmental change.

Plans could establish corporate targets for (say) the market share to be achieved within three years, a certain rate of return on capital employed, some specified percentage reduction in the labour force, greater efficiency in the use of working capital, lower aggregate expenditures, and so on. Achievement of these aims may require new investment or divestment, mergers and acquisitions, new product development, or entry to new markets. Objectives can be listed in order of importance and hence priorities assigned to the policies (and resources) required for their attainment. Each element of the corporate plan should have a direct and recognisable connection with the statement of the organisation's *raison d'être*. The financial, personnel, technical and other resources necessary to implement the plan must be listed and compared with the resources available, and stated deficiencies accompanied by a written explanation of how the shortfall will be met (and who will be responsible for this). The plan should set priorities for action, describe any changes in organisation structure that might be required, and include a timetable for its implementation. Then the minimum criteria that need to be satisfied before the plan can be regarded as a 'success' must be specified (eg quantitative targets for improvements in market share, reduced costs, or increased financial return over some predetermined period).

## Benefits of corporate planning

A firm with a corporate plan is better equipped to face up to change and hence to profit from new opportunities. Large businesses should find that coordination between divisions and subsidiaries is enhanced, that resources are allocated more efficiently, and that product policy — particularly product choice — is improved. Companies which prepare corporate plans can monitor their actual rates of growth (or decline) against predetermined standards, and can arrange their operations coherently and without one activity conflicting with others.

Operational plans are derived from the aggregate corporate plan, which provides a strategic framework within which tactics for achieving the global objectives specified at the corporate level may be devised. Operations can be varied as the plan is implemented according to feedback received and/or as environments alter.

Note, however, that the benefits of corporate planning are unlikely to be realised unless the exercise is taken seriously by the senior management involved, and middle and junior management are committed to the strategic objectives established by the plan. So top management should not set objectives hastily and without consulting subordinates, and subordinates themselves should be trained to appreciate the advantages that corporate planning can provide.

### Problems in corporate planning

Many senior managers are unable to cope with the volume and complexity of the information generated in corporate planning processes. They receive so much information in such diverse forms (sales forecasts, written reports, efficiency audits, bar charts, Lorenz curves, statistical analyses, etc) that they cannot identify clear priorities for action. The quality of information may be suspect, and the system for providing it might be extremely expensive.

Corporate strategies may be too successful. A plan to revolutionise the technology of a certain process might be brilliantly executed, but force the initiating firm into bankruptcy through the business's inability to finance the re-equipping of production lines necessary to implement the new methods (which competitors quickly copy). Equally, the introduction of a completely new product to a market creates opportunities for the firm's competitors to follow its lead — but more efficiently since competitors will have been able to observe and learn from the initiating company's mistakes.

## TAKING DECISIONS

Some people seem incapable of acting decisively, and when they do take decisions they are inconsistent, act hastily, and do not consider all the relevant facts. Prevarication causes muddle and irritates colleagues.

Others insist on becoming involved in all decisions, regardless of whose responsibility they ought to be. These people try to solve their colleagues' problems as well as their own — creating confusion, duplicating effort, and eventually preventing anything being fully resolved. Yet all management involves taking decisions, and your ability as a manager will be judged in large part against the quality of your decisions. The need for decisions arises from problems which, in a business context, might be 'strategic' (concerning the overall direction of the firm), 'tactical' (how to implement policy decisions) or 'operational' (relating to minor administrative matters such as the lengths of production runs, shift rosters or stock levels). Top management takes strategic decisions, lower levels are concerned primarily with tactical decision taking and control.

Often the decisions that you have to make can be dealt with quickly and without careful thought. The best choice might be obvious, or the consequences of a bad decision may be so trivial that only cursory attention to detail is required. For major decisions, however, a logical and systematic procedure is necessary; options must be listed and each one carefully considered. To the maximum possible extent, operational decisions should be taken automatically, according to predetermined criteria. Such 'programmed decisions' do not require the exercise of managerial judgement, initiative or discretion.

It is important to realise how problems can create opportunities as well as troublesome work. A vigorous and high-profile approach to problem solving will bring you to the attention of other people and, provided you are thorough and open in your approach, should enhance your career prospects in the long run.

For major decisions, adopt the following procedure.

## Analyse the problem

Decide what it is that you have to decide. A misstatement of a problem can result in inappropriate solutions being applied. For example, the problem of reducing your departmental expenditure might be interpreted as either how to reduce (say) stationery costs; or how to increase efficiency; or a redundancy problem involving the choice of personnel to be dismissed.

What is the true nature of the problem? Is it technical, financial, personal, or a mixture of these? Is the problem self-contained, or is it a manifestation of an underlying malaise? If the real problem is deep rooted, what are its fundamental causes? Collect and examine all the available facts. Determine which information is based on hard evidence and which on speculation.

## Plan a solution

Often major problems consist of a conglomeration of lesser, inter-related problems. Problems can result from unexpected occurrences, from events not happening as planned, breakdowns in communication, inadequate or misleading information, interpersonal conflicts, and a wide variety of other things. It is essential to pinpoint the precise nature of a problem, since only then may a lasting solution be imposed. If several people need to be involved in tackling the problem, then it is equally important to obtain a consensus on the cause of the problem and what the solution might involve. To identify the causes and true nature of a problem you need to consider:

- the symptoms which indicate the existence of a problem;
- the history of the situation;
- the opinions and feelings of the people involved;
- facts, figures, information and documents relating to the situation.

Dissect large problems into their constituent parts and deal with each part as if it were a separate problem. Prepare a list of the resources necessary to implement a successful solution, and compare these with the resources available. List the people who will be involved in the chosen solution and give them the information they need. Ask for views on issues — consult people in advance rather than simply informing them after decisions have been taken. However, only consult individuals whose views are directly relevant to the issue and/or will be personally affected by the decision — much time can be wasted in meaningless consultations with people who are only marginally inter-ested in a problem.

Next identify the barriers that might prevent a satisfactory outcome. Put down every constraint that occurs to you, regardless of how trivial it might at first appear (you can edit later) and determine how each barrier can be overcome.

If you are stuck for ideas you can 'brainstorm' a problem, individu-ally or with colleagues. The aim of brainstorming is to churn out ideas, without considering their feasibility. You simply list every idea on any aspect of the problem that comes into your head. Then, in another session, you go through the list of ideas assessing whether they are sensible, practicable, within your available resources, etc. Be as inven-tive and imaginative as you can; look at the problem from different angles instead of head on. You will find that one idea generates others and that ideas build on themselves.

## Consider similar problems

Problems similar to those currently being experienced might have appeared before but in a different form. If so, examine the consequences of the previous solution, since even if a particular problem has not previously appeared, a related or similar problem may have been settled. Solutions to kindred problems offer hints on how best to tackle the problem in question. Sometimes problems can be restated to make them resemble other problems previously encountered.

## Implement a solution

The selected solution should be made known to all affected parties and an action plan — with dates, specific targets and detailed work allocations — devised to ensure its implementation. Then the effectiveness of the solution must be monitored and remedial action taken if it does not produce the desired results.

Decisions are useless unless they are carried out. Ensure, therefore, that those selected to implement a decision not only understand it and what they must do, but are also committed to the decision and will not seek to undermine the intended outcome. It is useful if the people who took the decision are themselves involved in its enforcement. And where possible the activities needed to implement a decision should follow from clear directives issued at the moment the decision was made.

## Risk

Risk is involved in many management decisions, and the existence of risk sometimes causes supervisors to avoid or delay taking decisions in risky situations. The size of the risk must be compared with the expected benefits of a particular decision. Low-risk, high-return solutions are obviously preferable to high-risk, low-return options. Typically, however, a compromise between risk and return has to be struck, and the precise nature of the compromise will depend largely on the risk preferences of the person taking the decision. Some people enjoy assuming risk, others are highly averse to risky behaviour. Indeed, a few individuals find risk so exciting that they are prepared to forego satisfactory outcomes just to experience the exhilaration it provides.

You might 'take a risk' by hiring someone not seemingly suited to a particular job, by accepting a tight delivery date for a consignment of goods you know might not be ready on time, by making promises you cannot guarantee to keep, or by accepting someone else's promise when you know it might be broken. At what point does risky behaviour become irresponsible? Where do you draw the line between risk and potential return? A fondness for excitement and a tendency to act on impulse can cause you to behave recklessly, so always prepare a brief analysis of the risks involved in an important decision, and cover yourself by involving other people in risky choices. (If you are an exceptionally risk-averse person you might find you are more willing to select high-risk options when the decision is shared by a group.) Also, specify the minimum probabilities of success required of each option: this will help you to avoid rash behaviour and consciously decide whether a risk is worth taking.

# Part 2

# PEOPLE MANAGEMENT

# 5

# HIRING EMPLOYEES

Recruiting high-calibre people is one of the most critically important duties that, as a manager, you will ever be called on to undertake. It affects the long-term efficiency of the organisation, the quality of inter-personal relationships within it, the extent to which you can safely dele-gate work, and many other factors. Careful planning is essential, beginning with a precise specification of the type of person best suited to fill the vacant position.

## DESCRIBING THE IDEAL CANDIDATE

Your first job is to prepare a 'person specification' which defines the background, education, training, personality and other characteristics of the person best suited to fill the vacancy. In other words, you need to draft a pen portrait of the *ideal* candidate so as to provide you with a list of qualities to look for when preparing a short list of people to interview. The person you describe may not exist; but the process of drafting a person specification gives you a standard against which applicants can be compared. Schemes for categorising the various attributes required to perform certain types of work have existed for many years, usually presented in the form of a checklist describing the demands of the vacant job, as in the following example:

1. *Physical aspects of the work* Does the job require someone with exceptional strength or fitness (heavy lifting work for instance), or a specific physical appearance, dress, speech or manner (eg for a position as a salesperson or receptionist)?

2. *Need to communicate* Some work involves regular contact with others. Workplace supervisors, salespeople, receptionists, training instructors, etc need external appearances, manners and communi-

cation skills that are not so important for socially isolated jobs (long-distance lorry driving, for instance). Jobs with social interaction require agreeable people who mix easily. Such jobs are unsuitable for hostile, aggressive individuals.

3. *Formal qualifications* What is the minimum level of education and professional qualifications necessary for the job? It is important not to recruit people who are massively overqualified for the vacancy as they might quickly become bored and underperform, or leave the company.

4. *Experience needed* Should the person selected have personal experience of specific tasks, and if so for what periods and at what levels?

5. *Specific competences* Does the work require a person with particular abilities such as mathematical competence, manual dexterity, or the capacities to think quickly, assimilate large quantities of information, exercise mental agility and interpret complicated issues? Employees who cannot easily withstand stress should not attempt harrowing or emotionally arduous duties.

6. *Personal ambition* Repetitive production-line work is not intellectually stimulating; financial reward is probably the major motivating factor here. Other jobs present opportunities for creativity and self-development, and thus would be appropriate for people with drive, enthusiasm, self-direction and personal ambition.

Normally the person specification can be put together from the existing job description relating to the vacant post, plus your personal knowledge of what is needed. If you are in the unfortunate position of having no job descriptions for the workers in your department, you need to prepare them as quickly as possible. Job descriptions are necessary for general efficiency as well as recruitment reasons. They are required for many purposes, particularly appraisal (see Chapter 6).

## HOW TO WRITE JOB DESCRIPTIONS

To draft job descriptions proceed as follows:

(a) List the job titles and functions of all employees in the department, then specify to whom each one of them is accountable, and how many people each individual controls.

(b) Write down all the duties that *you* regard as important for each post. Then ask employees to keep daily diaries which detail all the tasks they undertake during (at least) a full calendar month, specifying the resources and equipment managed, and the frequency and purposes of their contacts with other individuals and departments.

(c) Compare these diaries with your original list of functions. Identify major discrepancies and seek clarification from the people concerned.

(d) Write out a complete description of each job, stating:

1. what is done, and the purpose and relative importance of the tasks undertaken;

2. how things are done;

3. who the job incumbent comes into contact with in the course of the job;

4. the experience, skill, knowledge and special qualities required;

5. how frequently the incumbent must do each task (rarely, occasionally or often);

6. the physical environment/special working conditions in which the work is undertaken;

7. any special circumstances or requirements (overnight travel or lifting heavy weights, for example) that might be encountered.

To define the relationship of one job to others, write out lists of points of similarity and difference between jobs, particularly in relation to the demands made on the worker, and to the pay, working hours, holiday and sick leave entitlements, and so on relevant to each position. Specify also the availability of overtime and/or bonus payments and how they are calculated.

Note the significance of the frequency with which certain tasks are undertaken. One job might require taking important decisions (those that would cost the firm dearly if they went wrong) two or three times annually. Another job might involve taking such decisions two or three times a week. It is useful, therefore, to divide a job description into sections for routine tasks, non-routine tasks, and tasks which are only rarely completed (when deputising for an immediate superior, for example). Likewise you should spell out the judgemental and managerial abilities expected from job incumbents: abilities to plan, coordinate, organise, etc. Finally, you need to state briefly the performance standards expected from the holder of the post.

## A simple example

Your completed job description for a particular position (an office junior in an advertising department, for instance) might look like the following:

| | |
|---|---|
| **JOB TITLE:** | Office junior. |
| **PURPOSE OF JOB:** | To provide routine clerical support to senior members of the advertising department. |
| **RESPONSIBLE TO:** | The head of marketing department's personal assistant. |
| **MAJOR DUTIES:** | Photocopying and collating. Sorting and distributing mail. Typing routine correspondence. Taking telephone messages. Using a mailmerge package. Filing hard copy and making entries to a database. Maintenance of records and files. Collection and collation of statistical information. Tidying up at the end of each working day. |
| **TRAINING:** | Standard two-day company induction. Four days on-job training within the department. Day release for up to one year for secretarial training will be made available. |
| **OCCASIONAL DUTIES:** | Receiving visitors and making coffee. Preparing graphs, bar charts and pie diagrams using standard graphics packages. Taking minutes in departmental meetings. Drafting correspondence. Making appointments for senior managers. Making travel arrangements. |
| **REGULAR CONTACTS:** | One other office junior in the public relations department. Head of marketing department's PA. Three senior advertising department executives. Secretaries to heads of departments of personnel and production. Mail room supervisor. Gate receptionist. |
| **EQUIPMENT USED:** | PCW. Photocopier. |

|  | Telephone system. |
|--|--|
|  | Word processing packages. |
|  | Database. |
|  | Graphics package. |

| **NECESSARY SKILLS:** | 30 wpm typing (no shorthand). Ability to audiotype and to load and use simple software packages. Knowledge of organisation of the marketing department. |
|--|--|
| **WORKING ENVIRONMENT:** | Busy open-plan office of 17 people. Will have own desk, chair, word processor and telephone. Moderate noise. No more than three hours' exposure to word processor per day. No unusual physical demands. |
| **SPECIAL REQUIREMENTS:** | Non-smoker. Must be willing to work up to one hour's overtime twice per week. Punctuality is essential. |
| **GENERAL:** | Incumbent should be numerate, well organised, capable of self-direction and able to exercise initiative. He or she needs to be well spoken and capable of dealing with irate customers over the telephone. Willingness to follow instructions promptly and efficiently is more important than judgemental/planning skills. |

# THE JOB ADVERTISEMENT

Once the ideal candidate has been described, the personnel department or the firm's secretariat should be able to draft and place a job advertisement in suitable media. Accurate job and person specifications lead to precise job advertisements and hence to fewer unsuitable applicants responding and less time wasted in sifting through applications. A good job advertisement will generate a small number of genuine and high-quality applications, not hundreds of speculative enquiries. Thus it must be quite specific about what the job involves.

Note the high cost of advertising vacancies via newspapers. Even in a local paper an eighth of a page box advertisement in a single issue can cost hundreds of pounds.

# THE LAW ON RECRUITMENT

When recruiting, you are not allowed to discriminate unfairly against members of a particular sex or racial group, and special provisions apply to rehabilitated criminals. However, there are no laws to prevent a firm refusing to employ a known trade union member (although it is illegal under the Employment Protection Acts to dismiss an employee for union membership once that person has been appointed), or from discriminating against applicants on the grounds of their sexual orientation.

## Sex and race discrimination

It is equally unlawful to discriminate against men or women, or against married (but not single) persons. An 'ethnic minority' is defined as a group distinguished from others by a sufficient combination of shared customs, beliefs, traditions and characteristics derived from a common or presumed common past, even if the distinctions are not biologically determined. Thus Jews and Sikhs have both been accepted as distinct 'ethnic' groups by the English courts under the Race Relations Act.

Indirect as well as direct sex or race discrimination is unlawful. Not only must the firm not treat one sex or ethnic minority less favourably when recruiting ('direct' discrimination), say by specifying that only males or whites will be employed, but also the employer must not impose any requirement or condition which adversely affects the prospects of a member of a particular race or sex when applying for a job. An example of indirect discrimination would be a condition that all job applicants must be over six feet tall for work where the employee's height is not important. This discriminates unfairly against women because not many females are taller than six feet.

## Exceptions to the legislation

For sex discrimination employers may lawfully discriminate in the following cases:

1. where the job requires a person of a particular sex for reasons of physiology, (eg modelling), authenticity (eg acting), or decency (eg a lavatory attendant);

2. jobs in a single-sex establishment;

3. employment in a private household, where the degree of physical or social contact or knowledge of intimate details might reasonably cause objection to the employment of a particular sex.

Such requirements are commonly referred to as 'genuine occupational qualifications' (GOQs). Comparable exemptions apply in the case of racial discrimination.

Note that it is lawful to recruit predominantly one sex or race on to a training scheme that seeks to redress an imbalance in employment of the races or sexes in a department or organisation where the imbalance has existed during the previous 12 months.

## Codes of practice

Throughout this book you will be referred to a multitude of 'codes of practice' on various employment matters. A code of practice is a document published by a government agency, professional body, trade association or other relevant authority which outlines model procedures for good practice in a particular field. Codes give examples of excellent and bad behaviour, and recommendations regarding how things should be done. Government codes of practice (eg those issued by the Equal Opportunities Commission, ACAS, or the Health and Safety Executive), are not legally binding, but are looked at by courts when adjudicating cases. Hence many codes need to be regarded as if they were legally binding.

Conduct that fails to correspond to a code issued by a government-funded body will normally be deemed improper if the issue comes before a court of law. A good example of this is the *Highway Code*, which is not a legal document of itself, but expresses powerful government-backed opinions on how road users should behave.

### The CRE and EOC codes

Both the Commission for Racial Equality and the Equal Opportunities Commission issue detailed advice on recruitment matters in their codes of practice for employers. According to these you should not impose unreasonable age limits when recruiting to posts where age is immaterial (such limits are unfair to women who are often unavailable for work during what would otherwise be the early part of a career on account of child-bearing and child-rearing responsibilities). You should, however, check job specifications to ensure that resulting job advertisements do not imply that applications from a certain sex or ethnic group will not be welcome, and make certain you are not demanding unreasonably high qualifications that only one sex or racial category is likely to possess. Further code of practice recommendations are that:

- job advertisements should appear in media likely to be seen by suitably qualified people from both sexes and all ethnic minorities;

- workers should not be recruited via personal recommendations of existing employees where the workforce concerned is wholly or predominantly white, black or Asian;

- firms should collect statistics on how many members of various minorities apply for jobs. Data is also needed on the proportions of women and ethnic minority candidates shortlisted for various categories of post, on how many are appointed, their participation in training schemes, how many are promoted, and when and why they resign.

Note that it would probably be unlawful to ask a woman interview questions relating to her child-bearing or other family plans or about the number and ages of her children, or to state in job advertisements that applicants should reside in certain areas (especially if there is low ethnic minority representation in these areas).

*Complaints of sex or race discrimination*

Complaints must be lodged with an industrial tribunal (see Chapter 9) within three months of the incident. A conciliation officer may be asked by both parties at this stage to settle the matter without a tribunal hearing, or may intervene on his or her own initiative. If a settlement cannot be reached in this way a tribunal will be convened to hear the case and, if it decides in favour of the complainant, may award damages (typically of quite low monetary value) to the complainant. Also the EOC or CRE may investigate allegations and institute legal proceedings and/or issue 'discrimination notices' requiring the employer not to commit further unlawful acts.

## Candidates with criminal records

Under the 1974 Rehabilitation of Offenders Act, a 'rehabilitated' person does not have to disclose to a recruiting firm the fact that he or she has a criminal record, provided the applicant's conviction has been 'spent'. And it is unlawful for an employer to deny someone a job solely on the grounds that the applicant has a spent conviction. If an applicant is asked to declare on an application form whether he or she has a criminal record, or is questioned about this during an interview, the applicant is entitled to deny ever having been convicted of the spent offence. A conviction becomes 'spent' following the elapse of a certain time period, although some convictions can never be spent (notably life sentences and other sentences of imprisonment for more than 30 months). Otherwise the period involved varies according to the gravity of the offence. Thus a prison sentence of up to six months becomes spent after three years; while sentences of between six and 30 months are spent after five years; a probation order is spent one year after it expires, and so on.

There are exemptions to the legislation, and candidates for certain jobs do have to reveal past convictions. The jobs involved are: lawyers, chartered accountants, medical practitioners, nurses, dentists, vets, prison officers, firearms dealers, social and health workers, and any form of work with children under 18. If a job applicant (or one of your existing employees) has a spent conviction that you know about, you must not reveal this information to anyone else since you could then be sued for defamation and/or the aggrieved person could make a formal complaint to the police — who might then prosecute you under the 1974 Act.

You may feel that this law is unfair on the grounds that you believe it is necessary to ensure that everyone you hire is trustworthy and reliable. Remember, however, that a person's criminal record might have arisen many years previously and involve only a minor offence. Moreover, criminal records are held only by those who were caught and punished at the time. It is hardly proper for such individuals to be punished again through not being able to get a job.

## PREPARING A SHORT LIST

Write out a list of the things you will be looking for in candidates under various headings of the person specification. For example, you might require a person with good eyesight but not physical strength, a certain educational certificate, experience in a specific industry doing a particular job, experience of supervising staff, emotional stability, the willingness to work shifts, and so on. Prepare a checklist of these and other relevant factors, and ask yourself how (indeed whether) they can be measured.

Divide your requirements under each heading into 'essential' and 'desirable' sections, checking carefully to ensure that all your 'essential' column entries are really necessary. Normally, the personnel department or the firm's secretariat will receive candidates' applications and scan them for those which meet the specified requirements. If there are insufficient applicants possessing all the necessary qualities, ask personnel to draw out all applicants who have (say) 80 per cent of the desired attributes, then if there are still not enough candidates 60 per cent, then 50 per cent. Thereafter it is probably not worthwhile pursuing the search for suitably qualified individuals at the salary offered and using existing advertising media.

## The problems involved in short lists

Difficulties arise in determining the suitability for short listing of applicants with widely varying backgrounds, experience and paper qualifications. For example, an older woman may possess certificates and diplomas with titles quite different to those obtained by a younger person. She may have been absent from the labour force for several years while raising children, and then may have worked in an industry unlike your own. How are you to compare her application with that of a young man who joined one of your immediate competitors straight from college a couple of years ago?

There are no straightforward solutions to this difficult problem, but there are some common factors to look for in an application form. For example, has the applicant a good record of passing examinations first time or were several attempts required? Are there observable gaps in the candidate's CV in particular subject areas (mathematics or English, for example)? Did the candidate drop out of particular courses? The fact that any of these are true does not necessarily mean the candidate is unsuitable, only that the issue should be further explored during the interview.

Examine the relevance of any particular set of qualifications to the advertised post, and look for evidence of the candidate's interest in attending job-relevant courses. A willingness to update in one area usually indicates a willingness to acquire further knowledge in others. How much responsibility did the applicant carry in his or her previous position? Can you identify a distinct pattern in the applicant's career, and if so how relevant is the vacant post to this career pattern? Did the applicant achieve promotion with previous employers, and how long did he or she remain in each job?

# INTERVIEWING

There is a single and simple golden rule to follow when conducting employment interviews. Since the purpose of an interview is to obtain information on candidates, then the interviewing technique which yields the maximum amount of information is the one to be adopted. Therefore it is necessary to put candidates into a state of mind in which they willingly disclose the maximum amount of information. This state of mind is possible only if candidates are comfortable, at ease, and do not feel intimidated. Uncomfortable, ill-at-ease candidates will not be as frank as those who are relaxed, confident and in full control of their responses. Hostile, overbearing interview environments with several interviewers aggressively firing complex questions at a candidate who is left groping for words will not encourage responses that are open and sincere. Candidates will be prevented from presenting themselves properly, and this will reduce the volume of data on which decisions can be based.

## Nervous interviewees

Everyone feels nervous in tense situations, since fear is a natural reaction to external threat. It signals the need for caution in hostile surroundings. Environments that do not frighten or intimidate enable interviewees to express themselves comprehensively and in uninhibited ways, so seek actively to create such an environment. Interview candidates promptly at the appointed time or, if delay is inevitable, offer an apology. The reception of interviewees should be friendly and constructive, with comfortable chairs and, if possible, no large table to create mental barriers between candidate and interviewers. If smoking is permitted, ashtrays should be available; if not, a sign to that effect should be prominently displayed. Interruptions from telephone calls, secretaries, etc disturb concentration and should not be allowed.

## Avoid theatrical situations

It is useful to have more than one person conducting the interview in order to obtain a balanced assessment. Thereafter, however, the number of people involved in the interview should be kept to the minimum, subject to the proper representation of all seriously interested parties. Overlarge panels create dramatic atmospheres more applicable to the theatre than an employment interview. Large panels (and any more than three is 'large') usually mean that managers in that organisation do not have enough work to do and seek to fill out their time by sitting in on job interviews for staff in other departments. Also the members of a large panel might ask candidates irrelevant and disconnected questions.

## How to proceed

Begin an interview with friendly, supportive and sympathetic remarks, starting perhaps with comments about the weather, travel arrangements, or similarly uncontroversial matters. Use the candidate's completed application form (or letter of application if your firm does not produce application forms) as your line of approach to the body of the interview, but do not ask questions that have already been answered on the form. Rather, seek supplementary information to probe the candidate's potential for effective performance in the advertised position. An interview is a matching exercise, comparing job requirements with a candidate's attributes. You can use the person specification to guide you through the interview and remind you of the attributes that you are seeking. However, taking detailed notes is not recommended because of its disturbing effect on the candidate's concentration.

Always assess candidates immediately after each interview, not together at the end of a long interviewing session. Important points arising from the early interviews will by then have been forgotten and the last one or two people interviewed might thus be placed at an advantage.

## The questions to ask

Open-ended questions, such as 'What made you decide to do that?' or 'Why did you enjoy that type of work?', are usually more productive in obtaining information than direct queries. Broadly worded questions invite the candidate to discuss feelings, opinions, and perceptions of events. Simple 'yes/no' questions will not draw out the candidate's views. Much of the skill of interviewing lies in listening — interviews should be discussions, not interrogations. Tell the candidate precisely what information is required, and give as much time as is necessary for a comprehensive answer. Never make critical or insensitive remarks during the interview.

Some managers behave most peculiarly when interviewing job applicants. They speak in pompous, unnatural accents; males dress in suits and ties even though normally they dress casually; they adopt formal and old-fashioned modes of address to others — people they have known for years and with whom they are on first-name terms are suddenly addressed as Mr or Mrs! Others seek to impress candidates with their importance. They discuss their own work, they moralise, and spend much of the interview expressing personal opinions on various issues, wasting time and contributing absolutely nothing to the quality of the interview.

## Be yourself

Act naturally when conducting a job interview — remember that the person you appoint has to work with you as you are, not as you transitorily appear while interviewing. Avoid the aggressive question; it serves only to intimidate and prevent the free flow of information. It is unfair for interviewers — who control the situation, who are on their 'home territory' and are not themselves subject to stress — to harangue and harass distressed candidates. It is sometimes argued that the deliberate creation of stressful environments is justified if the vacant job involves stress. But the ability to handle an aggressive interview proves only the candidate's ability to handle an aggressive interview; it does not necessarily reveal the capacity to cope with stress and aggression outside the artificially constructed interview situation.

## Stick to the point

Do not ask irrelevant questions, and avoid 'revealing' questions, ie those which disclose your attitudes and beliefs. An example would be the question, 'I like watching football, don't you?' The candidate will probably respond in a manner calculated to impress, regardless of opinions actually held.

Two other common interviewing mistakes are comparing candidates with yourself, since you hold an overinflated opinion about your own abilities and incorrectly assume that the candidate most like yourself is best suited for the job; and applying inappropriate selection criteria. The latter might involve males who interview females associating attractive physical appearance with work ability, appointing people the interviewer knows socially, or generally assuming that one desirable characteristic in an applicant means the person is equally worthy in other respects. Well spoken candidates, for example, are not necessarily industrious. Note how this phenomenon could work in the opposite direction — an interviewer may conclude (wrongly) that weakness in one area implies lack of ability overall.

# THE JOB OFFER

Select the successful candidate carefully. Do not allow pressure of work to force you into accepting unsuitable employees — they will probably underperform and create many difficulties in the longer run (need for extra training, counselling, perhaps even the need for a transfer to a different type of work). Equally, do not appoint someone who is obviously overqualified and who will become bored and frustrated in the advertised position. Try to fit the applicant to the objective needs of the job.

Following an offer of employment a number of legal and other formalities must be completed. All employees working at least eight hours a week are legally entitled to a written statement of terms and conditions of employment within eight weeks of starting work. Under the Trade Union Reform and Employment Rights Act 1993 the following information must be included in the written statement:

(a) names and addresses of employer and employee;

(b) job title;

(c) date of commencement and the date when continuous employment began;

(d) usual hours of work;

(e) the rate of pay and how and when payment will be made;

(f) terms and conditions regarding sick pay, holiday pay and pension schemes;

(g) grievance and disciplinary procedures;

(h) a note stating the employee's right to belong or not to belong to a trade union;

(i) length of notice to be given by either side;

(j) arrangements for working overtime;

(k) any collective agreements directly affecting terms and conditions;

(l) place(s) of work;

(m) for temporary jobs, how long the employment is expected to last;

(n) for employees working abroad, the period to be spent outside the UK, the currency of payment, any additional benefits payable in consequence of working abroad, and the terms and conditions relating to the employee's return to the UK.

Contracts of employment are important because they establish the existence of an obligation to pay wages, in return for a predetermined amount of work. Breach of a contract of employment will on the one hand provide the firm with grounds for fair dismissal, and on the other enable the worker to sue for unpaid wages.

The contract is the basis of the firm's disciplinary procedures and is the ultimate determinant of the work an employee must do. Note that a 'contract' is established the instant the successful candidate accepts your offer, verbally or in writing. The written statement which follows merely confirms the details of the arrangement — although it is permissible for the statement itself to refer the employee to other documents (booklets explaining superannuation schemes, grievance procedures, etc) where issues are examined in much greater depth. In the latter case, however, the documents referred to must by law be freely available to employees.

## Changes in the contract

Once the written statement is issued, the firm cannot alter its terms and conditions without the permission of the individual worker. If it does so it is in breach of contract and the employee can claim to have been unfairly dismissed. Therefore you cannot impose new shift rosters, working hours, changes in benefits or access to appeals procedures unless the alterations are covered by the contract or the worker agrees to them (in which case the firm must alter the contents of its written statement of terms and conditions within one month of the change).

Apart from the period of notice specified in the contract, certain minimum periods are imposed by law. The Employment Protection Act demands that at least a week's notice be given to a worker with more than one month's but less than two years' service, and one extra week's notice for each year of employment thereafter (so that, for instance, a worker with eight years' service is entitled to eight weeks' notice) up to a maximum of twelve.

# INDUCTION

Fresh recruits need to know where they should go for help if they experience problems. A new entrant should be told what to do if he or she:

- has a problem with money or understanding the wage system;
- has a medical problem;
- feels that working conditions are unsafe;
- does not get on with other people in the department;
- has difficulty with the work;
- is bullied or harassed;
- has a complaint;
- does not receive adequate training.

The problem is lack of time for transmitting this information, and the unsuitability of the environment in which inductions sometimes take place. No one is capable of absorbing large amounts of (perhaps uninteresting) information in one go, so induction should be staggered.

Try to make the recruit feel welcome. Do not repeat points already made at the interview or in the written job description circulated to candidates at the time of application; rather, expand on the information the newcomer already possesses. Explain the firm's organisation structure, the recruit's duties and responsibilities, training and promotion opportunities, and so on. At some point you will have to explain expected performance and quality standards, and the norms of behaviour and protocol already established within the organisation.

Initial induction is best undertaken privately away from the workplace. The recruit should then be introduced to the people with whom he or she is to work (write their names down on a piece of paper and give it to the recruit — names are quickly forgotten on first meeting) and to the person to whom he or she is responsible. This latter individual should be instructed to help the newcomer in every way possible and to be a friend and adviser during the first couple of weeks. The recruit should feel free to approach this person at any time in order to seek guidance on any problem. Arrange to see the recruit at the end of his or her first day, and again at the end of the first week to discuss any problems experienced during induction.

# 6

# EFFECTIVE PERFORMANCE APPRAISAL

As a manager you will from time to time be involved in assessing the quality of the work of members of your department, either informally or as part of a prearranged and methodical appraisal scheme.

Without doubt appraisal is here to stay, and the overwhelming majority of large organisations (public sector as well as private firms) recognise its advantages. Accordingly the ability to conduct effective appraisals has become a core management skill, and managers are increasingly assessed on their competence at conducting appraisals. Learning how to handle appraisals is excellent preparation for progression to higher levels within a company.

## What is appraisal?

Managers frequently make *ad hoc* judgements about employees, but are loath to discuss the grounds on which the opinions are based. Performance appraisal replaces casual assessment with formal, systematic procedures. Employees know they are being evaluated and are told the criteria that will be used in the course of the appraisal. (Indeed, knowledge that an appraisal is soon to occur could motivate an employee into increased effort aimed at enhancing the outcome of the assessment.) Specifically, appraisal is the analysis of employees' past successes and failures, and the assessment of their suitability for promotion or further training. Its advantages include the following:

(a) Boss and employee are compelled to meet and discuss common work-related problems. Appraisees become aware of what exactly is expected of them and of their status in the eyes of their line managers.

(b) Appraisal monitors the feasibility of targets set by higher management, who receive valuable feedback on problems encountered when implementing policies. Thus it creates a cheap and effective early warning system within the organisation's management information structure.

(c) It enables bosses to learn about employees and the true nature of their duties. Conducting appraisals helps you to remain in touch with the staff in your department. Unknown skills and competences might be uncovered. This data can be incorporated into the firm's human resource plan and hence assist in avoiding compulsory redundancies, in career and management succession planning, and in identifying needs for employee training.

A successful appraisal is one that results in:

- reasonable targets which are mutually agreed, not arbitrarily determined;
- recognition of the employee's achievements;
- clear identification of obstacles to improved performance (organisational problems as well as individual difficulties);
- enthusiastic pursuit of measurable objectives;
- two-way communication between boss and worker.

It is important for appraisal to be seen as a staff development exercise, intended to be helpful to everyone concerned, and not as a form of restrictive control or disciplinary measure. The purpose throughout must be to assist both individuals and the organisation in improving their performances.

## TYPES OF APPRAISAL

Appraisals should investigate the appraisee's strengths and weaknesses and seek to discover fresh opportunities for improving efficiency. The reasons behind successes or failures should be discussed, and the factors preventing better performance identified.

### Open-ended reports

The least satisfactory form of appraisal is to have the appraiser prepare an overall report on the employee's general abilities without going into detail over specific issues. In this case the appraiser writes what are in effect essays about members of his or her department, structured in whatever form and at whatever length the appraiser decides and using criteria selected by the appraiser. To help guide the appraiser's thoughts, an outline structure may be imposed with suggested headings for such things as technical competence, communications ability and willingness to cooperate with others.

Although a request for such a report compels a manager to think seriously about an employee's qualities, this form of appraisal cannot be recommended, for a number of reasons:

(a) many managers have difficulty in translating thoughts about a colleague into a formal written report — their command of language might be poor (causing them to fear being ridiculed for making grammatical errors), and they might have forgotten about important aspects of the appraisee's past performance;

(b) free expression requires careful preparation, and much time will be spent on drafting the report. Managers are busy people, and might fail to complete or treat superficially this time-consuming and troublesome activity;

(c) the chosen criteria might be ill defined or inappropriate, so that comparisons between the performances of one person and others become impossible.

## Checklists

More common (and far more satisfactory) than the open-ended report is the checklist approach to appraisal. Here the appraiser is required to assess each of several characteristics mentioned on a predetermined checklist in respect of each colleague. Headings for assessment could include punctuality, reliability, enthusiasm, productivity, speed of work, accuracy of work, and so on.

A problem is that some assessors rate nearly everyone as average for most categories. Therefore the system might insist that only a specified proportion of evaluations should be placed in central categories. The scheme may require that assessors award scores from one to ten for each attribute; or assessors might allocate workers to various grades of ability (for example poor, below average, average, above average, outstanding). Alternatively the assessor may be asked to place a tick alongside one of a number of statements about the appraisee's ability in a certain area. For example, in evaluating an employee's 'initiative', the selection might be from the following range:

(a) always needs to be told what to do;

(b) frequently asks for instructions;

(c) requires supervision only occasionally;

(d) rarely requires supervision;

(e) never requires supervision;

(f) offers new ideas, initiates activity.

This method enables appraisals to be undertaken quickly, cheaply and with a minimum of effort on the appraiser's part, but it can lead to hasty, careless and hence unfair assessments. Also the list of headings on the form may not be precisely relevant to an employee's work; a vast array of characteristics might be evaluated, yet only some of them *should* be considered. Office workers, for example, do not need to be physically strong. Possession of a postgraduate educational qualification is not essential for effective performance in mundane, repetitive, assembly-line jobs.

Apart from the headings for assessment previously mentioned (productivity, accuracy, initiative, and so on), an appraisal form might ask you to consider the following attributes and characteristics:

- knowledge, skills and/or formal educational qualifications acquired and/or utilised during the review period;

- abilities to delegate, plan, supervise, establish priorities, assume responsibility, cope with stress, exercise leadership;

- personal qualities: appearance, personality, disposition, enthusiasm, compatibility with colleagues, physical make-up (health and strength);

- critical faculties: creativity, judgement, problem-solving and decision-taking abilities;

- interpersonal skills: verbal and written communication, willingness to accept new ideas, relationships with colleagues.

## Analysis of specific incidents

A third form of appraisal involves managers reporting and analysing 'critical incidents' that have occurred in the course of an employee's work during the review period. Specific cases of outstandingly good or bad performance are isolated and discussed. This method tends to ignore the worker's overall average performance, since recent events may be overemphasised. Also employees might feel they are continually being 'spied on' by management.

In order to encourage bosses not to consider only the appraisee's performance immediately preceding the review, some critical incident schemes demand that the process should focus on just two incidents from the review period: one example of outstandingly good performance, and one of outstandingly bad. The causes of the incidents, and the roles of other employees in them, are then analysed in detail during the appraisal interview.

Frequent 'negative' incidents could mean incompetence, lack of training, poor motivation, that the person does not fully understand what is expected from the job, or that he or she has been let down by others. It is intended that the careful examination of these incidents will uncover key aspects of an employee's general performance — although it might not: critical incidents may be scrutinised, but the overall ability of the subordinate may not be properly assessed.

## Potential reviews

Another kind of appraisal is the 'potential review' which seeks to predict whether an employee is capable of taking on more demanding work, and the speed at which he or she is capable of advancing. Potential reviews are necessary in order to:

(a) inform workers of their future prospects;

(b) enable the firm to draft a management succession programme;

(c) update training and recruitment requirements;

(d) advise people of what they must do to enhance their career prospects.

The task is to match employees' abilities and aspirations with the firm's forecast requirements for higher-grade staff.

A fundamental problem here is the tendency of managers to assess colleagues according to successes achieved in their current jobs, rather than on their potential for higher-level work. Someone who performs quite adequately at one level might not perform so well if promoted to a more senior post. So employees may be promoted — on the basis of their achievements in successive jobs — to the point where they cease to be effective, and by then they already occupy senior positions where their incompetence causes enormous disruption. Potential reviews should therefore be conducted by people who are capable of recognising in others aptitudes for higher management work. Further difficulties arise when selecting the criteria to be used in assessing potential. These criteria should relate to the job specifications of the positions to which those under review hope to succeed.

A negative outcome to a potential review may damage the morale of the employee involved, and for this reason some firms conduct such reviews in secret. On the other hand, knowledge of a negative outcome could stimulate the person to greater efforts and activities aimed at remedying deficiencies. Also if the firm's human resource plan does not envisage promotion opportunities for a certain employee, it is really in the employee's own interests to be advised to seek alternative work.

## Self and peer group appraisal

Appraisal might be more useful to the appraisee, and lead in the longer term to greater efficiency, if it is conducted either by the employee or by a colleague of equal occupational status. Such appraisals may analyse issues more critically than when people fear the career consequences of admitting mistakes. Appraisees state — using any of the methods previously discussed — how they regard their performance, the adequacy of the training they have received, effects of alterations in job content, perceptions of key objectives, and future aspirations. They identify their own strengths and account for their failures and weaknesses, suggesting ways in which the firm might better use their talents, skills and recently acquired experiences.

There are, of course, problems with self-appraisal, including the following:

(a) Many people are quite incapable of analysing themselves. It is unusual for individuals to assess their own competence in other walks of life. At school, college, and during the early stages of a career the individual becomes accustomed to being directed and evaluated by others. The transition from appraisee to self-assessor might require skilled and detailed guidance by someone already competent in appraisal techniques. Most appraisees in lower-level positions will have received no training in self-analysis or appraisal.

(b) To the extent that appraisals form a basis for future career development, appraisees might overstate their successes while ignoring their failings.

On the other hand, employees are compelled to think carefully about the adequacy of their contribution, about barriers preventing improved performance, their future, and the quality of their relationships with others.

# SALARY ISSUES

It is a well established principle that salary assessments should take place well after performance and potential reviews have been completed. There are two reasons for this:

(a) The purpose of an appraisal is to seek ways of improving efficiency. If salary is discussed it inevitably dominates the conversation, to the detriment of fresh ideas for enhancing productivity.

(b) Salary levels are determined in part by market forces and union pressures independent of employees' abilities. Also it may be necessary to maintain wage parity between grades and departments. These factors require separate consideration.

# HOW TO CONDUCT AN APPRAISAL INTERVIEW

As a departmental manager conducting appraisals, you need to do four things:

- *assess* the situation confronting each appraisee;
- *diagnose* the appraisee's problems;
- *improve* the capacity of the person to improve performance;
- *monitor* the success of the action plan which the two of you agree.

## Starting the conversation

You need to listen, talk and reassure. Begin the interview with an outline of its purpose, and of the assessment criteria the company has chosen to use for the appraisal. The discussion should be serious and free from outside interruption.

Be friendly; do not threaten, bully, or even hint at adverse consequences resulting from the employee's behaviour. After some non-controversial remarks designed to put the appraisee at ease, offer an opinion of how well you think he or she has performed during the review period, focusing on the most positive aspects of the person's work. Then, having congratulated your colleague on successes achieved, ask whether he or she has any thoughts about how performance might be improved. This may well elicit a statement about problems experienced without your needing directly to point out any shortcomings that you have noticed.

## Criticism

If poor performance is something you are going to have to talk about and your initial remarks do not tease out difficulties, address the topic indirectly, concentrating on the issue rather than personal failings. The employee might not be aware of expected standards or that anything is perceived as wrong. Hence you should not appear to be judgemental, or to be brushing aside the employee's explanations of certain events.

Appraisals should not be used merely to criticise workers. Negative comments need to be counterbalanced by praise for a person's achievements; if nothing good can be said about an individual then he or she should not be in the department in the first place. Criticism should be low key and constructive. If you do have to criticise, support your remarks with concrete examples of when and how things went wrong. Suggest solutions for overcoming difficulties, and invite the employee to comment on the solutions you propose. Note, however, that you should never ignore unsatisfactory performance, which should be clearly identified and thoroughly discussed. Turning a blind eye to unsatisfactory performance creates precedents for the future and makes it seem acceptable to the person concerned.

Diagnose the causes of underachievement, but without mentioning at this stage the potential consequences of continuing poor performance. Instead, root out the histories of specific problems. Ask questions, and look for signs of distress or frustration as particular issues are discussed. Always emphasise that your role is to offer constructive support, not to make ill-considered criticisms. Give the colleague lots of opportunities to ask for your help and guidance, to air grievances and discuss anxieties.

## Questions to ask

It is easy to become depressed when conducting appraisals, especially if you have to complete a large number in a short time. Appraisees are in a reactive situation and normally will sit quietly and take their direction from you. Hence you need to exhibit a positive and reassuring attitude in order to get the conversation moving and encourage the employee to talk openly about his or her work. Discussion may be slow at first, so it may be useful to ask the appraisee a few thought-provoking questions to start the conversation on a high note. A good ice-breaker is to ask which aspects of his or her job the appraisee finds most interesting and which are least interesting. Another 'old chestnut' is the question, 'What do you think you will be doing in five years' time?' Further useful questions might be:

- Do you feel you are currently working to your full potential, and if not, how could your job be altered to ensure you can make maximum use of your capabilities?

- How relevant are last year's targets for the coming period?

- What fresh targets need to be established?

- Which of your personal objectives did you not achieve over the previous review period? What prevented your achieving them?

- Which of your abilities do you exercise most frequently in your present job?

- What training might you need in order to improve your performance?

- How can I (the appraiser) personally help you to improve your performance?

- How can the firm help you to improve your performance?

- What specific changes to your work would you most like to see?

- What have you done since your last appraisal to try to improve your performance, and your ability to complete higher-level work?

The usefulness of open-ended questions in employment interviews was discussed in Chapter 5. Open-ended questions (of the type 'How do you feel about . . . ?', for example) are equally worthwhile in appraisal interviewing situations as they:

- compel the appraiser to listen and comment on the appraisee's ideas;

- stimulate discussion and elicit important information and feedback;

- demonstrate the appraiser's concern to hear the appraisee's opinions.

Another valuable category of question for use in appraisal interviews is the 'reflective' question, whereby you deliberately interrupt the flow of the employee's remarks by repeating a point the appraisee has just made, but in the form of a question. An example is the question 'So you believe that . . . ?' A reflective question is a neutral response to a (possibly provocative) statement that does not require you to say where you stand on the matter being discussed. Also it enables you to check your understanding of the appraisee's position, since he or she will quickly interrupt if you have misinterpreted the point. Reflective questions, moreover, can then lead to useful open-ended discussions.

Needs for additional training might be identified from an employee's underperformance, or conversely from the fact that the worker is clearly ready for promotion and hence requires additional skills. Questions designed to elicit an appraisee's training requirements might include:

- How adequate has the training you have received so far been in helping you to complete your present duties?

- Have you thought about extra training?

- How can we help you to develop your capacity to do higher-level work?

## Rules for conducting appraisal interviews

Always prepare for an appraisal interview. Take your time and begin the groundwork well in advance of the date set for the interview. Think carefully about what you are doing (especially the aims of the exercise) and have all relevant documents to hand. It is equally important to ensure that the appraisee properly prepares for the appraisal and does not turn up not knowing how the interview is to proceed. Indeed, it may be useful to have a brief pre-appraisal meeting simply to outline procedural matters. At the pre-appraisal discussion you can point out that the matter has to be taken seriously, but that no harm is intended and the employee has nothing to fear.

Your preparation needs to cover the items to be discussed during the interview, notably:

- targets set at the employee's last and last but one appraisal;

- the worker's job description and its current relevance to what he or she actually does;

- the skills and competences required to complete the job;

- records of training undertaken and experience obtained by the appraisee during the review period;

- your own expectations of how the employee should have performed and how these might differ from the appraisee's expectations;

- specific instances of outstanding or poor performance.

Relatively unstructured interviews are probably better for appraisal purposes. The employee should be able to challenge the accuracy or relevance of the assessment criteria, as well as the fairness of initial targets and even your objectivity as an assessor. Always stick to the following rules:

(a) Apply identical criteria to the assessment of each employee in a particular grade. Avoid favouritism, bias and stereotyping (the creation of mental images of certain categories of people and then expecting all members of those categories to be exactly the same).

(b) Ensure that all necessary information is available, and use it all in your appraisal.

(c) Be as objective as you can in interpreting information.

Unfortunately managers sometimes interpret data in ways which lead them to conclusions they have already decided to make, seeing only what they want to see, hearing only what they want to hear. Equally, managers can underestimate the difficulty of things they personally find easy, and they sometimes notice and magnify in others their own personal failings.

Targets for future activities agreed during appraisal interviews might usefully form an integral part of a department's general action plan. It is therefore essential that the colleague's future progress towards achieving these targets is monitored, since unrealistically high targets initially set during performance appraisals will inevitably result in underachievement. Certain rules apply to target setting, as discussed below.

## SETTING OBJECTIVES

An objective could be stated in terms of achieving a certain standard (ie an ongoing performance criterion such as a specified departmental staff attendance rate or the attainment of minimum quality levels) that is to be maintained indefinitely; or as an *ad hoc* goal. The advantages of bosses and employees jointly setting personal objectives are as follows:

(a) it forces everyone in the department to think carefully about his or her role and duties, about why tasks are necessary, and how best to get things done;

(b) targets are clarified and mechanisms created for monitoring performance;

(c) crucial elements are identified in each job. This information is useful for determining training and recruitment needs;

(d) personal achievements of employees are recognised and rewarded;

(e) bosses and their colleagues are obliged to communicate — in consequence, bosses can quickly identify which employees are ready for promotion and the help they will need in preparing themselves for this;

(f) performance is appraised against quantified targets, not subjective criteria;

(g) there is forced coordination of activities — between departments, between junior and senior management, and between short-term and long-term goals.

The targets set should adhere to the following guidelines:

- Targets should be precise, unambiguous and (if possible) expressed numerically. Generic objectives such as 'increase profits' or 'cut costs' are not acceptable.

- Targets should relate to the crucial and primary elements of employees' jobs and not to trivial matters.

- Targets should be consistent.

- Each target should be accompanied by a statement of how it is to be achieved, by when, the resources necessary and how and where these will be acquired.

## Problems involved in setting targets

There are of course a number of difficulties associated with target setting, including:

(a) the danger of meaningless attempts to quantify activities that are innately unquantifiable. How, for example, can the objectives of an employee whose role is purely advisory be expressed in numerical terms?

(b) possible encouragement of a shortsighted emphasis on immediate quantifiable goals to the detriment of vague but nonetheless important longer-term objectives;

(c) difficulties created through individuals not being given the information, resources or authority necessary to complete the tasks allocated to them;

(d) the enormous amount of time consumed by regular consultations between bosses and the people who work for them. A dictatorial system whereby heads of department simply impose targets on subordinates, without consultation, might be more efficient. Moreover, firms operating in highly uncertain, rapidly changing market environments may need to alter their objectives so frequently that formal target-setting procedures become impractical;

(e) tendencies of managers to pay more attention to colleagues' personal qualities than to the work done by them;

(f) possible concentration of effort on the achievement of individual rather than departmental targets.

Seek consciously to take these problems into account when employees' objectives are being formulated. Most of the difficulties can be avoided (or mitigated), at least to some extent. A good way to assess the usefulness of objectives is to ask whether they pass the SMART test, ie targets need to be:

S pecific
M easurable
A greed between boss and worker
R ealistic
T ime related

Both parties should share a common perspective on the situation intended to exist after the achievement of objectives and on how soon results may reasonably be expected.

## ACTION PLANS

Typically the outcome to an appraisal will include:

- a clear statement of the employee's objectives for the coming period (six months or a year in most cases);

- a list of queries to be followed up and investigated;

- an agreement between appraiser and appraisee concerning the support and resources to be made available to the employee to enable him or her to achieve relevant targets. It is essential that you honour any commitments you make to the appraisee in relation to the provision of extra resources, training, help with specific duties, etc.

These and other outcomes to an appraisal should be incorporated into a precise statement of the actions to be taken by the employee in order to attain agreed standards and/or specific objectives. The action plan should be SMART (see above) and in addition:

- focus on just a few key objectives (no more than four in normal circumstances);

- identify performance criteria, ie definite yardsticks against which the success or failure of the employee's future performance may be assessed;

- be in writing;

- contain 'milestones' of progress to monitor the extents to which targets have been achieved at various points.

A problem that sometimes arises is that an employee has prepared diligently for an appraisal, has worked extremely hard and generally turned in an outstanding performance, but cannot be promoted or financially rewarded because no opportunities for this are currently available. Consequently the person may become demotivated and perform unsatisfactorily from now on. Note, moreover, that sooner or later everyone must reach a 'career plateau' from which there is little possibility of advancement. The higher up an organisation an individual progresses the fewer promotion opportunities exist, so that even the most able of managers will eventually exhaust their potential. Ideally the manager will now devote total effort to achieving excellence in his or her present job, although negative reactions might occur: apathy, resentment, loss of commitment to the organisation's goals, diminishing effort, etc.

In this situation you need, wherever possible, to:

- broaden the scope of the employee's assignments;

- extend the person's responsibilities;

- have the employee act as a role model for others (eg by involving him or her in the provision of training).

## LEGAL ASPECTS OF APPRAISAL

The 1976 Race Relations Act states that it is unlawful to discriminate on racial grounds in appraisals of employee performance. Likewise, the Sex Discrimination Act 1975 makes it unlawful, unless the job is covered by an exception (see Chapter 5), to discriminate directly or indirectly on the grounds of sex or marriage in the way they afford access to opportunities for promotion, transfer or training.

So a performance appraisal system could be deemed unlawful by an industrial tribunal, with consequent compensation to aggrieved parties and forced changes in the scheme.

## Codes of practice

Both the Equal Opportunities Commission and the Commission for Racial Equality issue codes of practice covering these matters. The CRE Code recommends that staff responsible for performance appraisals should be instructed not to discriminate on racial grounds, and that assessment criteria should be examined to ensure they are not unfairly discriminatory. Similarly, the EOC Code of Practice requires that:

(a) not only should assessment criteria be examined, but also performance appraisal schemes regularly monitored to assess how they are working in equal opportunity terms;

(b) the eligibility criteria for access to training, promotion and other benefits should be periodically reviewed to ensure there is no unlawful indirect discrimination;

(c) the relationship between performance appraisals and promotion should be specified, and reasons for exclusion from the appraisal system of any group of workers predominantly of one sex should be investigated;

(d) when general ability and personal qualities are the main requirements for promotion, care should be taken to consider favourably candidates of both sexes possessing different career patterns and general experience;

(e) policies and practices regarding selection for training and/or personal development should be examined for unlawful direct and indirect discrimination. Causes of imbalance in training between the sexes should be identified. Age limits for access to training and staff development should be questioned to ensure they are not unfairly discriminatory.

## The Model Equal Opportunities Policy

The Equal Opportunities Commission has suggested that in certain cases it might not be appropriate for male managers to interpret and grade female workers' qualities of initiative, assertiveness, self-confidence, leadership ability, etc, because men and women sometimes approach these facets of personality in different ways. Women appraisees, moreover, are often older than male colleagues of equivalent rank, and their role as child-bearer may have resulted in career interruptions and prevented them from undertaking formal management training and planned experience programmes at the same time as male contemporaries.

These problems led the EOC to issue a Model Equal Opportunities Policy which recognises the difficulties that can arise from male superiors ascribing particular personality traits to the criteria to be used in assessing a person's success in a managerial job. 'It is essential', the Model Policy states (sec.4(1)), 'that managers do not make pre-assumptions that individuals because of their sex possess characteristics that make them unsuitable for employment'. Among the many examples of inappropriate preconceptions quoted in this document are the assumptions that women:

- lack commitment;
- have outside interests which would interfere with work;
- are unable to supervise others;
- possess limited career intentions;
- are unwilling to undertake further training.

Female staff, the Model Policy argues, should be actively encouraged to discuss their career prospects with departmental heads. Also, written promotion procedures stating who is responsible for promotion decisions should be made available to all employees.

# TRAINING AND STAFF DEVELOPMENT

Executive managers frequently assist in the on-job training of the people who work for them, and sometimes have to devise complete training schemes. You need to be able to identify training needs, design on-job training programmes, instruct trainees, and evaluate the effectiveness of training methods. Training is necessarily intertwined with performance appraisal and promotion systems, and involves a wide range of instructional activities. The purpose of training is to improve employees' performances in their current jobs and/or equip them for more demanding roles. It is expensive: special instructors may have to be employed, external courses must be financed, internal courses require resourcing with materials, personnel and physical facilities. And there is no guarantee that trainees will actually benefit from participating in programmes. Employees are usually unproductive while undergoing training, and there are many incidental expenses (hotel accommodation, travel, meal allowances, etc).

## WHY TRAIN?

Putting aside questions of in-company staff morale, it might not make economic sense to spend enormous sums on training existing employees for higher-level work if competent people can be recruited cheaply from outside. Equally pointless is the (not uncommon) practice of training far more employees in a certain type of work than there are vacancies in that area. This policy, while ensuring a ready supply of qualified internal applicants whenever needs for a particular skill arise, causes high labour turnover as workers become increasingly frustrated at not being able to perform the work for which they were trained.

Indeed, 'overtraining' policies can backfire, resulting in shortages of trained internal applicants for higher-level jobs.

Training seeks to improve and develop the knowledge, skills and/or attitudes of employees. Apart from the benefits accruing to the individual worker (greater versatility, extra skills, etc), many advantages accrue to the firm. Employees become more flexible, the productivity and quality of work should improve, job satisfaction might increase (with consequent reductions in absenteeism and staff turnover rates) and the business need not fear the consequences of new technology.

## HOW TO IDENTIFY TRAINING REQUIREMENTS

In the first half of the twentieth century, skilled workers acquired their abilities through apprenticeships and college courses which equipped them with knowledge and skills sufficient for their entire working lives, while unskilled employees did jobs requiring little or no training. Today, however, few people can expect to do the same work in the same way for more than a few years, and the number of jobs available for totally untrained workers has declined. You should be able to identify training needs from:

- underperformance by workers, evidenced by low-quality output, lack of initiative, bad decisions or general incompetence;

- the acquisition of new and unfamiliar equipment or the introduction of new working methods;

- perusal of employees' job specifications to identify gaps between what they are doing and what they should be doing;

- analysis of the strengths and weaknesses of your department.

Some firms prepare 'skills inventories' classifying employees according to their qualifications, technical knowledge, experience and special abilities. Such data needs to be comprehensive, detailed, held in a form that allows easy crossreferencing, and regularly updated.

Training should never be regarded as punishment for inadequate performance. If it is, the individuals concerned will resent being put on a programme, will refuse to learn and thus will not benefit from instruction. Project to employees a positive image of the training function. The need for training in new skills and the continuous refinement of existing competences should be accepted as a natural feature of working life, and you can set a good example here through personally attending training courses.

# A TRAINING PLAN

Draw up a list of each of your employees' current activities and along-side each name write a brief statement of the functions you expect that person to be undertaking in 12 months' time. Then list all the new equipment you anticipate the department will acquire over the next year and who will operate it. For each individual, ask yourself what would happen to the department's work were that person suddenly to leave the firm, how quickly you would be able to find a replacement, and what training the new recruit would require. Recall examples of outstandingly bad performance that have occurred within the department over the last few months, and list their causes. Predict likely resignations, and specify the people best able to take over the work of employees who might resign.

You should by now have a clear indication of the department's current training needs and be in a position to plan a programme having regard for the long-term career aspirations of each of your people. Define the knowledge (what the employee needs to know), skills (what he or she must be able to do) and attitudes (how the worker should perceive the job) necessary for satisfactory performance in various positions. Then detail all the training inputs required to remedy current deficiencies. You now possess a 'training specification' from which a training plan may be devised. This plan should list all your training requirements and relate them to the company's stock of human resources. Trained personnel may be available in other departments, so interdepartmental transfers could save the cost of training. Jobs need to be analysed in terms of expected standards of performance, levels of expertise required, the costs and other consequences of not using trained personnel, and the feasibility of their being done by externally recruited staff who were trained elsewhere.

In drafting a training plan, difficulties arise in selecting appropriate programmes for particular individuals. A recruit may feel that he or she should be trained for management, whereas you might think that he or she should be trained for manual work. You need, therefore, to establish a training hierarchy whereby each employee moves systematically from one course to another within a unified staff development, planned experience and promotion programme. The successful completion of a course should be viewed as a stepping stone to another and lead to new career opportunities. The plan might cover (say) the next 12 months and should specify training objectives and anticipated expenditure.

# EVALUATION OF TRAINING

You will be most involved in on-job rather than off-job training, but you still need to be able to assess whether off-job programmes are worthwhile. Define the results you expect from training — what the trainees should be able to do, and by when. Do you want your staff to learn new skills quickly (and perhaps not as thoroughly as they could over a longer time), or do you want them to be trained gradually in anticipation of new working methods? Do you want workers' attitudes to change along with their skills and knowledge?

For manual workers the success of a training programme might be quantified in terms of better productivity, higher quality of output, less absenteeism, lower staff turnover, greater adaptability, fewer accidents and less need for close supervision. Unfortunately, improved performance in many jobs is difficult to express quantitatively in the short term. And some skills acquired on courses undertaken today might not be used until the future.

Training can improve workers' morale, create better interpersonal relationships, instil in employees a sense of loyalty to the organisation, and provide other intangible benefits. Note, however, that it is not sufficient merely to ask workers whether they feel more efficient as a consequence of attending a course; hard, objective evidence is also required. Courses which participants have particularly enjoyed (especially residential courses) may be popular not because of their intrinsic educational value but because of their 'holiday camp' atmosphere, recreational facilities, friendships established among course members, and so on. Always ask the question, 'What difference would it make if this training did not take place?' If the answer is 'not much', then you must critically reassess the value of your training activities.

Relate the outcomes of training to your initial objectives and your training plan. Isolate divergences and explain why they occurred. Interview people on completion of a course and ask them whether it was relevant to their work, whether it taught them things they did not previously know, whether is was too easy or too difficult, how well supported the programme was in terms of course materials, instructors, facilities, etc, and how they think the knowledge gained will help their future careers. Keep a written record of the answers, and repeat the interview after at least six months have elapsed since finishing the course.

## TRAINING METHODS

In general, the faster a trainee acquires knowledge the better, because lower costs are then incurred. To some extent, however, you 'get what you pay for' where training is concerned. If you expect a high level of performance after an employee has completed a course you need to devise the course more carefully than if little improvement in performance is required.

*Off-job versus on-job training*

On-job training at the workplace might involve verbal instruction, demonstration of how to use tools or equipment, or simply the trainee observing someone doing a job to get the 'feel' of its characteristics. Trainees usually perceive on-job instruction as immediately and directly relevant to their work, but problems arise in controlling the quality of training; good workers may be bad instructors and the workplace might not provide a suitable environment for the efficient transmission of skills. Work flows are interrupted during demonstrations, and bad working habits can be passed on. Therefore training is sometimes undertaken off the job — either externally in a college or training centre, or within the firm in a section of the premises specially reserved for such purposes. Trainees can then learn in a relaxed, non-threatening atmosphere, free from workplace pressures and distractions. Expert trainers may be employed full time, so that technically correct methods will be taught.

Off-job training consciously seeks to provide a learning situation where people acquire skills quickly, and are not seen making mistakes by departmental supervisors and other colleagues. Simplified equipment might be installed for training purposes, and professional, systematic, step-by-step instruction can be applied. Against these advantages are the higher costs of off-job training, the artificial nature of the environment in which work is performed (possibly causing some trainees not to take the training seriously), and potential conflicts between the way a trainee is shown how to do things on the course and how the same operations are performed at the actual place of work. Full-time trainers can lose touch with current working practices. Disputes commonly occur between managers (especially workplace supervisors) and instructors about how work should be completed. Also workers may have difficulty in adjusting from the easy-going, tolerant atmosphere of an off-job centre to the high-pressure environment of a production line or busy office.

Courses at local (or national) state colleges or private training centres may be of high quality, but are not necessarily of direct and immediate relevance to an employer's needs. The curriculum and syllabus are controlled by the college, not the firm. Staff are employed by the institution, and might be unaware of a firm's particular training requirements. However, attendance at an external course does bring people into contact with participants from other firms and thus encourages a broader approach to issues. And all the course planning and administration is done by the college.

## Techniques of training

Training programmes cannot succeed unless trainees want to learn. Trainees must recognise their deficiencies and see the training offered as a means for remedying them. People who stubbornly insist they have nothing to learn will not benefit from training.

Programmes should develop steadily, and not exceed the intellectual capacities of trainees. Each participant's progress on the course should be regularly monitored, and trainees should themselves be able to assess how well they are doing. If you have to devise a programme, make the training methods as varied and interesting as possible, and involve trainees in course planning as much as you can. Do not expect too much progress in too little time; failure to allocate sufficient time for absorption of instructional material can hinder learning in the longer run. Other basic principles of learning are that the trainee should:

(a) be presented with clearly defined targets;

(b) enjoy the learning experience and thus become involved with and committed to the programme;

(c) receive reinforcement of good performance, possibly through the allocation of higher grades;

(d) be able to transfer abilities learnt in relation to one task to the completion of other similar tasks, eg a person who has learnt word processing using one software package will quickly be able to operate another.

## Coaching

This involves an experienced instructor transmitting knowledge on a one-to-one basis. The instruction is immediate, direct, and the instructor is seen to be taking a personal interest in the trainee. Account may be taken of a trainee's special needs, and the pace of instruction can be varied to suit the trainee's capacity to absorb information. A trainee can repeat difficult operations, ask questions, and gradually gains confidence as the instruction proceeds. Against these benefits are the problems of a demonstration being wasted if the trainee fails to concentrate at crucial moments, so that the entire demonstration has to be repeated; and an incompetent instructor teaching incorrect working methods.

*Lectures*

The quality of a lecture depends largely on how much preparation the lecturer has undertaken, and on his or her skill in presenting information. Inarticulate lecturers are not effective. Equally, good lectures have little impact on students who are unwilling to learn. A lecture should emphasise major points, since only a few of the points made during a lecture (about 25 per cent at most) are remembered by the audience. Most people have difficulty in concentrating on a lecture for more than an hour.

*Programmed learning*

Programmed learning consists of the presentation of instructional material in small units (called 'frames') followed immediately by a list of questions that the trainee must answer correctly before progressing to more difficult work. The questions are an integral part of the scheme, and are usually designed in such a way that it is not possible to complete the programme without answering them. If an answer is incorrect, the trainee is immediately referred back to the appropriate point in the instructional material (usually a study manual) for revision. Frames are carefully ordered in a logical progression of knowledge and levels of difficulty. Trainees move at their own pace, become actively involved in the learning process, and can do their training independently without the presence of an instructor. However, much self-discipline is needed to complete the entire programme.

As more firms employ computer-assisted management methods it becomes increasingly attractive to base training on computer software packages. The program supplied in such a package will provide for instantaneous interaction between the package and its user, and contain numerous exercises for testing the trainee's comprehension of the material.

*Interactive video*

An interactive video consists of footage of a simulated interpersonal communication (often a conflict) that maps out the background to how the situation arose, portrays actors assuming various roles, builds up to a climax and then stops abruptly leaving the viewer to provide the next step. So, for example, the film might show a production operative just about to lose his or her temper and, at the crucial moment, invite you to say how you would resolve the situation. Then you discuss your proposed solution with colleagues.

*Case studies*

Case studies simulate real-life problems previously experienced or which are expected to occur in the future. Each member investigates and reports on an aspect of the case, and is expected to assess and criticise the work of colleagues. The aim is to encourage analytical approaches to problems and to develop participants' diagnostic abilities, focusing on general principles. The understanding gained while slowly studying the case should later be able to be translated into the ability to analyse and quickly solve similar problems in the future.

*Role playing*

Role playing requires each group member to act the part of a character in a certain situation. Often the character played occupies a role opposite to that of the real-life job of the participant. Thus, for example, a personnel officer might play the role of a trade union shop steward; a production manager pretend to be a salesperson; or a purchasing manager act the role of a representative of a supplying firm. Role playing forces trainees to see issues from alternative perspectives and points of view, albeit in artificial circumstances.

# STAFF DEVELOPMENT

Staff development seeks to improve a person's overall career prospects rather than train them to perform duties necessary for their present jobs. Hence it normally comprises a series of planned training activities and work experiences designed to improve a manager's performance and equip him or her for higher-level work. Activities might include attendance at courses, job rotation, understudying (ie spending a short period as a personal assistant to a more senior manager), attachments to project committees and special working parties, and the completion of longer-term academic qualifications in the management field. Programmes may cover:

(a) background knowledge of the company, its trading environment, products, production methods, markets and personnel;

(b) administrative procedures, the legal environment, specialist techniques;

(c) management methods, analytical skills, organisation, delegation and control, time management;

(d) interpersonal skills, communication, leadership and coordination;

(e) creative abilities, decision making and problem solving.

Note that some firms insist that managerial ability cannot be taught, and that management training courses are therefore a waste of time. They argue that few courses contain material that is directly relevant and immediately applicable to real-life management situations, and that normal competition between managerial staff should ensure the 'survival of the fittest'.

In firms which do train managerial staff, new approaches to training are increasingly common — firms want to develop the initiative, self-reliance, leadership and interpersonal communication skills of managers as well as their technical abilities. An interesting recent development in the training field has been the increasing use of outdoor management training, which assumes the existence of direct parallels between the personal qualities necessary for successful management and those cultivated through participation in outdoor pursuits such as rockclimbing, canoeing, sailing or orienteering. The essential demands of these activities — planning, organising, team-building, dealing with uncertainty, direction and control — are the same, advocates argue, as those needed for management.

## TRAINING ADMINISTRATION

All governments take a keen interest in training and regularly initiate new schemes and systems. In 1990, responsibility for coordinating industrial training in various geographical areas passed to Training and Enterprise Councils (TECs), which consist of local company managing directors and other senior business executives (who participate on a voluntary basis) plus a salaried civil servant. There are about 80 TECs in the UK. Their task is to provide the country with a skilled work-force. To achieve this they contract training providers (eg local colleges) to deliver courses and other training that correspond to specifications laid down by the area TEC. The aim is to match the training provided to the needs of local businesses. TECs do not themselves run training courses.

The other major event in the training field over recent years was the establishment of the National Council for Vocational Qualifications (NCVQ), a government body set up to implement a national system for vocational qualifications and to determine standards of occupational competence on a national level. Examining bodies desiring NCVQ accreditation must develop courses that satisfy NCVQ criteria, which are laid down by 'lead bodies' for various industries or occupations. A lead body is a committee comprising representatives of professional bodies, government departments and major businesses connected with the industry or occupation concerned. Its role is to devise criteria for measuring the competence of employees in a particular field. NCVQ does not itself award certificates or diplomas. Rather, it 'hallmarks' approved qualifications, indicating thereby that the holder has attained a certain prespecified level of knowledge, skill and understanding of a certain subject.

NCVQ-approved qualifications have to be competence based, ie the training undertaken must contribute directly to a person's ability to complete a job. Thus courses need to cover all the 'elements of competence' associated with a specific type of work. Elements of competence are descriptions of actions, behaviours, outcomes, or knowledge of what should be done in a workplace situation. These elements are then collected into 'units of competence' that form the basis of an NCVQ-recognised award. Each unit of competence is accompanied by 'performance criteria', ie definitions of what trainees should be able to do on completion of the training.

# 8

# SPECIAL PROBLEMS

This chapter deals with a number of common disciplinary and counselling problems facing managers who have to control other people.
Some of these are widespread and familiar (persistent absenteeism
and/or lateness, for example); others (such as alcohol and drug abuse
by employees, helping individuals who are HIV positive, dealing with
theft and vandalism) are among the most serious issues confronting
modern society. Organisations cannot close their eyes to these problems and must ensure that their managements are given adequate training and advice to cope with them. Fortunately a number of
government-sponsored codes of practice exist to guide managers on
how best to cope with these problems. Their contents are outlined in
the following pages, together with general advice.

## ABSENTEEISM

The cost to British industry of employee absenteeism is alarming.
Estimates suggest that the average UK worker takes 11 days off per
year, and that on any given day up to 7 per cent of the workforce of a
typical large British company will be absent — four times the rate
among UK industry's leading international competitors. Britain is
losing 200 million working days each year to deliberate non-attendance.

Specific losses attributable to absenteeism include reduced production, sick pay, the need for additional overtime to cover for absent
workers, problems resulting from having to reschedule projects, failure
to meet deadlines and additional clerical and supervision expenses (telephone calls, administering statutory sick pay, etc). Absenteeism also
generates less tangible costs, including low morale among colleagues
who see others 'swinging the lead', loss of team spirit (critically important in today's business world), plus overwork and stress for certain
individuals (perhaps causing these people then to be absent).

A number of factors contributing to high rates of absenteeism have been identified, including job dissatisfaction, individual inclination not to attend work, and bad personal relationships within groups of workers. Other factors include poor physical conditions, boredom, inadequate supervision, stressful environments and/or inconvenient working hours. Further determinants are said to be:

- travelling difficulties and/or distance from work;

- a person's general state of health;

- the sex, age, and length of service of the employee (young people and females have higher absenteeism rates on average than others, long-serving workers lower rates);

- availability of sick pay;

- whether an employee has extensive family responsibilities.

## Tackling absenteeism

The first and perhaps most important thing to do to control absenteeism is to maintain careful records that identify individuals and types of work with the highest absenteeism rates. Thereafter you need see whether it is possible to redesign employees' jobs to make them more interesting (by giving people a wider variety of tasks to perform or greater responsibility, for example); to introduce job rotation, flexitime and job sharing arrangements in appropriate situations; or perhaps to increase employee participation in decision making. Recruitment and selection procedures should always try to determine job applicants' attitudes towards absenteeism from work.

The ACAS Code on Disciplinary Procedures (see Chapter 9) has a separate section on absenteeism which — after incompetence — is perhaps the commonest source of disciplinary action. Unauthorised absenteeism from work is a breach of contract in that the absent worker has reneged on the obligation to be at work during contractually agreed working hours. Occasional unwarranted absences do not normally justify dismissal (unless there are strict rotas, safety hazards or demonstrable interruptions in production due to absenteeism). And even if the absenteeism (or lateness) is persistent, action can only be taken after formal written warnings (the ACAS Code recommends at least two) have been issued and full disciplinary procedures invoked.

The first written warning might be a confirmation of a formal verbal warning. It should state that on a certain date you warned the individual (a man, say) about his absences from work, that he provided no excuse for his behaviour, and that you expect him to improve — otherwise you will have no choice but to invoke the disciplinary procedure. The next letter will remind the employee of the first, will point out that attendance has not improved and specify the dates the employee was unjustifiably absent. In closing the letter you should state that if he is again absent without good cause within (say) the next three months then a final warning may be issued and that any absenteeism after that could result in dismissal. The final written warning will refer to the previous warnings, and again specify the dates of further absences. It should point out that previous warnings were ignored, that no satisfactory explanations have been offered (but that if any exist you should be informed immediately) and that he will be dismissed if he is absent without permission during the next three months. The next time he is absent he should be suspended pending a full disciplinary hearing as outlined in Chapter 9.

Paragraph 38 of the ACAS Code recommends that absences should be investigated promptly, that the worker should be invited to explain his or her absences indicating any mitigating circumstances, that domestic circumstances should be taken into account where relevant, and that if — following warnings — the employee's attendance does not improve then his or her age, length of service, past performance, likelihood of reform, availability of alternative work where attendance is not so crucial, and the effect of absences on the firm's overall operations should all be taken into account when deciding an appropriate course of action.

A sanction must be 'reasonable' in the context of the circumstances of the offence. Actions taken should be recorded on the worker's personal file, with full details of the offence and the reasons for your decision. However, the Code insists that except in special circumstances (agreed between management and union), records of breaches of disciplinary rules should be discarded after some predetermined period of satisfactory conduct.

## Keep absenteeism in its proper perspective

Although employee absenteeism is troublesome, annoying and financially expensive, it is important not to become obsessed with the issue. Monitoring and checking the validity of each and every absence can be enormously time consuming, and proving that a particular absence was improper may be virtually impossible. Also the constant questioning of employees on these matters could create an oppressive, unpleasant and unproductive working environment. More important are employee attitudes and the creation of an organisational environment where people feel that it is wrong to take time off without justification.

### Creating the right climate

A work environment conducive to low rates of absenteeism will normally be one in which:

- managers at all levels within the organisation visibly set a good example in relation to absenteeism;

- absenteeism is openly discussed (during appraisals, for example);

- employees with poor attendance records are given genuine help in overcoming their absence problems;

- management does not shirk from taking justifiable disciplinary action against workers with bad absence records;

- employees with excellent attendance records are openly praised and rewarded so that they can act as role models for other workers;

- every employee is given personal responsibility for something;

- the tasks undertaken by employees are varied and interesting.

## ALCOHOL ABUSE

It is, of course, none of your business how other people conduct their private lives. Yet some problems experienced by colleagues outside working hours — problems related to alcohol or drug abuse, for example — will almost certainly affect their performance at work. Departmental managers confront these situations directly. You cannot avoid becoming involved if members of your team cease to function effectively because of personal difficulties.

There are numerous agencies, special clinics, professional counselling services and advisory bodies to assist people afflicted by the illness of alcoholism. Yet the simple fact is that victims rarely seek outside help unless compelled (or heavily encouraged) to do so. Instead, they look for informal help, relying on friends and colleagues — like yourself — whom they already know and trust and with whom they feel confident. You are, like it or not, an important part of the afflicted person's life-support system.

## Consequences of alcohol abuse

Excessive drinkers generally have higher rates of absenteeism from work, are unpunctual, take more sick leave, and are involved in more industrial accidents than non-drinkers. Their ability to concentrate and sustain effort is affected and, in the longer term, their physical health is damaged. Alcoholics are more than ten times more likely to contract cirrhosis of the liver than non-drinkers, and are likely to suffer from inflammation of the pancreas, various ulcers, gastritis, and several types of blood and neurological disorders. It is reasonable to expect that alcoholic employees are less productive than others and, at the managerial level, less competent to take important decisions.

Alcoholism is a disease, requiring proper treatment if it is not to become worse. Yet those affected are not usually able to give up drinking independently; the more a person needs to stop drinking the less he or she is likely to be able to do so. If a member of your team abuses alcohol it is almost certain that your section's work will suffer since the effects of alcohol persist during the (working) hours the individual is not drinking. His or her intellectual capacity declines, as does the ability to communicate with others and the accuracy of perceptions of other people's attitudes. Alcoholics are typically unreliable, prone to irrational behaviour and frequently depressed.

Most problem drinkers have jobs, but on average are also five times more likely to be absent through sickness, and three times more likely to experience an accident than other workers. The danger is that since heavy drinkers are often personally likeable people, and because of the positive image that social drinking enjoys, problems such as frequent lateness, missed meetings, uncompleted work, etc will initially  be ignored. But when an employee's drinking reaches the point where he or she is unable to work efficiently, the worker is arbitrarily dismissed! You should try to prevent this from happening. Apart from your losing a colleague, the firm also loses all the training and expertise embodied in the employee. And bear in mind that the circumstances which caused your colleague to begin drinking heavily might one day apply to you.

Indications that someone has a serious drink problem include regular late arrival at work with a hangover, irritability, forgetfulness, inattention, lunchtime drinking followed by poor performance in the afternoon, and personality changes. Alcohol is a short-term stimulant but long-term depressant. Immediately after a drinking session the individual may be sociable and alert, but not for long. Work efficiency declines, and with it the worker's self-esteem. He or she will apologise repeatedly for letting you down. But the problem will worsen, until eventually the individual will not be able to undertake any routine duties without first having a drink.

### How to deal with an alcoholic employee

There is little point in warning alcoholic employees about the likely consequences of continuing drunkenness, since warnings simply upset them and cause them to feel even more wretched and inadequate than before — and thus more likely to seek relief in drink. Equally, however, you should *not* put up with drunken behaviour, otherwise the afflicted person will get worse, placing intolerable burdens on working colleagues.

As alcoholics deteriorate, their behaviour causes them to become unpopular with workmates, leading to social isolation, self-pity and hence further alcohol abuse. At first you may be tempted to protect your colleague, believing that the problem is temporary and bound to improve. Indeed, you might expend a great deal of energy on covering up, finding excuses for his or her non-appearance at committees, explaining absences, and so on. But in the end you are bound to fail. Accept that your colleague is ill, and look to a proper and established procedure for dealing with the problem.

### The DHSS code of practice

The UK Department of Employment, the DHSS and the government Health and Safety Executive have jointly issued a set of guidelines (under the title *The Problem Drinker at Work*) for dealing with alcoholic employees. These guidelines recommend that firms have an alcohol policy and that:

(a) the policy should be agreed jointly by management and workers' representatives, not arbitrarily imposed;

(b) alcoholism should be regarded as a health rather than a disciplinary problem (although a disciplinary matter may have initiated the procedure). Personnel needing assistance should be assured of appropriate aid and support;

(c) individuals seeking help should *not* face the possibility of losing their jobs, nor should their terms and conditions of employment be altered;

(d) either the firm should offer treatment via its own medical services or, if it does not possess sufficient resources for this, refer the case to a specialist treatment unit.

Like all government-backed codes of practice and policy recommendations, HSE guidelines do not carry the force of law but, when adjudicating cases, courts and tribunals will ask whether they have been
followed. Thus although drunkenness on the job and/or diminished
work performance due to the effects of drink do provide and always
have provided grounds for 'fair' dismissal under the headings of
'misconduct' or 'incapability' (see Chapter 9), tribunals — under the
influence of HSE recommendations — increasingly lean towards interpreting alcohol abuse as a sickness rather than as a disciplinary offence.
Chronic sickness leading to poor performance at work can itself lead to
'fair' dismissal, but tribunal decisions have established that a definite
procedure must be followed in this case:

(a) The position should be discussed with the worker to ascertain
whether there is any chance of improvement.

(b) Proper medical advice must be obtained, and the worker given the
chance to refute the medical opinions stated (perhaps by presenting
evidence from another qualified medical practitioner).

(c) The employer must consider whether any other post is available or
likely to become available where the worker's ill-health would not
be a problem.

Note, however, that the above procedure need only be followed if the
employee has a bad record for sickness for which he or she is not
responsible. Thus while tribunals have insisted that alcoholics — as
'sick' people — should be treated with patience and consideration, no
tribunal would (I presume) ever decide that alcohol abuse was not the
individual's own fault. Another factor militating against problem
drinkers is that under the 1974 Health and Safety at Work Act,
employers have a statutory duty to provide a safe working environment, as well as their being under a common law duty to take 'reasonable care' to ensure the health and safety of employees. Alcohol abuse
impairs judgement, encourages slapdash approaches to safety, and
causes accidents. An employer who does not act against an excessively
heavy-drinking employee may be accused of breaching — by neglect —
health and safety law.

A firm's alcohol policy should apply equally to all grades of staff, not
just management. It should be written, and widely circulated specifying
the help available and the procedure for obtaining (confidential) assistance.

# AIDS

The numbers of employees of both sexes contracting the HIV virus are, alas, increasing sharply and today no company can assume that none of its workers will succumb to the illness. The best advice for managers who have to deal with members of staff who are HIV positive is that they follow the Department of Employment (DOE) guidelines on this matter, published under the title *AIDS and Employment* and available from HMSO. These guidelines include model procedures for employers to follow and which seek to help firms avoid unfair discrimination. Specific recommendations stated in the guidelines are that:

1. victims shall not be required to disclose the fact that they have the virus (unless there exist genuine risks of infecting other workers); and

2. employees with AIDS-related diseases shall not be treated differently to anyone else suffering from a serious illness.

The dismissal of those who are HIV positive because other workers refuse to work with them will normally represent unfair dismissal, unless there is a demonstrable risk of spreading infection (eg if the employee works with blood products).

# THEFT

Theft by employees is a significant cause of financial loss to many companies. Some employees, moreover, steal from fellow workers, creating an atmosphere of mistrust, suspicion and unpleasantness within the firm. Thieves are occasionally caught; and it is usually the head of department who must deal with the matter in the first instance.

## Meaning of theft

'Theft' is defined in law as the dishonest appropriation of someone else's property with the intention of permanently depriving the other person of that property. But it is not 'dishonest' to appropriate property if the person taking it genuinely believes that the property belongs to him or her, or believes that the owner has given or would give consent to its removal. Great ambiguity can therefore arise over whether something has been 'stolen' when — as is common in many firms — employees have free access to materials or equipment and frequently take work off the premises, including work taken home in the evenings or at weekends. Similarly, occasional 'borrowing' of small amounts from petty cash or a till is considered acceptable in many firms, with the proviso, of course, that the money is quickly repaid. Nevertheless, theft means taking anything that does not belong to the taker if he or she has no intention of giving it back. So using the telephone at work for personal calls, keeping things that are found, even not returning excess change to a customer, are all cases of 'theft'.

## Dealing with a thief

In principle, an employee who steals may be fairly dismissed on the grounds that such conduct causes irreversible damage to the business. There is, however, much legal ambiguity in this respect. If the theft is serious and the case against the worker strong, then he or she may be dismissed under existing legislation provided the employer carries out a 'reasonable' investigation into the circumstances of the theft. An immediate investigation is essential because if the matter is reported to the police and the employee consequently charged, the trial might not be scheduled for many months in the future and any interviews with witnesses conducted by the firm's representatives during the interim could be construed as interference with the course of justice. A conviction for theft not connected with the worker's employment might still be grounds for fair dismissal, as long as the firm can demonstrate that its public reputation would suffer or that trade or insurance terms would be adversely affected by the continuing employment of the convicted person.

## Why people steal

Why do people steal? There is no simple answer to this question. Indeed, it is a question that has perplexed philosophers, theologians, psychiatrists and the penal authorities for generations. Among the more common causes of theft by employees are the following.

(a) *Hatred of the employing institution* — a desire to 'get one's own back' for perceived injustices (low pay, being passed over for promotion, poor relationships with colleagues and/or management, etc) committed in the past.

(b) *Shortage of money* — caused by circumstances not related to work or through low wages inducing the employee to 'top up' his or her wages by stealing from the firm.

(c) *The 'Robin Hood syndrome'* — a desire to punish better-off colleagues for being better-off. Thieves often justify this notion by saying that most people are insured against theft, or that wealthier colleagues can afford to lose small amounts.

(d) *Temptation* — caused by poor security (unlocked offices, valuables left lying around) leading to 'opportunistic' theft.

(e) *Excitement* — the exhilaration of taking risks and not being caught.

## Counselling an employee caught stealing

Suppose there is an outbreak of stealing within your department, and that you catch the person responsible (a young man, say). If it is a first offence and the extent of the theft is not too serious you will probably want to give him a second chance, on both moral and efficiency grounds (cost of recruiting a replacement, loss of skills and experience embodied in that man, waste of training expenditures, etc). He must repay whatever he stole, but thereafter should be counselled to discover the causes of his errant behaviour and to encourage in him the desire to amend his ways.

A good way to begin an interview with the thief is to have the man describe, in detail, what he did the day before the theft occurred, how he felt on the morning of the day the offence was committed, and his thoughts and actions after the event. This simulated action replay will help both of you to understand the core motives underlying his behaviour, and the patterns of interpersonal interaction associated with the theft.

To gain an understanding of your subordinate's state of mind, ask him to list the people from whom he would *not* steal. Would he steal from his parents, his wife and children, his immediate workmates, yourself — and how does he explain differences in his willingness to steal? How far is he prepared to go? If he is prepared to steal a colleague's umbrella, would he steal the same colleague's wallet, or his or her car? Would he be prepared to enter a workmate's home and steal from there? Would he steal from workmates' families? Ask him if he would steal from his own close friends if he were absolutely certain of not being caught. Ask whether he would only steal only small amounts from friends, but large amounts from others. Answers to these questions may provide valuable insights into why your subordinate steals. It may be that he steals during moments of emotional distress — just after arguments with colleagues, for example. Is his behaviour compulsive, or does he feel it can be controlled?

Next, point out the potential financial cost of his behaviour. Add up the value of the items you know he has stolen, and deduct this amount from the value of (say) two years' loss of wages (emphasise the difficulties a thief, without work references, will experience in getting another job) less his estimated social security benefit. Then mention the shame, humiliation, loss of occupational status, etc associated with being dismissed for theft. Tell your subordinate to list all the things he finds attractive about stealing (excitement, financial benefits, etc) and all the reasons for not stealing (fear of discovery, a police record, loss of status in the eyes of other people, and so on). Ask whether he still thinks that stealing is worthwhile.

## Suspension of employees suspected of theft

For more serious situations the usual procedure is to suspend a suspected thief (on full pay) pending a preliminary investigation. However, you should only do this if you are dealing with an apparently open and shut case. The fact that a person is suspended implies guilt, and he or she will carry that label even if subsequently proven innocent. Nevertheless, suspension is better than summary dismissal because it avoids legal complications.

After the preliminary investigation, the employee should either return to work, or be dismissed — it is not generally possible to suspend a worker without pay (say until a criminal prosecution has come to court) unless this provision is formally embodied in his or her contract of employment, since refusal to pay wages constitutes a breach of the employment contract and is therefore tantamount to dismissal. Hence a worker suspended without pay can claim unfair dismissal in an industrial tribunal; and this case will be heard quite separately from and independent of the criminal proceedings. It could even be possible for someone to be found guilty in a criminal prosecution, but for a tribunal to rule that the worker has been unfairly dismissed. For example, the 'theft' may have been trivial but the firm wished to 'make an example' of someone and in so doing acted — in the view of the tribunal — in an 'unreasonable' manner.

## Searching and detention

An employee suspected of theft cannot legally be searched without his or her consent unless the search is conducted by the police, or agreement to submit to a search is incorporated into that person's contract of employment. In the latter case, refusal to be searched constitutes grounds for fair dismissal. The firm's own vehicles can be searched at will, but a vehicle owned by an employee cannot be searched without the employee's permission. You cannot arrest and detain an employee unless you have 'reasonable grounds' for suspecting that he or she has committed a criminal offence. Otherwise the worker can sue your firm for wrongful arrest and imprisonment.

Unless you have been properly trained in these matters, do not attempt to extract a written statement from anyone who is not willing to provide this voluntarily. Statements are obviously useful, as they can be presented in evidence in legal proceedings. Someone who admits a theft might therefore be invited to sign a document confirming verbal statements in order to clarify issues and prevent subsequent arguments about who said what. But a court will not accept as evidence any statement obtained through bullying or oppression.

If during your initial interview with the suspected thief you start writing down what he or she says — with a view to using these notes in a subsequent prosecution — then you are obliged to tell the suspect of this intention and you should take a note of the point at which you issued the warning. All internal disciplinary procedures must follow the rules of natural justice (see Chapter 9).

## SEXISM

Sexism at work may arise from inappropriate perceptions of the role of women, or from institutional barriers in relation to recruitment, selection of employees for training or promotion, operation of appraisal and grievance procedures, etc. Among the special problems sometimes confronting working women, the following are particularly worthy of mention.

- The need to balance continuity of employment (and hence the acquisition of skills and experience during the early stages of a career) against requirements to take time out from the workforce for child-bearing and initial child-rearing. A woman who leaves the workforce for (say) four or five years in order to have a family is then that many years 'behind' her male contemporaries when she resumes her career. Note how management recruitment and development programmes are typically designed for young college leavers rather than for slightly older women with families.

- The assumption that family commitments will cause a woman to take more time off work than male colleagues.

- Possible discriminatory sexual stereotyping by existing male senior managers, who might assume that a woman's role is to look after home and family and not to manage organisations.

- Lack of female role models for women managers to emulate. The higher a woman rises within an organisation the fewer female colleagues of equivalent rank she is likely to have.

- The existence within some organisations of exclusively male networks and informal communication systems which provide help and support to male employees but not to women.

Practical measures for avoiding sexual discrimination at the workplace include:

- monitoring the numbers of men and women at various grades within a department to check whether there is roughly equal representation and, if not, the precise identification of the reasons for disparities;

- conscious recognition by management that older women who have taken time out for child-rearing duties are just as valuable to the firm and have exactly the same capacities for acquiring skills and useful work experiences as their younger male colleagues;

- encouraging female staff to attend courses and to apply for promotion;

- organisation of work schedules, responsibilities and functions in order to allow female staff greater flexibility in their working hours, especially during school holidays.

It is especially important that male heads of department do not participate in sexist conversations among their male subordinates, do not share sexist jokes, and make it known that they will deal sympathetically with women subordinates' complaints of sexual harassment via grievance and/or disciplinary procedures.

## RACISM

Departmental managers may experience the effects of racism either through complaints received from ethnic minority workers, or through a racist (or sexist) atmosphere created by unpleasant remarks, racist 'jokes', unofficial segregation of racial groups, and covert discriminatory practices. Some organisations now incorporate anti-discrimination clauses into their disciplinary codes, with explicit provision for the suspension, and ultimately the dismissal, of staff who engage in discriminatory behaviour. Without doubt, formal rules can prevent some discriminatory practices, but they do not necessarily change attitudes towards various racial groups. Rules against racially or sexually abusive language are especially useful, since abuse of this nature inhibits minority group employees from participating enthusiastically in work groups and encourages non-acceptance of minorities by the existing staff.

You should never participate in racially offensive conversations, and you must not be seen to be influenced by racist remarks. Listen sympathetically to grievances from affected minority group individuals, and visibly support them in pursuing their complaints. Examine your induction courses and procedures to ensure that all new entrants are made equally welcome regardless of race, sex, or indeed any other distinguishing characteristic (physical disability, for example). How many ethnic minority workers are employed in less attractive jobs? Do they receive on average lower pay than other employees, and if so, why? How many of your direct and immediate colleagues — the ones with whom you share confidences and jointly take decisions — are from ethnic minorities?

Ask yourself, honestly, whether you expect different standards from minority group employees. How do their qualifications compare with the level of work they undertake? Are your ethnic minority subordinates less inclined to discuss their work with you, or to approach you with problems, and if so, why?

## Application of disciplinary procedures

The Race Relations Act 1976 makes it unlawful to discriminate racially in the operation of disciplinary procedures, for example by victimising (ie treating less favourably) a person for having complained about racial discrimination or having given evidence about such a complaint. The Commission for Racial Equality's Code of Practice recommends that in applying disciplinary procedures consideration should be given to the possible effect on an employee's behaviour of the following:

- racial abuse or other racial provocation;
- communication or comprehension difficulties;
- difficulties in cultural background or behaviour.

In particular, required standards of behaviour should take account of the cultural and religious needs of certain ethnic minorities. For example, a Sikh should not be disciplined for having long hair and a beard or for refusing to abandon his turban to comply with company uniform requirements.

Test cases in the courts seem to have established the principle that special considerations apply to constructive dismissals in race (or sex) harassment situations. Thus if a worker complains that he or she has been racially abused and insists that you discipline the offending worker, and you refuse or demonstrably fail to apply appropriate sanctions against the culprit, then the victim of the harassment can resign, claim constructive unfair dismissal, and will almost certainly win compensation.

The 1975 Sex Discrimination Act (Sec.4(1)(2) and (3)) similarly renders illegal the disciplining of individuals for having complained or helped others to complain about sex or marriage discrimination. And it is illegal to dismiss someone on the grounds of sex or whether or not they are married. Paragraph 32(a) of the Equal Opportunities Commission's Code of Practice recommends that care be taken to ensure that members of one sex are not disciplined or dismissed for 'performance or behaviour that would be overlooked in the other sex'.

# DRUG ABUSE

Some people turn to drugs other than alcohol (or tobacco for that matter) to help them cope with the stresses of work or other social circumstances. Others use drugs because they are attracted to drug-related lifestyles. Yet more are enticed by the state of euphoria that certain drugs provide. Persistent use of drugs, whether taken under medical prescription (as with tranquillisers and certain antidepressants) or illegally (use of heroin for example) may affect adversely the user's performance at work. While drugs in the short term enable users to overcome anxiety, tension, and perhaps even significant emotional distress, their protracted use causes dependence — eventually to the extent that users cannot survive a single working day without their use. All addictive drugs affect judgement, perception and the ability to concentrate. Tranquillisers cause doziness and lethargy; heroin, cocaine and other psychotic drugs have profound and lasting physical and mental effects.

Use of narcotics relieves anxiety, creating feelings of detachment from everyday worries and great personal wellbeing. Addiction may or may not be physical (depending on the nature of the substance used) but will always have a psychological dimension.

## Effects of persistent drug use

Among the many harmful physical effects of the persistent use of non-prescribed narcotics are frequent nausea and vomiting, severe loss of appetite leading to rapid weight loss, lack of energy and loss of interest in surroundings; dangers of blood and liver infections, plus the danger of contracting HIV caused by injection into the bloodstream using shared dirty needles; plus a variety of illnesses associated with impurities in the substances with which the drug is mixed.

Physical dependence is evidenced by unpleasant withdrawal symptoms when the drug is no longer available. These begin 8–24 hours after the last dose and are characterised by feelings of great anxiety, physical weakness, aches and pains similar to those experienced with a bad attack of 'flu, plus diarrhoea. More severe withdrawal symptoms include acute cramp, inability to sleep or eat, and alternately shivering and sweating. The worst phase is usually over in 24 hours, but in extreme cases it can last for over a week. Yet despite these horrors, ex-drug users frequently return to the habit after their physical addiction has gone — users become psychologically addicted to the drug, missing the mental euphoria it creates. The drug acts as a sedative that blocks out mental anguish; it blunts the central nervous system and thus generates a false sense of emotional wellbeing. In consequence, ex-users crave for the relaxed peace of mind, exhilaration and freedom from worldly cares that the narcotic artificially provides.

## The drug user at work

Drug problems at work are sometimes compared to alcohol abuse. The analogy is inappropriate, for two reasons:

1. Whereas the sale and consumption of alcohol are entirely legal, the possession of narcotic drugs is a criminal offence. Drug users, therefore, will not normally discuss their habit with non-users.

2. Lay people typically feel they lack sufficient knowledge of drug-related addictions to be able to do anything of practical value to help. Everyone experiences alcohol, but few people have experienced non-prescribed illegal drugs. Thus whereas many managers feel confident and at ease when discussing alcohol, they feel great discomfort when discussing drugs. A head of department might honestly believe he or she can influence a heavy drinker into giving up alcohol, but despair at the prospect of helping someone to abandon hard drugs.

Consequently, employees who would be helped if they were alcoholics — in accordance with a procedure similar to that previously outlined — are summarily dismissed for job inadequacy caused by drugs. This is a pity, because much can and needs to be done to help drug-addicted employees. Drug abuse in Britain is growing alarmingly. And as drug usage expands, manifestations of drug abuse will be increasingly evident at work.

The fact that someone is seriously abusing hard drugs will soon become apparent: loss of interest in personal appearance, weight loss, frequent absences, slow and halting speech, drowsiness and inability to concentrate, and a collection of symptoms very similar to those experienced with a heavy cold — coughing, reddened eyes, running nose, and so on. Behaviour in general will change.

## Helping an employee on hard drugs

Conventional disciplinary measures are essentially useless in the case of serious drug abuse. Drug addicts rarely cease to be addicts for fear of suspension or the sack, but drug abusers do often want to be rid of their habit (usually because of a crisis: an overdose, being arrested by the police, acute lack of money, etc). You will encounter a colleague's drug abuse either through a single dramatic incident that clearly indicates he or she has a drug problem affecting performance at work; or you will notice signs of drug abuse. In the former case, counselling should occur immediately and by compulsion. In the latter situation you will have to raise the subject yourself. Do this frankly and as quickly as possible. The following guidelines might be useful for counselling someone who is clearly using hard drugs:

1. Maintain total confidentiality. Apart from the legal implications of drug abuse, society overall does not yet accept that drug addiction is as much an illness as a misdemeanour; so drug abusers are harassed much more than heavy drinkers. You will not be able to help unless the confidentiality of the conversations you have with the afflicted person is guaranteed.

2. Point out the benefits of breaking the habit (even if the person involved is an 'occasional' user with only a light addiction) no matter how distressing the experience. A hard drug takes everything from the user, yet offers little of lasting value in return. It temporarily suppresses the natural emotional defence mechanisms (anxiety, depression, etc), but at a fearful price in the longer run. Without the drug — which itself has severely debilitating and dangerous physical effects — the addict becomes ill and experiences great mental anguish. And the physical effects are felt intensely because deprivation increases the body's sensitivity to pain.

Likely responses from an occasional user are that narcotic drugs are less physically damaging than tobacco or alcohol (which in aggregate terms is true); and that although hard drugs are illegal, no one has the moral right to prevent others from regulating the state of their own mind.

The counterargument is twofold. First, as a manager you are concerned only with performance at work and you cannot allow the person's work to continue to decline (as it surely must) for the sake of other members of the team. Secondly, narcotics are vastly more addictive than other drugs, including tobacco and alcohol. Occasional light use is extremely likely to degenerate to more serious addiction. And if the employee had not been adversely affected by the drug the two of you would not be having the conversation!

## Giving up

Another point to emphasise is the frequently ignored fact that (according to the UK Institute for the Study of Drug Dependency) most people who give up drugs do so of their own accord, and without medical supervision. Gradual cutting down is possible, given some self-control, for light users. You must of course advise your colleague to see a doctor or otherwise seek specialist help, but equally you have to be prepared to recognise that many drug users are not willing to go this far, since to do so requires them to admit openly their dependence on the drug.

Thereafter, the victim must seek independently to change his or her lifestyle (as must the dried-out alcoholic). Without a personal commitment, no one else can help. The individual must avoid contact with other drug users, responsibilities have to be faced, fundamental causes of emotional distress confronted. These longer-term adjustments are not, and cannot be, any of your concern. All you can do is offer sympathy and support during the immediate transition.

# VERBAL ABUSE AND PHYSICAL VIOLENCE

Violence occurs when someone hits another person, no matter how lightly, for any reason whatsoever. It is an offence for which employees may be fairly dismissed, but the test of 'reasonableness' must always be applied. Thus, for example, an employee might challenge a dismissal for fighting on the grounds that it was merely self-defence against an unprovoked attack using the minimum force necessary. The dismissal would be 'fair' only if you could prove that this was not the case. Other matters that must be considered when assessing 'reasonableness' are whether the violence was serious (horseplay among employees is unlikely to justify dismissal); and the status of the employee (did, for example, the aggressor attack a supervisor, a senior manager, a subordinate, or a fellow worker of equivalent grade — a tribunal would probably consider it unfair to dismiss a lower-ranking person for fighting with a supervisor who is not also dismissed). You need to collect all the facts relating to the incident, statements from witnesses and from the people involved (particularly in relation to provocation), the extent of retaliation, and whether there was racial or sexual abuse.

## Threatening behaviour

Swearing at people and other forms of threatening behaviour short of physical violence might also justify dismissal, provided it is serious and persistent and you act 'reasonably' when deciding to dismiss. The dismissal itself will be for 'misconduct'; which (as mentioned in Chapter 9) is a legally nebulous term. Thus whether misconduct has actually occurred is more a question of fact than of law. Each set of circumstances must be considered separately, especially in relation to the following points:

(a) Is this the first time the employee has engaged in violence and/or abuse and threatening behaviour? If not, were previous incidents ignored and if so, why?

(b) Is the offence (particularly if it only involves swearing at someone) substantial in relation to the employee's job? Can it really be said to have disrupted working relationships or staff harmony, and to represent in effect a repudiation by the employee of his or her contractual obligation to serve the employer and work properly?

(c) Were there any extenuating circumstances, such as ill-health, or the worker being under emotional stress at the time of the incident?

(d) Has the employee expressed remorse for the action?

Disciplinary action is legally justified in the case of bad language only if it is so wilfully offensive that it may reasonably be assumed to distress the person to whom it is addressed. Thus a tribunal might rule that words used in the company of somebody occupying one occupational status (a female senior manager, for example) are unacceptably disagreeable, whereas the same words used in other circumstances (if, for instance, a worker abuses another of the same grade) are words used 'as a matter of course' and therefore acceptable.

Violent acts committed outside working hours could justify dismissal, but only if the incident can be proved to have affected the reputation of the employing firm. For example, a man working with young children might be fairly dismissed if he is convicted for child molestation in circumstances entirely unconnected with work. Note the difficulty of justifying a dismissal for a non-work-related disturbance without a criminal conviction.

## Dealing with an abusive or violent employee

As a manager, your most likely involvement with violent or abusive acts will be concerned mainly with disturbances resulting from provocation, or from bad interpersonal relationships which have deteriorated over a considerable period of time. The demeanour of one person may aggravate another. Perceptions that somebody is deliberately uncooperative, fractious, insolent or failing to show respect can lead to abusive confrontations.

Paradoxically perhaps, many abusive people lack skills of personal assertion. They are not able to cope with stressful and distressing situations without becoming aggressive — rather than dealing with troublesome people in assertive, forthright, but nevertheless polite and detached ways (see pages 218–222 for more on assertiveness). A small financial outlay on sending such an employee on a short assertion training course may be a sound long-term investment resulting in a better, more productive worker able to exert proper self-control.

Otherwise, the best way you can assist is by helping an abusive person to explore and understand his or her own aggressive feelings. Three things are required:

(a) development of that person's awareness of the effects on others of a violent or abusive act;

(b) counselling to discover the situations and people that the aggressive person finds annoying (and why) — and how that person perceives the attributes and characteristics of the individual that he or she has abused or attacked;

(c) implementation of a programme, with clearly defined objectives, for exercising self-control.

## Counselling

To counsel an abusive employee you could begin by asking the person (a young woman, say) to list all the times she lost her temper during the previous two months, and to describe what exactly caused the loss of temper on each occasion. Ask her to specify the worst thing she would be prepared to do to another person — how violent or abusive is she prepared to be? Would she, for example, hit someone with a bottle, or with a knife? Are there any people she would never abuse or hit — a parent, children, a pregnant woman, a disabled person, and why would she not attack such individuals? If she can restrain herself in those contexts, why can she not exercise control in others?

This conversation may well tease out several aspects of the woman's aggressive nature that previously she was not aware of, and may induce some measure of remorse. Use this as the basis for a meeting between her and the person she abused. Invite her to apologise to the injured party. Also suggest to her that from now on she keeps a diary recording all losses of self-control, outbursts of temper and feelings of aggression. Each entry should include an attempt to explain how the situation occurred and why she felt upset.

She needs to learn that abusive incidents do not 'just happen'; they result from identifiable, and usually predictable, combinations of events — many of which can be consciously avoided.

## Vandalism

Vandalism is violence against property rather than against people. Although seemingly motiveless, it usually results from deeply felt resentments, anger, frustration and a feeling of not being able to control events. Wilful damage to premises is the most visible form of vandalism, although acts of vandalism can cover a wide range of activities — from outbreaks of graffiti, defaced posters, cigarette burns on carpets and furniture, through to unmitigated criminal damage. The latter extreme — criminal damage — means deliberately or recklessly destroying or damaging property which belongs to another person, or damaging or destroying one's own property in such a way as to endanger other people (eg racing a private car around the firm's car park damaging other vehicles in the process). Note, however, that it is permissible to damage other people's property in self-defence, or if the person committing the damage genuinely believed the owner had given or would give permission. It is sometimes difficult to distinguish criminal damage from an honest mistake.

Most 'vandalism' is directed against communal parts of institutions (graffiti on walls, broken windows, etc) rather than personal property. Vandals perceive such communal parts as 'impersonal', and they are easier to attack without being caught. Various forms of vandalism may be distinguished, ranging from vandalism associated with theft (damage is done as a corollary to unlawful gain), through sabotage to production lines in order to have a rest from work, to the destruction of property as revenge for a personal grievance, to simply 'messing around' without malicious intent. Malicious vandalism results from feelings of failure, boredom and frustration.

Vandalism, therefore, may indicate the absence of adequate grievance procedures, or breakdowns in communication, or the inability of employees to participate in decisions that fundamentally affect their working lives. Dealing with a vandal is akin in many respects to dealing with a thief, and the techniques discussed earlier might be applied, although it is especially important in the case of vandalism to root out the cause of the behaviour, since the factors that motivate one person to commit a destructive act (resentment over recently imposed working conditions, for example) might also affect other employees.

# DEPRESSION

Depression is a significant cause of staff absenteeism and/or workplace underperformance.

## What is depression?

Depression means permanent feelings of dejection and apathy. The cause of work-related depression may be exogenous (with an external origin), such as failure to achieve an important objective or disappointment at not gaining promotion; or endogenous (within the person), resulting perhaps from feelings of hopelessness, personal inadequacy and inability to cope. Depression manifests itself in abnormal sleep patterns, listlessness, lethargy and agitated behaviour. Loss of appetite and libido may also occur. Depressed people tend to avoid contact with others, and not interact in socially conventional ways.

In work contexts, depression is worsened if employees perceive that they have no control over depressing situations. Participation in decision making, provision of training and staff development opportunities, job rotation, and involvement of individuals with teams (rather than working in isolation) may therefore alleviate some depressing circumstances. Long working hours can cause depression. They restrict social interaction outside work and leave little time for leisure, or indeed for simple rest and recuperation.

## How victims of depression react

People react to unpleasant events in different ways. Thus being passed over for promotion may cause one person to become angry, another to become depressed, a third to breathe a sigh of relief at not having to assume extra responsibility. If this incident is followed by a belief that promotion will never come then the affected individual might experience despair; whereas belief that the decision was fundamentally unfair could lead to an outburst of anger. So whether an event causes depression depends crucially on how it is perceived, and you may be able to assist colleagues in this respect by helping them to clarify issues and see them in a proper perspective — a reinterpretation of a depressing incident might transform its psychological consequences.

Depression is a wretched experience and those who have been severely depressed greatly fear its recurrence. Paradoxically, therefore, the dread of becoming depressed in future can itself cause feelings akin to depression.

## Helping a depressed colleague

Severe mental depression is, of course, a serious illness requiring specialist medical treatment, possibly involving the use of prescribed drugs. However, convincing someone to seek proper medical advice can be difficult. If you have a colleague who is acutely depressed, try pointing out that depression is today recognised as a 'legitimate' medical illness and that it can be cured. Many severely depressed people are perplexed and confused by their emotions; they feel physically ill, but are reluctant to seek proper medical advice because of the absence of physical signs of illness — there is no rash, bruise, cut or other dramatic visible manifestation to show the doctor. Depressed people do not understand themselves, and typically do not expect others to understand them either.

Exude confidence when you begin discussions with a depressed colleague, and suggest that he or she can almost certainly look forward to a recovery. Comment that everyone becomes depressed occasionally, and that given what has happened to the employee, he or she has every right to feel miserable. If the depression is 'situational' and not especially distressing, you may well be able to 'talk your colleague through' the experience. Reassure the person that his or her reaction is reasonable and that he or she is not behaving irresponsibly or without good cause: look for rational justifications for your colleague feeling depressed.

For serious endogenous depression, however, do actively encourage your colleague to see a doctor. Say this directly — your advice will probably be welcome because seriously depressed people do not enjoy being depressed, and will gladly accept the possibility of alleviation.

Even today, depression is not a socially 'acceptable' illness, and sufferers are often deeply ashamed that it happened to them. It is easy, therefore, for a depressed person (wrongly) to feel isolated, misunder-stood and entirely alone. Just by listening, by offering support and company during moments of crisis, you can play an important and valuable role in assisting that person objectively to reappraise his or her situation, dispassionately and without attributing blame.

# 9

# FIRING EMPLOYEES

In Britain (as in all other European Community countries) it is not legally possible to dismiss employees casually. Certain formalities must be followed and adhered to exactly if the dismissal is not to go to court and be declared wrongful or unfair. As a manager you are quite likely to be involved in the implementation of disciplinary and dismissal procedures at some time or other, so it is essential that you possess a working knowledge of the legal aspects of the situation. The main points are as follows:

1. In law, the only person normally entitled to sack an employee is the chief executive of the organisation. This authority can (and usually is) delegated to lower levels (a divisional manager or personnel department, for example), but ultimately the decision to dismiss may have to be confirmed by the managing director of the business.

2. Verbal and written warnings must be given before a dismissal (with some exceptions as explained below).

3. The employer is legally obliged to be reasonable at all times and to apply fair and just procedures.

4. Dismissal has to be the last resort, when all other possible measures have failed.

5. A dismissed worker should have the right of appeal.

## NOTICE

Independent of the period of notice specified in a person's contract of employment, certain minimum periods are imposed by law. The UK

Employment Protection Act demands that at least a week's notice should be given to a worker with more than one month's but less than two years' service, and one extra week's notice for each year of employment thereafter (so that, for instance, a worker with eight years' service is entitled to eight weeks' notice) up to a maximum of twelve weeks.

# DISCIPLINARY INTERVIEWS

The first step in the disciplinary procedure is to establish what precisely the employee is alleged to have done wrong. Is there an up-to-date rule book? If so, are its procedures clearly defined? Have disciplinary incidents been properly recorded?

## Formal and informal warnings

Note the important distinction between formal and informal warnings when documenting disciplinary events. In law, an unrecorded 'informal' warning cannot be used to justify disciplinary action following a repetition of the offence. Informal warnings are precisely that, ie off-the-cuff reminders not to behave in a certain way. Vindication of disciplinary sanctions requires detailed cataloguing of misdemeanours as they occur, plus the issue of formal *written* warnings outlining the likely consequences of continuing errant behaviour. Moreover, miscreants must be informed that incidents have been recorded.

## Starting the process

In practice the disciplinary process normally starts with an interview conducted by the employee's head of department. These interviews are necessarily more formal than other types of interview because of their legal implications. You have to be able to demonstrate that a disciplinary interview was conducted reasonably and that, even if there is some deficiency in your interview technique, the outcome to the interview would still have been the same.

Do your homework before the interview. Identify the rule or convention violated, and ask yourself whether a breach actually occurred; whether the breach is serious enough to warrant further action; and whether the real reason for taking action is the breach of the rule and not some other reason. Check the accused person's record, looking particularly to see if similar conduct has previously been overlooked or condoned. Prepare a list of possible outcomes to the interview, and the consequences of each. Confirm with your own boss that you possess the formal authority to impose appropriate sanctions and that senior management will back you up if disagreeable consequences ensue.

Never conduct a disciplinary interview when you are angry, tired, depressed or otherwise emotionally upset. Allow a reasonable 'cooling-off period' before discussions begin, although not too long — people quickly forget the details of events. Arrange for the interview to be conducted in private and without interruption. Preface your remarks with a precise specification of the allegations and, because it is a formal occasion with potentially damaging consequences for the accused person's career, outline the possible repercussions of the interview. Do not pretend that the interview is a 'friendly chat' when in fact its outcome will be recorded and perhaps used to justify disciplinary action. If action beyond an informal warning is likely, the employee should be given a written statement of the allegations as well as being told about them verbally.

Next outline the procedure that will be followed, and ask whether the worker wishes to be represented by a 'friend', who might be a trade union representative, another employee, or an outside person if the firm's disciplinary rules allow for this. If so, the meeting must be adjourned to arrange representation. In any event, the worker should always be given time to prepare his or her case, to request production of relevant documents, to locate witnesses, and to study allegations in depth.

Ask for an explanation of the worker's actions. Investigate facts. Find out exactly what happened and why. Where there is conflicting evidence and/or the accused denies having committed the offence, you will have to reach a decision on what took place *before* deciding on disciplinary action. You should have a copy of both the firm's disciplinary rules and the employee's personal file beside you for quick reference during the interview. If the offence is admitted, ask whether there are any special circumstances to justify the person's behaviour.

## THE ACAS CODE

ACAS (the government Advisory, Conciliation and Arbitration Service) publishes a Code of Practice on disciplinary procedures. The Code (entitled *Disciplinary and other Procedures in Employment*) is available from HMSO and is updated periodically. Failure to observe the Code does not render the firm liable to legal proceedings, nor does it make a dismissal automatically unfair, but the Code is admissible in evidence before courts and industrial tribunals and if any of the Code's provisions appear to a tribunal to be relevant for deciding any question arising from the proceedings, then the provisions of the Code will be 'taken into account in determining that question' (Employment Protection Act 1975, sec.6(11)). The Code recognises that the maintenance of discipline is a management responsibility, but emphasises the desirability of involving workers' representatives when drafting procedures.

### Company rules

Under the ACAS Code, employers should indicate the forms of conduct that are considered unacceptable, and in what circumstances. Rules should be particular rather than universal and justified in terms of the objective requirements of a job. Thus, for example, smoking may reasonably be prohibited in a food shop, but not on an open-air building site. The Code accepts the difficulty of specifying precise rules to cover all circumstances, but states that rules should not be so general as to be meaningless. It suggests that each employee be given a copy of the rules and have them explained verbally as part of an induction programme. Employees should be informed of the consequences of breaking rules, particularly those rules which if broken may result in summary dismissal.

### Dismissal procedures

Paragraph 10 of the ACAS Code recommends that procedures should be in writing, specify to whom they apply and what actions might be taken, be fast, and contain the provisions that:

(a) a worker's immediate boss cannot dismiss that person without referring to senior management (the levels of management authorised to take various forms of disciplinary action should be clearly specified in the procedure);

(b) individuals should be informed of complaints against them and be given the opportunity to state their case before decisions are reached;

(c) the accused has the right to be accompanied by a trade union representative or by a fellow employee of his or her own choice;

(d) employees should not be dismissed for a first offence (except for gross misconduct) and disciplinary action should not be taken until after an investigation. If the worker is suspended during this period the suspension should be with pay, and the procedure should state how pay will be calculated;

(e) full explanations should be given for any penalties imposed, the right of appeal should exist and the procedures for appeal should be fully explained to the individual.

The Code distinguishes between informal verbal warnings for minor infringements of rules, and formal written warnings issued following serious offences. Formal warnings should set out the nature of the breach of discipline, the likely consequences of further offences, and should state that the warning constitutes the first stage of the formal procedure.

If misconduct is repeated, a second and final written warning should be issued containing an unambiguous statement that a further recurrence of the offence will lead to whatever action (suspension, dismissal, or some other sanction) has been determined. Assuming the errant worker's behaviour does not improve, the next step is suspension or dismissal accompanied by a written statement of reasons for the action taken and details of right of appeal. The law expects you to 'act reasonably at all times'. This means taking into account the worker's past record, any extenuating circumstances, and whether the worker was fully aware of the standards required and of the consequences of misbehaviour. Other factors to be considered (paragraph 16) are:

- the employee's age, position, length of service and general performance;

- whether domestic or similar problems make it appropriate to reduce the severity of the disciplinary action taken;

- what action was taken in similar cases in the past.

## Appeals

Appeals procedures are dealt with in paragraphs 23–27 of the ACAS Code, which suggest that appeals should be considered quickly, that time limits for lodging an appeal should be immediately transmitted to the individual concerned, and that appeals should be heard by a higher level of authority than took the original disciplinary action.

Wherever possible, the appeal should be considered by independent people who are not the immediate bosses of the manager who decided to dismiss the worker. The procedure should spell out the actions that may be taken by those hearing the appeal, and enable any new evidence to be made known to the employee.

Existence of an appeals procedure demonstrates management's commitment to fair play. The 'convicted' employee is given the opportunity to explain why he or she believes the original decision was wrong, and it shares the burden of taking unpleasant disciplinary decisions. Moreover you are more likely to take proper disciplinary action against errant employees when you know they have the right of appeal. Independent arbitration might be an appropriate means of reaching a final decision, provided both parties agree.

## Natural justice

Courts and tribunals expect all in-house hearings to adhere to the 'rules of natural justice'. These rules are not embodied in any statute, but have been established through legal custom and practice, case law and precedent over the years. Natural justice requires that:

(a) accusations are supported by evidence;

(b) the accused person is informed of the full details of the complaint;

(c) any committee convened to hear the case acts in good faith, fairly and without bias;

(d) the employee is allowed to state a case, to hear the evidence given against him or her and is able to question witnesses;

(e) the accused is allowed the right of representation and has full access to all information and documents;

(f) the committee hearing the case should not include the other party to the dispute.

A breach of the rules of natural justice does not necessarily render a dismissal unfair, provided you acted reasonably and the outcome to the proceedings would have been the same had all the proper procedures been followed.

## Probation and appraisal

The ACAS Code recommends (paragraph 45) that employers actively seek to pre-empt disciplinary problems by minimising the risk of poor performance and by 'creating conditions which allow employees to work satisfactorily'. In particular, probationary employees should be told what is expected of them, targets set should be 'realistic', and the consequences of failure to meet required standards should be fully explained during induction procedures. Regular performance appraisal is suggested (paragraphs 46–47), so that when people do not come up to standard the cause is likely to be their own carelessness, negligence, idleness or misconduct rather than incompetence in the long run.

## THE LAW ON DISMISSAL

In general, dismissal is the termination of employment by:

(a) the employer, with or without notice; or

(b) the employee's resignation, with or without notice, when the employer behaves in a manner that demonstrates refusal to be bound by the contract of employment. This is termed 'constructive dismissal', and means the employer is behaving so unreasonably that the worker has no alternative but to quit; or

(c) the failure of the employer to renew a fixed-term contract.

Dismissal without notice is known as 'summary' dismissal. This might occur when a worker's behaviour makes the fulfilment of a contract of employment impossible. Examples are theft, persistent drunkenness, violence, abusiveness to colleagues or customers, wilful disobedience, or incompetence that immediately causes damage to the employer's business.

### Unfair dismissal and wrongful dismissal

There is an important difference between 'unfair' dismissal and 'wrongful' dismissal. Unfair dismissal can only happen when the person dismissed is an 'employee' of an organisation (in the sense defined by the 1978 Employment Protection (Consolidation) Act, which deals with these matters) and certain eligibility criteria apply. At the time of writing, a worker is able to claim unfair dismissal only if he or she has worked continuously for an organisation for at least two years full time, or two years part time doing at least 16 hours a week, or five years part time doing at least eight hours a week.

Continuity means the absence of gaps in the worker's service of more than a week, although holidays, time off for sickness (up to six months at a stretch), and 'normal' layoffs (teachers' long summer vacations, for example) do not break continuity. A series of short-term contracts, issued one after another, will build up a worker's continuity to exactly the same extent as a single contract for a longer period. Thus a worker employed on renewable one-year contracts is regarded in law as equivalent to someone on a permanent contract after the appropriate number of years has elapsed. If there is any doubt about eligibility to claim unfair dismissal (which results in the case being heard in an industrial tribunal rather than an ordinary civil court) then you or your colleagues in the personnel department should seek professional advice. The precise meaning of 'unfair' dismissal is given on pages 150 to 153.

'Wrongful dismissal', in contrast, may be claimed by any dismissed worker, regardless of length of service — a worker who has been with the firm for only a few days may be 'wrongfully' sacked. This occurs when the worker is dismissed with insufficient notice, and results in civil proceedings in a county court. The aggrieved party sues for damages equivalent to the actual loss incurred. There are major differences in procedure between county courts and industrial tribunals, and whereas costs in the latter are intended to be minimal (and in normal circumstances are never awarded to the other side), costs in the county court can be enormous.

## Grounds for fair dismissal

The Employment Protection (Consolidation) Act 1978 lists four major reasons for which staff may be fairly dismissed: genuine redundancy, gross misconduct, inadequate performance, or 'some other substantial reason'.

## Redundancy

A worker is 'redundant' when the firm no longer requires work of the type done by that person. Thus it is a worker's job that is redundant, and not the particular worker. Note therefore the common misuse of the term 'redundancy': managers often say they are going to make someone redundant, when what they really mean is that they intend to dismiss the worker for incompetence. If an employee is no longer required in one section but instead of being made redundant is transferred to another section of the firm and displaces another employee who is dismissed, then the latter employee is 'redundant'.

Acceptance by an employee of another job in the firm will prevent the employee from claiming he or she is redundant, even if that job has inferior conditions, prospects and pay to the previous job. If the worker refuses the offer of another job in the firm, that person will only be regarded as redundant if the alternative job is inferior to the previous job, unsuitable to his or her skill and training, or an unreasonable distance from the person's home. If a worker accepts another job within the firm as an alternative to being made redundant then he or she has the legal right to spend up to four weeks in that job before deciding whether to accept it, without forfeiting the right to a redundancy payment if the alternative job turns out to be unsuitable.

## Legal rules on redundancy

A number of important legal rules (embodied in various Employment Protection Acts) apply to redundancy. Firms must:

- give adequate warning of intended redundancies and consult with the recognised union (ie the union they normally deal with) before the redundancies are implemented;

- seek alternative work for those threatened with redundancy;

- give the workers involved time off on full pay to look for other jobs;

- use fair and objective criteria when selecting employees for redundancy. These criteria could reasonably include the ages, lengths of service, capabilities, qualifications, experience, and past conduct of all the employees who might be involved, taking into account each person's suitability for alternative employment within the organisation. Race and/or sex discrimination is illegal when selecting people for redundancy. Selection criteria must be disclosed to the firm's trade unions and timetables for layoffs clearly stated;

- stop recruitment, ban overtime, introduce short-time working, and insist that all employees over normal retirement age retire. Volunteers for redundancy should be sought. As far as possible, the workforce should be cut through natural wastage rather than compulsion.

Redundancy payments must be given to redundant employees who have completed at least two years' continuous service with the employing company. The worker receives one and a half weeks' pay for each year of employment (up to a maximum of 20 years) in which he or she was over 40 years of age, one week's pay for each year of service between 22 and 40, and half a week's pay for each year between 18 and 21. There is an upper limit on the total value of a 'week's pay' that may be awarded. Redundancy payments are not taxable.

*Misconduct*

The term 'misconduct' has no legal definition — each case must be considered on its individual merits. Gross misconduct (theft, violence, etc) justifies summary dismissal in certain circumstances; but the law insists that you 'act reasonably' at all times, and it is up to you to prove that misconduct vindicating dismissal actually occurred. You must be able to specify where and when the misconduct took place and how it affected the worker's job and/or workmates. Then you have to demonstrate that the worker's past record was taken into account, and how exactly the organisation suffered on account of the event. Also you need to show that the dismissed person was not selected unfairly from others who were equally guilty, that dismissal rather than some lesser action was required, that formal warnings were issued, proper investigations carried out, and that a fair dismissal procedure was followed — including the right of appeal.

## Incapability

Inadequate performance (incapability) means that the employee cannot satisfactorily complete his or her work, or does not have the qualifications for the job. Note that a sick employee may be 'fairly' dismissed on these grounds, although industrial tribunals expect the employer to discuss the position with the worker concerned to ensure that the illness will in fact prevent effective performance, and to seek less demanding work for the sick employee.

Nevertheless, employers are entitled to dismiss any worker whose skill, aptitude, health or physical or mental qualities are not up to the demands of the job — but the employing firm must show that it acted reasonably at all times. Thus you should have given that person written warnings of his or her inadequacies, offered the chance to improve (preferably with the offer of help and training), and have followed a proper procedure. If you promote somebody who turns out to be useless at the higher level of work, you should offer the opportunity to revert to a less arduous job before dismissing that employee.

Always keep documentary evidence of an employee's incompetence and *do not* write glowing references for a worker immediately prior to dismissal, since such documents can subsequently be used as evidence against your allegations of inadequate performance.

## Other substantial reasons

Other reasons for fair dismissal include disruption of staff relations, 'organisational efficiency' (although the meaning of this must be established in each individual case), or a temporary job coming to an end — provided the impermanent nature of the work was fully explained to the worker when the employment started. A good example of this is laying off a worker who was engaged to cover the absence of a woman taking maternity leave. You may also dismiss someone if the continuation of that person's employment would cause you to break a law (for instance, if one of your drivers lost his or her driving licence); and you can fairly dismiss any worker who goes on strike. Note however that *all* striking workers must be sacked and not just some of them, unless there are extenuating circumstances (such as certain strikers being convicted for violence on picket lines).

## Compensation

If you dismiss someone unfairly your firm will have to pay compensation and/or reinstate the worker. Usually an industrial tribunal which finds that a dismissal is unfair will first, if the employer agrees, make an order for the worker to be reinstated, ie restore that person in the job as though the dismissal had never happened, or re-engaged, ie return to his or her previous employer but in a different job. If the employee does not wish to return to the former employer, if reinstatement or re-engagement is judged by the tribunal to be impracticable or if the employer refuses to comply with an order for reinstatement or re-engagement, then monetary compensation must be paid by the employer. It consists of:

(a) a basic award calculated in the same way as redundancy pay; and

(b) a compensatory award assessed by the tribunal as being just in the circumstances, taking into account what the employee has suffered in hardship or in company benefits lost;

(c) a special additional award, usually of between 13 and 26 weeks' pay, is given when the employer refused to comply with an order for reinstatement or re-engagement.

## Automatically unfair dismissals

Tribunals will hold that some dismissals are automatically unfair, and the victims of these sackings do not always have to satisfy the same eligibility criteria for being able to claim unfair dismissal. Three circumstances give rise to unquestionably unfair dismissal: sacking a pregnant woman simply because she is pregnant; dismissal for union membership or activity or for refusing to join a union; or dismissal of workers when a business changes hands — unless significant technical, economic or organisational changes warranting the dismissal of staff also occur at the same time.

## Following instructions

Note finally that although you are entitled to expect the people who work for you to cooperate and to obey all your reasonable, lawful and non-dangerous instructions, all the orders you give must be covered by the worker's contract of employment. A worker is entitled to disobey you if an instruction is not essential to his or her work, as evidenced by contractual conditions of employment. And even if it is, the dismissal is warranted only if the disobedience is wilful and important to the employee's work. Written warnings should have been issued, and previous disobedience of similar instructions should not have been ignored. Dismissals for disobedience should not occur too long after the event or accusations of victimisation are likely.

A worker is perfectly entitled to refuse to accept a change in the terms and conditions of his or her contract (pay, hours of work, shift systems, etc) provided the change is fundamental. Thus, for example, a requirement to change departments might not be deemed fundamental, whereas a change in the location of a worker's job from one part of the country to another probably would (unless this was explicitly provided for in the contract). Also a worker may legitimately refuse to work overtime not agreed via a written or implied contract of employment.

The duty to obey has been strengthened by court decisions which have established that it is reasonable for a manager to demand that workers inform on colleagues' misbehaviour. Suppose, for example, that a spate of thefts has occurred within your department. You cannot identify the culprit, but can prove that other workers know who is stealing from the firm. It seems that now you are legally entitled to insist that your subordinates name the thief, and may dismiss them all if they refuse.

## Action short of dismissal

Action short of dismissal means any sanction imposed on a worker other than the sack. Examples are demotions, failure to promote certain employees, denial of pay increases, refusing requests for time off, loss of increments, allocation of unpleasant and/or low status duties, and so on. These actions are lawful provided they do not discriminate unfairly with respect to race, sex or marital status, are not intended to penalise someone for joining or wanting to join a union, or becoming involved in union activity, or for refusing to join or withdrawing from a union (1982 Employment Act 10(4)).

Victims can seek redress not only from their employers, but also from individual employees (including union representatives) who pressurise employers into taking unfair action short of dismissal. Cases are heard in industrial tribunals, which decide how much compensation the employer and the people bringing the pressure on the employer should pay. Note, however, how useful an action short of dismissal (a demotion, say) can be in offering an errant worker the chance to reform.

## TAKING DISCIPLINARY ACTION

Disciplinary actions in well managed firms will be few and far between. They represent failures on the organisation's part: failures of recruitment, induction and appraisal systems; of communications systems; and of management's ability to motivate employees. Paragraph 16 of the ACAS Code suggests that precedents should be followed when imposing sanctions (to ensure consistency of decisions and the avoidance of unfair discrimination) and that consideration is given to whether the written disciplinary procedure indicated the form of disciplinary action that would result from the misconduct.

The Code considers formal verbal warnings to be appropriate for minor offences — formal in the sense that they are recorded on the employee's personal file, with the employee being advised that the warning has been recorded. If the offence has occurred before, you should consider writing to the employee stating (as suggested by the ACAS Code, paragraph 17) the precise nature of the offence, the likely consequences of a further repetition, and what improvement is required and over what period.

Following a further repetition of the misbehaviour, you need to decide exactly what action to take. In reaching this decision, take account of paragraph 50 of the Code which pleads for special consideration in certain situations.

If the source of the disciplinary action is substandard work, then before imposing a sanction:

- mention the inadequacy and remind the employee that he or she has a responsibility to achieve the required standard;

- try to remedy deficiencies through better communication, extra training, encouragement, etc;

- give the employee adequate time for improvement, especially if he or she has recently been promoted and is having difficulty coping with higher-level duties;

- ensure that the fault does actually lie with the employee and that adequate warnings have in fact been issued.

In the case of illness, accident or advancing age, try (paragraphs 51–52) to find alternative work for the employee. For a sick employee, seek to establish the person's precise medical condition. Allow a 'reasonable' time for recovery and, where possible, reorganise departmental workloads and/or engage temporary staff to cover the worker's absence. Ask the sick employee whether any residual incapacity is likely after returning to work. If so, look for suitable alternative positions where medical defects will not be important. Where there is doubt about the nature of a disability, ask for the employee's permission to consult his or her doctor and also to seek independent medical advice. And inform the worker the instant that a medical condition seems likely to put his or her job at risk. Workers suffering allergies should, if possible, be found work away from the source of the allergy (paragraph 35). The Code recommends that when employees become mentally rather than physically ill their relatives should be consulted to check on their progress.

# INDUSTRIAL TRIBUNALS

Workers who believe they have been unfairly dismissed, or subjected to sexual or racial discrimination, or who wish to register complaints under a variety of other employment regulations and statutes (including health and safety and equal pay legislation) may initiate actions in industrial tribunals. These are independent courts consisting of three persons: two lay members (one from each side of industry — employers' organisations and trade unions) plus a legally qualified chairperson. Procedure in tribunals is meant to be informal relative to other courts (members wear ordinary clothes, not wigs and gowns). Nevertheless, a body of case law has arisen around statutes interpreted by tribunals (particularly the Employment Protection Acts), precedents have been established and much legal jargon unfamiliar to the lay person is used. This is particularly noticeable where one party to a dispute is represented by a solicitor or barrister (or both) while the other is not.

## Initiation of a case

A case begins when a complainant (referred to as the 'applicant') completes form IT1 (called an 'originating application') which he or she obtains from a Post Office, job centre, Citizen's Advice Bureau, or the DHSS. The form is easy to complete and requires only brief particulars of the applicant and the alleged offence (unfair dismissal, for example). IT1 is then sent to the local office of the industrial tribunal (the address is provided with the form) where it is photocopied. One copy is sent to ACAS and another to the employer (called the 'respondent') who must complete and return another form, IT3. The latter is known as a 'notice of appearance', and is sent to the employer with the copy of the originating application. Again, form IT3 requires only brief details of the employer's defence.

Copies of the completed IT3 are sent to the applicant and to ACAS. An officer of ACAS then attempts to settle the matter out of court. He or she will offer to visit the complainant at home to discuss the case and will offer to speak to the employer. ACAS officers act only as intermediaries and are not allowed to take sides. If no out of court settlement occurs a date is then fixed for the tribunal.

## Further particulars

Having seen an outline of the other party's case, either side may request 'further and better' particulars of its substance. For example, if an employer states that a worker who alleges that he or she was unfairly dismissed was actually sacked for incompetence, the worker may demand precise details of the supposed incompetence. An employee accused of being persistently late can ask for the dates of his or her supposed lateness. If a party refuses to supply further particulars, the other side can ask the tribunal to order their provision. Refusal to obey such an order results in that party not being allowed to present a case when the tribunal convenes. This means that only one side of the story is heard, so normally the party presenting the case will win. Similarly, both sides may request copies of documents that are relevant to the proceedings, eg contracts of employment, internal memoranda concerning disciplinary action, letters to outside persons (excluding legal advisers), work rotas, and so on. As with 'further particulars', a party can apply for a tribunal order for such documents to be produced, with similar consequences if the order is not obeyed.

Copies of all the documents to which either party intends to refer during the hearing must be sent to the other side a 'reasonable' time before the hearing takes place. Usually, the tribunal itself will want to receive copies of relevant documents before the hearing. Witnesses can be called to give evidence (on oath) and may be subpoenaed by the tribunal if they are reluctant to attend.

## Initial hearings

If there is doubt about the tribunal's ability to hear the case (if, for instance, the employer alleges that the complainant has not completed the necessary amount of continuous employment to claim unfair dismissal) then a 'preliminary hearing' may be called at which the tribunal will investigate its powers to hear the case. Also if having quickly examined the superficial facts of the situation the tribunal feels that one party's case is certain to fail — say because a dismissal was obviously unfair, or because a disgruntled worker has initiated a case frivolously or vexatiously simply to annoy the employer knowing full well that it cannot succeed — then a 'pre-hearing assessment' will be convened to establish agreed facts and, if appropriate, warn one of the parties that its case will probably fail. If the party receiving the warning wishes to proceed with the case, it may do so (before a different tribunal in order that the eventual outcome is not prejudiced) but may if it loses be ordered to pay the costs (normally each side must bear its own costs, and tribunals are extremely reluctant to award costs to one of the parties even if the other party has been warned of this possibility at a pre-hearing assessment). Under the Employment Act 1990, tribunals are empowered to require an applicant to pay a deposit of up to £150 if a pre-hearing review considers a case to have been brought frivolously, vexatiously or to be entirely unreasonable.

### Procedure in tribunals

Usually the employer (or the employer's representative) speaks first at a tribunal hearing, although in sex and race discrimination cases the applicant normally begins. A brief opening statement is presented, witnesses are called and examined, crossexamined by the other party, and then questioned by members of the tribunal. Then the other side makes an opening statement and calls witnesses, and then both sides sum up. The tribunal may alter the order of proceedings to suit particular circumstances. At the end, the tribunal privately considers its decision which is announced either on the spot or, if complex legal issues are involved, within a couple of days. Reasons for the decision are later confirmed in writing. Appeals are allowed and are heard first by the 'Employment Appeals Tribunal' and then by higher courts.

### Appearing before a tribunal

As a manager, your most likely personal contact with an industrial tribunal will be as a witness on your employer's side. In this case, you will enter the room where the tribunal is to be held as one of several members of your firm's party and sit just behind the person who is to present the employer's case. The three members of the tribunal sit facing the court behind a long table on a dais about a foot higher than the rest of the room. On being called you sit behind a table at right angles to the court, swear to tell the truth, and are then questioned in turn by your firm's representative, the other side, and by members of the tribunal. You must recount events, give dates and times, confirm the existence of documents, etc. An important difference between an industrial tribunal and other courts is that hearsay evidence can be allowed in a tribunal. Also you can be asked leading questions, and may be allowed to read a prepared statement on a complex point. All parties sit while speaking.

Many cases, especially those where only limited evidence is available, are won or lost on the standard of presentation of witnesses. If you are in the right, and tell the facts honestly without omission or embellishment, you should make a powerful impact. Speak slowly (the tribunal members will be taking notes by hand), clearly, and take care not to repeat your points. Mention only relevant matters, do not be sarcastic or aggressive. In particular, do not make unpleasant remarks about the complainant — project yourself as an agreeable, reasonable and objective person. You should, of course, be well dressed, clean and tidy.

## Proving the allegations

Documents are the best means of proving a case, and the more comprehensive your records the better. For example, in a dismissal case you should have copies of carefully worded written warnings, memoranda to the personnel and other departments, written evidence of your having actively tried to avoid the dismissal (say through offering extra training, a change of department, detoxification help for an alcoholic, etc) and of your being reasonable at all times. If a worker was sacked for bad timekeeping you need written evidence (time cards, for instance) of all the times the person was late. The firm's representative will lead you through your evidence. You will then be crossexamined by the other side, which will challenge your version of events and seek contradictions in your evidence.

The chairperson of the tribunal should ensure that you can give your evidence without being harassed or bullied — although you must answer all relevant questions. Be sure you fully understand the applicant's complaint, and why that person feels so aggrieved that he or she is prepared to go through the harrowing experience of an industrial tribunal. Assume that the other side will ask the questions you least want to answer, and check that you have sufficient information to deal with them. Points deserving special attention include the following:

(a) Did you possess the formal authority to do whatever you did (eg dismiss the worker) and did you have written evidence of this authority at the time the action was taken?

(b) Were all provisions of relevant codes of practice strictly followed? If not, why not?

(c) Is any crucial evidence missing? Do you have all the documents necessary to support your statements?

The better prepared you are and the more logically you present your material, the more impressive your evidence will appear. Do not express opinions about the meaning of laws on particular issues. This is the role of the tribunal and the representatives of the contesting parties. Be prepared, however, to explain company documents and procedures. While doing this bear in mind that internal administrative systems mean little to outsiders, so avoid technical jargon and ensure before the hearing that you can describe, simply yet comprehensively, any company-specific procedure that you might need to refer to when giving your evidence.

# 10

# EMPLOYEE RELATIONS

Unless you work in a very small business you will almost certainly have to deal with employee representatives (union workplace representatives, staff association members, or individuals representing others for the purpose of voicing *ad hoc* complaints) at some time in your career. Large firms usually have set rules to govern the procedures for employee representation, for the conduct of negotiations over wages and conditions of work, for resolving disputes and conflicts, and for a whole range of grievance and disciplinary processes. Rules may be formal or informal; written or agreed verbally; internally formulated or imposed from outside (via laws or government agencies, for example).

## DEALING WITH UNIONS

Sometimes managements deliberately encourage employees not to join unions in the belief that unorganised workers are easier to control than union members. This in fact is a questionable assumption, since management itself can benefit considerably from the unionisation of its workforce. Conflicts between management and labour occur even without a union, and these conflicts still have to be resolved. Negotiation with unions can be most effective in determining pay and conditions and settling disputes. Bargaining with individual workers over pay absorbs much time and effort, and results in a myriad of petty differentials which cause friction and resentment among the staff. And pay agreements negotiated with recognised union representatives — apart from determining the wages of all employees — can usually be expected to stick, at least until the next round of negotiations.

Meetings between management and unions can be useful for discussing issues wider than just pay and conditions, and might create a sense of participation among employees. Unionised workforces may feel relatively secure in their jobs, and thus be more willing to cooperate in the redeployment of labour. Note also that if unions are not recognised, labour will still make its voice heard — possibly in disruptive ways (high rates of absenteeism and staff turnover, non cooperation, lack of effort, etc).

Yet many managers still regard trade unionism unfavourably, associating it with selfishness, extremism, unwarranted strikes and so on. Managerial prerogative, they argue, is reduced, decision taking is delayed by consultation, and labour costs increase. Simultaneous negotiations with several different unions can be tedious and difficult, and the unions involved might not agree among themselves. Other objections are that unionisation might disrupt existing (harmonious) staff–management relations; will 'formalise' disputes procedures, creating unnecessary divisions between management and labour; and could encourage conflict.

# INDUSTRIAL DISPUTES

There are many causes of dissatisfaction at work: low wages, poor physical working environments, absence of job satisfaction, denial of promotion or training opportunities, speeding up work flows, and so on. To resolve grievances, impartial — preferably independent — procedures are required. These might include the following:

(a) *Formal plant-level or national agreements* specifying how grievances should be resolved. Invariably, departmental managers are closely involved in grievance procedures. Indeed, many procedures explicitly state that the worker's immediate supervisor should be approached in the first instance. If the grievance remains unsettled, then typically the worker will nominate a representative (often a trade union representative) who takes up the case. The union representative will discuss the matter with the manager concerned and — if settlement is still not forthcoming — with higher levels of management.

(b) *Establishment of joint negotiating committees* (works committees) that meet at a predetermined interval to deal with problems which have arisen since the last meeting. Both sides promise not to take industrial action before a matter has been discussed in the works committee.

(c) *Arbitration agreements* which provide for the appointment of an independent referee to hear and adjudicate cases. Parties agree in advance that the arbitrator's decision must be final. Each side nominates potential arbitrators, and a mutually acceptable name is chosen. The work of ACAS is important here, and is worthy of further consideration.

## ACAS

The Advisory, Conciliation and Arbitration Service was established in 1974 and given a statutory identity in 1975 via the Employment Protection Act. Its role is to improve industrial relations. ACAS will conciliate an industrial dispute if asked to do so by one of the parties (or by the government). All applications to industrial tribunals (see Chapter 9) are automatically referred to ACAS, which tries to achieve out-of-court settlements. ACAS seeks to discharge its responsibilities through the voluntary cooperation of managements, unions, and complaining employees; it has no independent statutory powers to compel parties to behave in a certain way. There is no charge for the majority of ACAS services.

Advice is offered on request or on ACAS's own initiative to any employer, worker, staff association or trade union on any matter concerned with industrial relations or employment, regardless of the size of the organisation. Advice is available in each of the following areas:

- negotiating machinery, bargaining arrangements, procedures for settling disputes and grievances;

- consultative and participation agreements, trade union recognition;

- communications and the disclosure of information to trade unions;

- labour turnover, absenteeism, human resource planning, productivity bargaining, hours of work and other conditions of employment, payments systems and job evaluation;

- industrial relations and employment legislation, including the law on unfair dismissal, sex and race discrimination, equal pay, recruitment, selection and induction;

- disciplinary, dismissal and redundancy procedures;

- training in industrial relations.

# GRIEVANCE PROCEDURES

UK employment protection legislation requires that all written contracts of employment (see Chapter 5) contain details of the employing organisation's grievance procedure. This does not mean that an employer *must* have a grievance procedure; only that if it exists then its particulars must be communicated to employees via the contract of employment. The mechanism for invoking the procedure should be set out, stating full details of to whom the employee should complain, and the process of appeal should the employee not obtain satisfaction. If a firm does have a grievance procedure, but the worker is denied knowledge of its existence, then he or she can refer the matter to an industrial tribunal which can order details to be revealed. These revealed details then bind the firm 'as if' they had been included in the original contract of employment. However, tribunals cannot interpret the meaning of words used in describing procedures.

## The case for formal procedures

Serious discontent can arise from seemingly trivial incidents. Often grievances relate to personal relations within a section, although they might equally emerge from almost any aspect of the employee's work: terms and conditions of employment, holiday arrangements, status and authority, treatment by managers, working conditions, etc. No organisation is so well managed that its employees never need to complain, and even if the firm is objectively a good employer, staff may still feel that complaints are justified. Well constructed grievance procedures enable firms to resolve complaints quickly, fairly, and without industrial action.

Formal procedures minimise the risk of inconsistent decisions. The employer is seen to be trying to be fair. And of course, the absence of formal procedures will severely prejudice an employer's case if the grievance eventually results in legal proceedings.

A grievance 'procedure' is an established set of agreed rules for enabling management, the aggrieved employee and his or her representative to settle a complaint. The rules will restrain both sides from behaving irresponsibly, provided both sides are committed to their application and have confidence in their impartiality. This presupposes that employees have knowledge of the rules and how they should be interpreted. There are several advantages to formal procedures, including the following:

(a) Each side has a common understanding of how a grievance will be received and processed. Indeed, the very act of drafting agreed

procedures normally involves consultation with employee representatives and will include a wide-ranging discussion about the nature
of the grievances likely to arise.

(b) Since promotions, resignations, transfers and retirements of staff
mean that the managers and union officials who deal with grievances change periodically, there is need for continuity in procedures
— made possible by the existence of written rules.

(c) Written rules clarify important matters such as who has authority to
take decisions in settlement of disputes, the time scale for register-
ing a grievance, how an appeal should be lodged, and so on.

(d) Subsequent misunderstandings about what was discussed and
agreed during the hearing of the grievance will be minimised if the
hearing is recorded and follows a set of formal rules.

(e) Employees have the security of knowing that whenever major problems arise they can air their concerns to the highest levels of
authority within the organisation. Management is compelled to
consider the consequences of its actions in the context of their
possibly resulting in invocations of the grievance procedure.

## The case for informality

Although informal application of *ad hoc* custom and practice can lead
to ambiguity and inconsistent decisions, it may in some circumstances
be more efficient than a formal procedure. Formalisation reduces flexibility, since precedents established through following formal rules must
be adhered to in future cases. A 'mini' legal system will build up
around the procedure, with its own protocol, norms, case law and rules
of interpretation. It becomes impossible to 'turn a blind eye' to certain
practices, no matter what the circumstances.

Managerial prerogative is necessarily affected by the existence of a
grievance procedure, since departmental managers and supervisors —
who occupy 'front-line' positions in management's contact with the
work force — are liable to have their decisions challenged. Grievance
procedures can be used tactically as part of a wider industrial relations
offensive (a union might for example instruct its members to invoke
the procedure whenever possible in order to inconvenience the
management and hence pressurise it into conceding a pay claim), or
vexatiously in order to draw attention to a secondary issue. Moreover,
formalisation does not remove the underlying causes of grievances, it
merely changes the forum in which grievances are discussed.

Grievances might be dealt with faster and more equitably if they are settled 'on the spot' without formal provision for appeal to higher authority.

## Equal opportunity considerations

The 1975 Sex Discrimination Act makes it unlawful:

> to victimise an individual for a complaint made in good faith about sex or marriage discrimination or for giving evidence about such a complaint. (S.4(1),4(2) and 4(3))

'Victimisation' means treating someone less favourably than others simply because that person is claiming a statutory right or is helping someone else to do so. Likewise, sections 4(2) and 2 of the 1976 Race Relations Act prohibit discrimination in the operation of grievance procedures invoked by individuals complaining of racial discrimination and/or harassment. The Act is particularly concerned to prevent employers from disciplining workers who raise grievances concerning discrimination. Also, the Commission for Racial Equality's 1984 Code of Practice (issued under the 1976 Act) insists that employers should not:

> ignore or treat lightly grievances from members of particular racial groups on the assumption that they are oversensitive about discrimination. (Sec. 1.22)

Moreover, trade unions are obliged under the Race Relations Act (S.11(3)) to offer the same help to members of all racial groups in the processing of grievances.

## Grievance interviews

A grievance interview must be handled in a different manner to a disciplinary interview. In the first place, there is no presumption of a party's 'guilt'. Your task is to establish the facts and, assuming the complaint is valid, to remedy the grievance. If the complaint fails, you must convince the complainant that your decision is fair, and based on objective criteria. So you must be strictly neutral in your approach. Do not try to 'perform well' during the interview — aim for a satisfactory outcome rather than an impressive display of your negotiating skills.

Note also that initially you will be dealing with the complainant on a one-to-one basis. It is within your authority to reject a grievance in the first instance; but someone else will adjudicate an appeal against the decision. It is essential, therefore, that your first response is based on hard, factual evidence — preferably backed by witnesses and written documents.

Another important difference between grievance and disciplinary interviews is that you cannot *prepare* for the former because you will probably have little prior knowledge of the nature of the grievance until it has been explained.

*How to proceed*

One way to conduct a grievance interview is as follows:

(a) Ask the complainant to state the background to the case and (importantly) what he or she would like to see done to resolve the problem.

(b) Explore the facts. Take a note of the names of witnesses to incidents, and of any documents that might help to resolve the case.

(c) Attempt a preliminary definition of the nature of the problem. Identify any company rules, policies or procedures the breach of which might have caused the complaint. Ask the complainant whether he or she agrees with your interpretation of the problem. If there is disagreement, isolate the differences of opinion. State your position as clearly and simply as you can.

(d) Either suggest a solution to the problem or — if you believe the grievance is unfounded — explain carefully your reasons for rejecting the complaint.

(e) Record your decision, or a failure to agree, in a written statement approved by the complainant. A 'failure to agree' should highlight the contentious issues. Outline the procedure for appeal.

## HANDLING CONFLICT

Usually conflicts at work arise in one of two categories: conflicts between your function and those of others, or conflicts with higher authority or with employees. To resolve conflicts you might appeal to higher authority to impose solutions, compromise, or (assuming you are empowered to do so) impose your own will. The latter encourages retaliation and discourages free interchange of information and ideas. However, imposed solutions are frequently better than compromises (even if the solutions established are not popular) since compromises satisfy neither party to a dispute.

It is often easier to deal with conflicts between other people than those involving yourself. Third-party disputes can be approached objectively and without presumption, and you are better able to identify symptoms of distress. Look for breakdowns in communication and unwarranted arguments between individuals, for unnecessary — perhaps even harmful — competition between functions, and for inflexible, insensitive attitudes towards other employees. Further indicators of impending conflict are people deliberately withholding information from each other, abuse of colleagues behind their backs, excessively formal relations between individuals, and unwarranted criticism of the quality of other people's work.

In seeking to resolve conflicts between colleagues, relate their behaviour to the objectives of the teams to which they belong. Objectives provide solid criteria for decisions when arbitrating disputes. Clarify the person's formal role as specified in the firm's organisation chart or manual, and offer interpretations of people's roles where opinions differ. Define job boundaries, and ask each side to detail why they consider the other's behaviour to be unreasonable. Initially you should speak to the disputants individually, but in so doing ask each party to suggest items for the agenda of a meeting to settle the dispute. Ask each side to empathise with the other's position.

## Is your department working as a team?

To establish whether the members of your department are acting as a team ask yourself the following questions:

(a) Are people willing to express ideas and opinions regarding working methods, etc openly and in a non-antagonistic way?

(b) Do 'territorial disputes' frequently break out among department members, with individuals insisting on 'doing their own thing'?

(c) Are conflicts resolved quickly and amicably?

(d) Do employees seek to develop their skills and learn about each other's duties?

# NEGOTIATION

Negotiation is an important management skill, and it is essential that you are able to negotiate effectively. You might negotiate with employee representatives, with colleagues in committees, safety representatives (see Chapter 12), with other departments and possibly with customers and suppliers. Elements of negotiation may also enter into performance appraisal interviews and procedures for the control of grievances.

## Negotiation and consultation

Negotiation differs from consultation in that whereas the latter results in a unilateral decision imposed by yourself (albeit taking into account the views of other people), 'negotiation' implies decision taking through an agreement which both sides are obliged to keep. Typically, consultation is not adequate for subjects that involve conflict and/or deeply divided views. The essence of negotiation is compromise; you seek the agreement of the other side to as many of your demands as possible.

Willingness to negotiate presupposes a willingness to forego various objectives — there is little point in offering to negotiate if you are totally inflexible in your aims. It is important therefore to distinguish clearly between issues on which you will negotiate and those about which you are prepared only to consult.

## Effective negotiation

To bargain effectively you need a clearly defined set of negotiating objectives, a thorough understanding of the feelings and motives of the other side, and a well prepared negotiating plan which sets out the strategy and tactics you intend to adopt.

Analyse the opposition's case, the justifications for its position, the costs of conceding to its demands, and the extent of the opposition's support from other parties (eg support for union representatives on the part of the union rank and file). Check the validity of the facts the opposition is likely to put forward in support of its claim. What does the opposition really want, and how far is it prepared to go in securing its objectives?

Certain conventions have emerged among those who negotiate on a regular basis, intended to facilitate efficient bargaining. These are the following:

1. Once an offer has been made it should remain on the table until the situation changes or unless it was made conditional on some reciprocity that is not forthcoming.

2. All aspects of items on the agenda shall be negotiable, unless one of the parties has previously indicated its unwillingness to discuss certain matters.

3. Negotiators should negotiate only with each other and not make secret appeals to the people the other side represents.

4. Confidential conversations between opposing representatives should not be repeated during formal negotiations.

Observance of these simple rules puts neither side at any disadvantage, yet creates a robust and 'professional' working environment.

## The opening statement

Usually proceedings begin with one of the parties (normally the side which initiated the negotiation) making an opening statement outlining its objectives and offering facts and opinions designed to convince the opponent of the justice of its case. If you are the person who opens the discussions, then begin by stating your perceptions of the issue, and suggest a solution. Do not specify how much you are willing to concede, or impose any final demands. Experienced negotiators recognise that negotiations rarely involve 'all or nothing' situations; and even if your position is strong you should always allow your opponent to 'save face'.

Deliver the opening statement enthusiastically and with conviction. Deal with the more obvious objections to your statements during the introduction, state the facts as you see them, quoting examples and precedents, and emphasise the strongest aspects of your case. Predict in advance questions likely to arise from your opening statement, and provide answers to them before they are asked. The other side then makes its presentation and bargaining ensues.

## Need for caution

The side making the initial opening statement has an advantage in that it can determine the general context in which the negotiations take place (their tone, the way in which subjects are discussed, coverage of issues, and so on). It is important that you do not respond to your opponent's opening statement hurriedly or in a manner that relates more to his or her presentation than to your own predetermined position. If it is clear that the two sides see the situation from entirely different perspectives, you should still proceed with your prepared opening statement. Not only will this emphasise the differences in your positions, but it also gives you time to absorb the introductory comments of the other side. Do not make a counteroffer at this stage — to do so legitimises your opponent's aspirations. Make your offer at the end, not the beginning, of a negotiation. And always set your initial offer within the limits of your predetermined strategy.

## Dubious negotiating practices

Lax and amateurish approaches to negotiation are an expensive luxury, and you need to be fully aware of some of the dubious negotiating practices that individuals with extensive experience of negotiating might apply. For example, a common (though reprehensible) tactic is to agree to a demand in general terms but deliberately fail to establish procedures whereby the settlement can be implemented. Several months then elapse before the non-implementation is noticed, and more time passes before complaints are registered. By then, the personnel involved in the original agreement might have left the organisation, and new negotiations to secure its implementation have to begin all over again. At these fresh discussions, the party that initially agreed to the demand might argue that circumstances have changed and that the terms of the settlement can no longer apply!

Another questionable practice is the deliberate confusion of issues by introducing additional items to a negotiating agenda which are then discussed in parallel with the major matters for which the negotiating session was originally instituted. An agreement to one item on the agenda might then be made conditional on the achievement of a settlement on another. And to secure the latter you might have to make unanticipated, undesirable concessions. Agenda items are 'traded off' against each other.

### Tricks of the trade

Deflecting the opposition from its original purpose is one of many 'professional fouls' employed by skilled and determined negotiators. Some other commonly used 'tricks of the trade' are listed below:

(a) Conceding the existence of weaknesses in a certain proposition and then offering compromises based on your interpretation of their significance.

(b) Creating diversions and systematically confusing seemingly clear issues.

(c) Criticising the motives of the person presenting the argument rather than discussing the issue or giving reasons for decisions.

(d) Insisting that a certain practice is common in other firms, industries or situations when in fact it is not.

(e) Congratulating the other side on the logic of its arguments, or flattering the incisive rationality of its presentation, but then suggesting conclusions to these arguments which directly contradict the opponent's position.

(f) Introducing irrelevancies into the argument, drawing false analogies, and putting words into the other party's mouth knowing full well they will object and then waste time in correcting your (knowingly) false interpretations of their statements.

(g) Deliberately confusing an issue to such an extent that it seems reasonable to establish a subcommittee to investigate and deal with its implications. The establishment of a subcommittee is usually fatal for the problem under discussion.

(h) Presenting one's own unashamedly disgraceful behaviour as the consequence of a carefully considered, rationally justified moral position.

(i) Making broad generalisations knowing they will be challenged. Selecting untypical particular instances to 'prove a point'.

Clearly, lasting and satisfactory agreements are possible only if the parties negotiate in good faith. There are innumerable ways to disrupt and undermine negotiations; and disruptive tactics may themselves be a part of the negotiating strategy of one (or both) of the sides. Be aware of these unpleasant (but common) manoeuvres; but recognise that they are ultimately destructive — they may result in short-term 'victory' for one of the participants, yet might fail in the longer term as other parties realise they were duped, and hence retaliate. You should adopt a principled approach. Do not provoke your opponents. Treat them with courtesy and respect; yet be fully aware of the tricks they might pull.

Once an agreement has been reached, insist that it be written down and that named persons be made responsible for its implementation. Set a timetable for the activities required to execute the agreement and establish a procedure for monitoring progress towards the goal. Settlements should of course be implemented in the form in which they were agreed.

*Failure to agree*

All negotiations eventually end, if only with a failure to agree. Therefore both sides have an interest in establishing common ground. Look for analogies and precedents, and how others have resolved similar issues. A useful way of approaching an agreement is to ask the other side the question, 'What would happen if ...', and then proceed to outline certain concessions you might be prepared to offer (entirely without commitment at this stage) in return for various reciprocities. The opponent might then make a similar hypothetical proposal, and you will both have a broad understanding of how a settlement might be achieved. Then you begin to trade concessions, hoping that the (minor) concessions you offer will be matched by more significant concessions from the other side. Your aim is to elicit major benefits at minor cost.

Remember always that the opponent expects to go away with something and that settlement is most unlikely without at least a minimal *quid pro quo*. Make your opponent's decisions easy: suggest alternative ways for presenting the settlement to the outside world, offer some interpretations of your proposals which make them appear beneficial to the opponent. Try to appear as if you have yielded to your opponent's pressure, even when you have not.

# 11

# WAGES

## INTRODUCTION

It is not uncommon for managers to be asked by the people who work for them to explain how the latter's wages have been calculated. New recruits in particular are frequently astounded to find that nearly half their gross pay is lost through tax, national insurance, superannuation and other stoppages, and typically they turn to their departmental managers for advice. So you need to understand how deductions from wages arise, and be able to communicate such information clearly and precisely.

### Wages and salaries

In the past, important distinctions existed between 'wages' and 'salaries', but today the words are used interchangeably, reflecting the convergence of methods for paying white-collar and blue-collar employees that has occurred over the last 30 years. A salary was defined as a fixed annual amount, paid monthly. Wages in contrast were variable weekly payments (usually made in cash) that fluctuated in value through overtime, bonuses, and piecework rates. Salaries were determined individually; wages through management/union collective bargaining. Nowadays, however, many salaried workers are unionised and paid according to union negotiated salary scales, with annual increments; while large numbers of wage earners now receive relatively stable, time based earnings.

## INCOME TAX

Workers may be 'employed' by an employer, in which case they pay 'schedule E' tax, deducted by the employer under PAYE (see below), or they might be self-employed and pay their tax under 'schedule D'. The essential differences are that a wider variety of allowances is available under schedule D, and PAYE is deducted weekly or monthly whereas tax on profits from self-employment is paid in two equal instalments on 1 January and 1 July each year. The overwhelming majority of workers are taxed using PAYE under schedule E.

Disputes sometimes occur between the Inland Revenue and firms and/or individuals concerning whether particular types of work should be regarded as 'employment' or as 'self-employment'. A number of well established tests are applied by the Inland Revenue (and ultimately by the courts if it comes to this) in order to determine the matter; namely whether the person doing the job:

- controls how it is done, without undue interference from the engaging company;

- determines his or her working hours;

- is subject to internal grievance and/or disciplinary procedures;

- is 'integrated' into the firm's overall operations;

- is provided with a uniform, tools or equipment.

In cases of doubt the Inland Revenue usually comes down on the side of a person being an employee rather than a self-employed 'contractor'.

## PAYE

The 'pay as you earn' scheme enables employees to pay their tax gradually over the year, and places the responsibility for tax collection on employing firms. All individuals are entitled to claim certain 'allowances' which are fixed annually by the government in the Finance Acts that follow each year's budget. Allowances include a 'personal allowance' and relief on some mortgage interest, life assurance premiums, and the costs of working overalls and/or the tools of one's trade. These allowances are deducted from current annual earnings to give 'taxable income'. Once a year the individual completes a 'tax form' listing his or her allowances. The Inland Revenue then converts these allowances into a tax 'code' which is transmitted to the employer, who has already been issued with tax 'tables' showing how much tax is to be deducted from the monthly (or weekly) earnings of workers on various tax codes.

## An example

Suppose that a male worker claiming £5000 allowances is allocated a (fictitious) tax code '5'. If his annual earnings are £15,000 his taxable income is £10,000. Let the rate of tax for someone earning this amount be 30 per cent, so that (£10,000 x 0.3 / 12) = £250, the amount to be deducted each month for someone earning £15,000 a year on tax code 5. In other words, if monthly earnings are £1250 (that is, £15,000 / 12) then, according to the tax tables issued to the employer, £250 must be deducted from the wages of that employee as long as he is on tax code 5. Were his wages to increase to £2000 a month (ie £24,000 a year) then his taxable income rises to £19,000 and, at a 30 per cent rate of tax, he must now pay £475 a month (that is £19,000 x 0.3 / 12). Thus under the heading 'code 5' the tax tables will show that £475 must be stopped from wages of £2000 a month, and so on. Note that new employees who have not previously earned any income (school leavers, for example) pay no tax at all until their aggregate earnings have exceeded the value of their tax allowances, so that a new recruit with (say) £5000 of allowances pays no tax until £5001 has been earned, moving then on to PAYE.

At the end of the tax year (5 April) the employer must issue to each worker a form 'P60' which is a statement of pay and tax deducted during the year. When an employee leaves, the employer has to issue to that person a form P45 stating the pay and tax deducted during the year up to the date of leaving. A copy of the P45 is sent to the Inland Revenue. On beginning a new job the individual hands over his or her P45 to the new employer who then applies the tax code stated on it to the employee's monthly (or weekly) earnings. If the worker has no P45 the firm notifies the Inland Revenue on form P46.

The firm is legally responsible for maintaining records of cumulative pay and tax deducted ('sheets P11') and for sending a monthly cheque for all tax stopped from employees' wages together with a P30 'Remittance Card'. Annual totals must be declared by the employer to the Inland Revenue on form P35, the 'Annual Declaration Certificate'. Employees are informed of their tax codes on form P2, 'Notice of Coding' which is sent to them after they complete a tax form.

## NATIONAL INSURANCE

There are four types of national insurance contributions. Class 1 contributions are paid by employees. They are based on a predetermined percentage (varied from time to time by the Chancellor of the

Exchequer) of the worker's earnings — up to a predetermined ceiling (varied annually) so that there exists a maximum amount of Class 1 contributions that any person is obliged to pay. Two types of Class 1 contributions exist: contracted-out, and not contracted-out. The latter is higher than the former.

Contracted-out employees belong to company pension schemes approved by the Department of Health and Social Security. Members pay lower Class 1 contributions because the company scheme will give benefits which relieve the State of the burden of providing these benefits in the employee's later life. Non-contracted-out employees paying the higher rate now automatically belong to the State Earnings-Related Pension Scheme (SERPS) unless they subscribe to an approved private pension scheme (which need not be attached to any one employer).

## SERPS

Employees in SERPS pay approximately 2 per cent extra on their Class 1 contribution, and their employers pay an extra 3 per cent. SERPS will create improved retirement, widows' and invalidity pensions — accumulating over an individual's total working life. It will provide a 'basic' pension, common to all individuals, plus an additional pension dependent on earnings above a specified lower earnings limit.

## Other NI classes

Class 2 contributions are for the self-employed. They are flat-rate and do not vary with earnings. The range of benefits available from them does not include the additional pension to which Class 1 contributors are entitled under SERPS. Class 3 contributions are voluntary and designed for people who, for various reasons, are not contributing under Classes 1 or 2 but who wish to accumulate sufficient contributions to qualify for a limited range of benefits. Class 4 contributions are paid by self-employed people on their profits between certain levels.

## Role of the employer

The great majority of people pay Class 1 NI contributions. Added on to the contributions paid by the employee is a further (and larger) amount contributed by the employer. If the employer is not contracted-out then the employer's contributions are normally higher than if an approved company superannuation scheme is in force. Employers are responsible for deducting NI from workers' wages and paying this (together with PAYE) to the Inland Revenue which then passes it on to the DHSS. To calculate contributions, the firm uses tables supplied by the DHSS, each containing weekly and monthly amounts under three headings: A — for 'standard' rate contributions, B — for widows and older married women who sometimes pay contributions at a reduced rate, and C — for individuals over the normal age of retirement (in which case no contribution from the firm is required).

# STATUTORY SICK PAY

Another source of confusion to many employees is the computation of statutory sick pay (SSP). Currently the situation is that firms are responsible for paying state sickness benefit to their employees for up to 28 weeks during any one period of entitlement. The company pays the worker his or her SSP and must bear the cost. Part-time workers who earn more than a certain threshold are entitled to SSP, and there is no length of service qualification. Payment is only made for absences of more than three days and for whole days not parts. Note, however, that if two or more periods of incapacity to work fall within a period not exceeding eight weeks they become 'linked', so that waiting days occur only within the first period of incapacity. Statutory sick pay is paid for each day of following periods.

## Reporting illness

Everyone who pays Class I National Insurance is eligible for SSP. It is up to the worker to inform the employer that he or she is ill, within seven days of a day of incapacity unless there is a 'good cause' for the worker not being able to do this. Evidence of sickness must be supplied to the employer via a doctor's statement on a prescribed form, unless the sickness is for less than seven days in which case no medical evidence need be forwarded. Should an employer refuse to pay SSP, the worker is legally entitled to demand a written justification of the employer's decision. The issue is then referred to a DHSS adjudication officer. SSP is liable to tax and employee's National Insurance.

## Medical suspension

Schedule 1 of the 1978 Employment Protection (Consolidation) Act lists a number of health and safety hazards which, if they result in injuries to workers with at least one month's continuous service with a firm, entitle them to a week's pay for each week of 'suspension' on medical grounds for a maximum of 26 weeks. If the firm offers alternative work which the injured employee is capable of performing, and he or she turns this down, then no payment need be made.

## GUARANTEE PAYMENTS

The Employment Protection (Consolidation) Act 1978 also gives employees, who have been laid off or put on short time because of a shortage of work, the right to continue to receive pay for a limited period, ie for up to five days in any period of three months.

## MATERNITY PAY*

Under the Trade Union Reform and Employment Rights Act 1993, a woman must not be dismissed because of her pregnancy. Maternity pay must be paid to the woman by the employer. There are two levels of payment: 'higher' and 'lower'. If the woman has worked with the same employer doing more than 16 hours a week for at least two years (five years if she has worked between 8 and 16 hours a week) she can claim from her employer the higher rate of 90 per cent of her normal weekly pay (less the value of state benefit) for six weeks, plus the 'lower' rate (set by statute) for up to 12 further weeks. Women with between six months' and two years' service are entitled to the lower rate (of state benefit only) for up to 18 weeks. In the latter case, the money is paid by the employing firm, which then reclaims it from the Department of Health and Social Security.

All pregnant women are entitled to 14 weeks maternity leave and to return to their original job thereafter, regardless of length of service. This may start, at the earliest, eleven weeks before the expected week of childbirth and is subject to the woman giving her employer 21 days' notice.

If the employee wishes to return to work before the end of the 14 week leave period, she must give seven days' notice. During the 14 weeks, the woman is entitled to all contractual benefits, except remuneration (unless she has completed two years' continuous service with the employer, as outlined above).

### The qualifying week

To qualify for statutory maternity pay the woman must have accumulated 26 weeks' continuous employment by the 'qualifying week', ie

---

\* The government has announced that from October 1994 all women with more than six months' service with an employer will receive 90% of their average earnings for six weeks, followed by statutory maternity pay for another twelve weeks. Women with less than six months' service will receive statutory maternity pay only.

the 15th week prior to a pregnant employee's expected week of confinement. Also the woman must still be in employment with that employer during the qualifying week, although employment for a single day within that week will suffice to meet the condition.

## Notice of maternity absence

As stated, pregnant workers are legally required to give their employers at least 21 days' notice of the date they intend to start their maternity absence. Notice must be in writing if the employer so requires. If less than 21 days' notice is given the employer has discretion over whether to accept the shorter period and, if the shorter period is not accepted, no statutory maternity pay need be offered. In the latter case the woman may demand a written statement of the employer's reasons for not accepting the shorter period and may then appeal to the DHSS that it was not reasonably practicable for 21 days' notice to be provided.

## Other maternity rights

All pregnant women — regardless of length of service — are legally entitled to paid time off to attend 'reasonable' numbers of ante-natal appointments. However, firms are entitled to ask to see letters confirming that female employees are actually pregnant and that appointments have in fact been made. Note that you cannot fairly dismiss a woman for reasons 'connected' with pregnancy. Therefore dismissal of women suffering from emotional tension brought on by pregnancy, or suffering from post-natal depression, or who miscarried and were consequently ill, is unlawful.

## Rules on reinstatement

Following the birth of the child, an employee who has completed two years' continuous service (or five years, if she has worked between 8 and 16 hours a week) is legally entitled to return to work up to 29 weeks after her confinement (with a possible four week extension on medical grounds) and to be reinstated in her old or an equivalent job. For women without the required length of service, the 14 week rule applies. The woman must give notice of her intention to return. In the former case, this notice must be in writing and submitted at least 21 days before taking maternity leave and, if the employer writes to the employee within seven weeks of her confinement asking for confirmation of her intention to return to work, she must reply within 14 days.

# PEOPLE MANAGEMENT

## THE LAW ON PAYING WAGES

The Wages Act 1986 removed all previous restrictions on employers paying their workers by means other than cash (or cheque or credit transfers in appropriate circumstances), although the actual method of payment is a matter for negotiation. Under the Act it is generally illegal to deduct money from an employee's pay or for the firm to require the employee to pay back money received in wages except in the following circumstances:

(a) Deductions for income tax and national insurance; or if a court has ordered that part of a person's wages be paid to a third party (eg to settle a fine or money owing under a court judgement).

(b) Payments requested in writing by the employee, such as trade union or sports clubs subscriptions.

(c) Agreed deductions for lateness or poor work, provided the agreement is incorporated in the employee's contract of employment.

(d) Accidental overpayment of previous wages or expenses.

(e) For retail employees only, deductions to make good cash shortages (eg money missing from the cash till) or stock deficiencies. 'Retail employment' means anyone involved in the sale and supply of goods or services. Hence the Act covers not just shop assistants, but any employee handling cash transactions with customers — bus conductors, milk deliverers, booking office clerks, bank counter staff, etc. Deductions must not exceed more than 10 per cent of the wages due on any one pay day (except the last pay day before the employee leaves the firm) and the deduction must be made within twelve months of the detection of the shortage or deficiency.

## ARE WAGE INCREASES A GENUINE INCENTIVE?

In a word, 'yes', although by how much varies from person to person. The point is that monetary wage increases can be used for so many purposes: to buy goods and services, to change lifestyle, support a leisure activity, etc. Also a pay rise is an explicit recognition of a person's occupational competence; pay rises awarded for excellent performance can greatly increase a worker's commitment and general morale. This itself can be a motivating factor. Comparison of a person's wages with the wages of others enables the individual to relate his or her job to other jobs within the organisation and externally.

*182*

There can be no doubt that relations with colleagues, pride in the quality of one's work, group cohesion, and so on are major motivators, but wage increases remain a primary factor.

## Wage differentials

That pay increases are important for the motivation of employees is evident from the frequency of the grumbles that arise from the petty (and not so petty) wage differentials that often exist within a large department. As a manager, you may well encounter disgruntled employees who complain that they are receiving inappropriate rates of pay. It is useful, therefore, to list in advance reasons which explain wage differentials between various employees in order to deal with any queries that arise. Differences might be due to:

- age;
- length of service;
- training received;
- basic qualifications;
- level of skill required;
- responsibilities assumed;
- frequency with which higher-level work is undertaken;
- stress associated with a job.

Ultimately, employees' wages are determined by the forces of supply and demand. In the shorter term, however, management will seek to ensure that differentials between salary grades are 'consistent' (within existing parameters which could eventually change through market pressure) and rationally determined.

## Salary structures

Ideally, salary structures should allow for progression through a scale that coincides with the level of attainment of the salary earner at any given point, should have a rationale that is understood by the staff, and should be cheap and simple to operate. Unfortunately, modern systems tend to be complicated, and in consequence may fail to achieve any of these objectives. Two major factors explain the intricacy of many contemporary schemes: tax efficiency, and the confidentiality of amounts earned. The UK tax system offers enormous savings to both the company and the employee through paying staff via fringe benefits rather than in salary as such. Also a remuneration package comprising many components will be unique to the individual and, unless that person chooses to tell colleagues how much exactly the package is worth, staff will not really know how much other people earn. Different people are prepared to work for different levels of reward. Thus an extra (and valuable) fringe benefit might be offered to one employee who demands extra remuneration, but not to others — so that the existing basic salary structure is not disturbed.

If serious complaints do emerge it is important to identify the root cause of the dissatisfaction. Has the employee reached the top point of a grade without being promoted and if so, why was promotion withheld? Is extra training needed? Is the person incompetent — is there an adverse comment on his or her personnel file? It may be that the individual's job is fundamentally dissimilar to those of the colleagues with whom that person is making a comparison. List and explain the reasons for allocation to the particular grade, and if the worker then decides to invoke a grievance procedure pursue this in the usual way; it is better to bring the complaint into the open than to have a perpetually dissatisfied and demotivated employee.

## EQUAL PAY FOR WORK OF EQUAL VALUE

Britain's Equal Pay Act was revised in 1984 to enable individuals to claim equal pay relative to a member of the opposite sex employed by the same firm who does work of equal value as determined by a job evaluation study (see below). This legislation was designed to enable women who perform jobs not usually done by men (typists, office cleaners, etc) to claim fair rewards for their contributions. Hence a woman need not identify a man who is doing identical work for the firm on higher wages, she just has to demonstrate that her job is worth the same in terms of its 'demands'. Such demands might relate to the effort, skill, responsibility assumed, working conditions, or decision-taking capacities required for effective performance.

The amended Equal Pay Act emphasises that the relevant yardstick in determining equal value is whether the jobs are equivalent with respect to the demands made on the employee when doing the job, rather than the perceived value of the work to the employer. In other words, it is the nature of the work actually done that matters.

### Assessing equal value

To investigate whether two jobs in your section are of equal value (bearing in mind that if they are and if they happen to be undertaken by members of the opposite sex, your firm could be open to legal action if they are not paid equally) you should:

1.  list all the common elements in the two jobs;

2.  list all the differences between them;

3.  assess the extent to which such differences can be set off against each other in terms of the demands they make on the worker.

Then list all the differences which in your view cannot be offset, and for each difference specify why the difference is important and why exactly it causes one job to be more valuable (in terms of the demands made on the worker) than the other. The Equal Opportunities Commission's guide to the amended Equal Pay Act offers a number of examples of possible similar and dissimilar demands made on the workers undertaking two hypothetical jobs. These are reproduced below.

### Examples of similar demands

| Job A | Job B |
|---|---|
| Responsible for contact with public | Responsible for staff |
| Lifts heavy weights occasionally | Lifts small weights continually |
| Diagnoses machine faults | Analyses written reports |
| Checks stocks and orders replacements | Checks work done by subordinates and allocates tasks |
| Uses drilling machine | Uses typewriter |
| On feet most of day | Has to concentrate on numbers |

### Examples of dissimilar demands

| Job A | Job B |
|---|---|
| Drives a van | Examines customer complaints |
| Sweeps up | Chooses fabric for new designs |
| Decides shift rosters | Responsible for packing and despatch |

Finally, prepare an explanation of the pay differential between the two jobs.

Cases that go before tribunals are judged on their individual merits, although all rely heavily on the results of independent job evaluation studies. Already such studies have determined that the work of a factory nurse was of equal value to that of a skilled fitter, that a secretary's work had equal value to a scientific assistant's, that an administrator's job was equal to a data analyst's, and that the demands made on a seamstress were of equal value to those made on a fork-lift truck driver. Other pairings have involved quality controllers and technical trainers; and the comparison of catering assistants with drivers.

# JOB EVALUATION

Job evaluation is a means of ensuring equitable rates of pay and conditions of service. It concerns the appraisal of the relative value of a job compared to other jobs undertaken within the organisation, focusing on the characteristics of each job rather than on the personal attributes of the occupants of specific positions. Its purposes are to establish a hierarchy of graded posts according to their objective worth to the business (so that individual occupants of these posts may be fairly rewarded); to remove pay anomalies and petty differentials; and to reduce the number of separate grades of pay.

If it is done properly, job evaluation avoids inequitable job structures thus removing the source of disputes over pay relativities. Also, clearly defined job hierarchies facilitate the implementation of rational promotion systems that specify precisely all the qualifications and personal attributes needed for an individual to advance to the next higher grade. All jobs of equivalent value will be equally graded and rewarded, regardless of their departmental locations.

The argument against job evaluation, of course, is that the systematic allocation of employees to rationally determined grades, each possessing its own clearly defined characteristics and level of responsibility, might encourage inflexible attitudes and an unwillingness to complete duties not strictly covered by the job specifications emerging from a job evaluation exercise.

## Legal aspects of job evaluation

Under the 1984 amendments to the Equal Pay Act any person is entitled to the same remuneration and conditions of service as a member of the opposite sex who is doing similar work, or 'work which is of a similar value', as judged under a job evaluation exercise. If a job evaluation has *not* already been undertaken within the organisation the employee has the legal right (regardless of length of service, current grade or part-time or full-time status) to apply to an industrial tribunal for an order (which is legally enforceable) that a job evaluation be carried out by an independent expert appointed by and reporting to the tribunal. This evaluation will consider the effort, skills, responsibility, requirement to take decisions and so on attached to the post, and the demands made on the individual worker in this job compared to jobs done by the firm's other workers.

To stand up in law, any job evaluation scheme must be 'analytical', ie it must make genuine comparisons of all the relevant factors associated with the jobs under consideration and not simply rank jobs according to general, subjective criteria. Normally, analytical methods involve the allocation of points to the constituent features of each job. The greater the total number of points awarded, the higher the status (and wage) of the post.

# 12

# HEALTH AND SAFETY IN THE WORKPLACE

## THE LAW ON HEALTH AND SAFETY AT WORK

The main statute governing employee health and safety is the Health and Safety at Work Act (HSAWA) of 1974, which imposes on employers a general duty to ensure so far as is 'reasonably practical' the health and safety at work of all employees. Breach of this duty can lead to a criminal (rather than civil) prosecution. Any firm employing more than four workers must, under the Act, prepare a written statement of its policy on health and safety and bring this to the attention of employees. Plant, machinery and other equipment must be safe and well maintained, and all arrangements for handling, storing and transporting articles and substances must be safe and free of health hazards. Importantly, your employer is obliged to provide the supervision, instruction and training needed to ensure health and safety. Firms are statutorily obliged to check that all aspects of the workplace are safe, including means of entry and exit, machinery and equipment, and the working environment (fumes, dust, etc).

The Act is administered through a Health and Safety Commission which is a watchdog body that delegates its powers to a national Health and Safety Executive (HSE). The latter issues codes of practice which, while not legally binding or enforceable, are looked at by courts when adjudicating cases. Find out whether the HSE has issued a code of practice relevant to your industry and if it has, ensure its recommendations are implemented. This demonstrates unequivocably that you are taking 'all reasonable precautions' to ensure health and safety within your department.

# YOUR PERSONAL POSITION

Your position as someone who takes decisions that may be in breach of a legal duty is usually (but not always) covered by the doctrine of 'vicarious liability', which holds that since you are an employee of an organisation, then your employer is liable for civil (but not criminal) wrongs that you commit in the course of your employment, not you personally. The phrase 'in the course of employment' means acts authorised by the employer or, where they are not formally authorised, where actions are so closely connected with employment that they are incidental to the employee's work. Only if your action is clearly outside the scope of your employment will you be personally liable for your deeds.

It is critically important to note, however, that any person (including a head of department) who acts in an executive capacity is personally liable for offences committed under the Health and Safety at Work Act if that person consented to connive with the commission of the offence or if it was attributable to his or her neglect. 'Consent' means agreeing (actively or passively) to the offence; 'connivance' occurs if you become personally involved in committing the offence; 'negligence' means acts or omissions that lead, directly or indirectly, to the offence.

## Position of employees

Section 7 of the Act states that employees must take 'reasonable care' to ensure they endanger neither themselves nor others at work. Thus your subordinates are legally required to cooperate on health and safety matters — although note that it is *your* responsibility to ensure that instructions are carried out. For example, if protective clothing is necessary then not only must the firm provide it (free of charge) but also you must make sure that it is worn, if necessary by disciplining workers.

# SAFETY REPRESENTATIVES

If a recognised trade union so wishes it can appoint 'safety representatives' at places of work. The union does not need management's permission for this, but the union must be 'recognised' by the employing firm for the purpose of collective bargaining. So if management does not permit a union to operate within the company the union has no legal right to appoint safety representatives.

In businesses that do recognise trade unions, it is for the unions themselves to decide the procedure for selecting safety representatives, whose functions include:

(a) investigation of hazards, accidents and dangerous occurrences, and making representations to management on matters arising from these investigations or on any other safety issue;

(b) meeting outside inspectors and receiving information from them;

(c) making formal inspections of the workplace every three months or following accidents or dangerous occurrences;

(d) inspecting and taking copies of any relevant information (accident reports, for example) that the employer is statutorily obliged to maintain.

## Inspections

You should positively welcome the appointment of safety representatives in your department, and cooperate with them at all times. Active involvement of employees in safety matters helps to prevent accidents, acts as a check on the efficiency of the firm's safety records and procedures, and generally improves morale. Inspection is an essential part of a representative's duties. Departmental managers are entitled to accompany the representative during inspections, but the Act gives that person the right to confer with his or her union members in private as the inspection proceeds. Notice of an inspection need not be given if an accident or dangerous incident has just occurred.

Following an inspection, the safety representative has to complete a report, one copy of which must be sent to you (as management's representative). The report (books of standard inspection report forms can be purchased from HMSO) will contain a blank section headed 'remedial action or explanation' which you must fill in prior to returning the report to the representative. If you obstruct an inspection or fail to provide necessary information the representative can call in an HSE inspector who possesses legal powers to inspect, and this person will disclose to the representative the information you initially withheld.

## Facilities for safety representatives

Under the Health and Safety at Work Act, your firm must furnish such 'facilities and assistance' to representatives as they may reasonably require in order to complete inspections. The Act does not specify the meaning of this, although the Trades Union Congress has issued its own Code of Practice, recommending that safety representatives be provided with:

(a) use of a room and a desk with facilities for storing correspondence, inspection reports, etc;

(b) access to a telephone, typewriter and photocopier;

(c) a noticeboard, and use of the internal mail system;

(d) access to test equipment and copies of all relevant statutes, regulations, HSE Codes of Practice, etc.

If a firm refuses to make any facilities available at all, the union can bring a case against your firm in an industrial tribunal.

*Time off work*

Safety representatives are legally entitled to 'reasonable' time off work on full pay to carry out safety duties and attend union safety training courses. You must be given proper notice of a representative's intention to attend a course, plus details of the course and a copy of the syllabus. Only if the firm offers a comparable course internally may a request for time off be denied.

## SAFETY COMMITTEES

Should any two safety representatives so require, the firm *must* establish a 'safety committee'. The request has to be in writing and the committee must be set up within three months of the date of the letter. 'Notes of guidance' on the operation of such committees have been issued by the Health and Safety Commission (HSC). These recommend that the committee should consider welfare matters as well as health and safety, analyse trends in accidents, diseases, etc, and investigate specific incidents. It should also develop safety rules and become involved with safety training. According to the HSC notes, the number of management representatives on the committee should not exceed the number of employee representatives, and the management side should be knowledgeable about safety matters and possess 'adequate' executive authority. Note that safety representatives are not accountable to the committee, only to union members — and they do not have to obey its commands. Nor does the existence of a safety committee (which might include medical doctors, nurses and other expert members *ex officio*) imply that safety issues should not be subject to collective bargaining between management and unions.

Many firms employ a specialist safety officer to represent them on safety matters. Full-time safety officers (unlike union safety representatives) are not protected against criminal liability if they fail in their duties.

# SAFETY POLICY

It is in your own interests to pay meticulous attention to health and safety matters; legally and in view of the fact that this will reduce the number of accidents occurring within the department. Accidents are expensive. Not only do they disrupt operations; they also incur the costs of sick pay, investigations, training of temporary replacement workers, and so on.

Seek consciously to identify hazards, and to inculcate in others a respect for safe methods of work. Never authorise or even condone unsafe working practices — try instead to incorporate safety checks into the departmental management system. Be seen to investigate all accidents, and regularly inspect machinery and equipment. Insist on 'good housekeeping' within the department, and that all accidents (no matter how trivial) are reported.

## An accident prevention checklist

Accident prevention is critically important for the smooth running of any organisation. Ask yourself the following questions in relation to your own department:

1.  Do the staff possess the right attitudes towards safety at work? Are they safety conscious, and if not whose fault is this?

2.  Has every employee been given the training necessary to operate equipment?

3.  Are there any payment incentive systems in operation that might encourage workers to cut corners where safety is concerned?

4.  Has the correct equipment been provided to enable workers to complete their duties satisfactorily?

5.  Have you identified potential safety hazards within your department?

6.  Does the firm have set procedures for dealing with employees who circumvent safety rules? If not, then such procedures need to be formulated.

## Reporting accidents

There are government regulations compelling employers to report all serious accidents (and other accidents involving more than three days' absence from work) within seven days. Failure to comply with the regulations is a criminal offence. They demand that the firm inform its local authority environmental health department immediately (normally by telephone) following a death or serious injury arising from an accident, or whenever a 'dangerous occurrence' — an over-turned crane or a burst pressure vessel, for example — takes place. Note that under the regulations, self-employed people and individuals receiving training for employment are covered in exactly the same way as employees. Approved report forms may be purchased from commercial stationers or from HMSO (form F 2508). Records of accidents, dangerous occurrences and outbreaks of certain specified industrial diseases have to be kept for at least three years.

## The accident book

Accident reports are useful for identifying and preventing the recurrence of dangerous activities. Also, formal records are needed to investigate subsequent claims for compensation from injured employees. Every firm employing more than nine persons, or less than nine if the firm is covered by the Factories Act 1961, is legally obliged to keep an accident book. Reports should be completed as quickly as possible after the incident (before memories fade) and give full details of the victim (age, sex, occupation, etc) and of the accident (time, date, circumstances). It should list witnesses, describe the injuries sustained, first aid administered, and note whether (and if so, when) an ambulance was called, and when the ambulance arrived and departed.

The cause of the accident should be stated, with details of whether safety rules were followed, whether protective clothing was actually worn, machinery properly guarded, etc. When completing an accident report, take a note of what the victim was doing at the precise moment the accident occurred, and whether, in the opinion of witnesses, the employee was partly to blame. Copies of the report should be circulated to the worker and his or her union, to safety representatives and to the personnel department. Collectively, accident reports should be analysed to identify recurring causes and the effects of changes in machinery, working methods, paces of production, shift work patterns, etc on accident rates.

*External inspections*

HSE (and other) government inspectors visit firms' premises periodically to ensure they comply with various legal requirements. Inspections also occur following complaints by workers or members of the public and after serious accidents. If an inspector finds that an offence has been committed then he or she may either inform the employer on the spot of the unsatisfactory item and later ensure that remedial action has been taken; or serve an 'improvement notice' compelling positive action within 21 days, or a 'prohibition notice' forcing the firm to cease a risky activity; or prosecute the firm before magistrates.

The policy in most cases is to prosecute only if the law is deliberately and persistently flouted. Appeals against improvement or prohibition notices are heard by industrial tribunals. Typically, appeals are based on the grounds that it is 'not reasonably practical' to comply with the notice — for example, if the risk of injury were extremely small and the financial cost of complying with the order extremely heavy.

# THE EC HEALTH AND SAFETY MANAGEMENT DIRECTIVES

A number of important new sets of health and safety at work regulations came into effect in early 1993 in consequence of the UK's implementation of six 1992 EC Directives on health and safety matters. The 1992 regulations on display screen equipment are discussed on page 198. Other regulations in the package are as follows.

*Management of Health and Safety at Work Regulations 1992*

These require employers to complete risk-assessment exercises intended to identify any dangers to the health and safety of their workers or anyone else likely to be affected by the firm's operations. Preventive and protective measures must be specified and a plan for putting them into effect drawn up. Firms with five or more workers have to maintain a permanent record of the risk assessment. The regulations also require employers to establish procedures for dealing with health and safety emergencies and to appoint 'competent people' (who may be outside consultants) to devise and implement the measures necessary to ensure that the firm is complying with health and safety law. Existing UK health and safety legislation is reinforced and extended in the following respects:

1. Employees (including temporary workers) must be given clear information about risks, in language they can easily understand.

2. Firms must ensure that workers are trained in safety matters and capable of avoiding risks. Health surveillance mechanisms have to be provided wherever necessary.

3. Employees are legally obliged to report dangers and to follow safety instructions.

### Provision and Use of Work Equipment Regulations 1992

'Work equipment' is defined under these regulations as including everything from hand tools to complete factories or refineries, while 'use' means every aspect of equipment operation, servicing and cleaning. Employers are obliged to make sure that equipment is suitable for its intended purpose and that it is only used in appropriate ways. When selecting equipment, employers must take into account working conditions and the hazards of the workplace. Proper training and information relating to the equipment must be given to workers.

### Manual Handling Operations Regulations 1992

These require employers to identify unavoidable handling risks in terms of the size, shape and weight of the load, the handler's posture while performing operations and the ergonomic characteristics of the workplace (space available, humidity, etc). By law, hazardous manual handling operations must be avoided wherever possible.

### Workplace (Health, Safety and Welfare) Regulations 1992, and the Personal Protective Equipment at Work Regulations 1992

The purpose of these two sets of regulations is to tidy up and consolidate a large number of existing pieces of legislation currently spread over several different statutes. They concern such matters as the working environment (lighting, ventilation, room space per worker and so on), facilities (toilets, rest areas, drinking water, etc), removal of waste materials, cleaning and maintenance of protective clothing and equipment, and the design and approval of new personal protective equipment.

## OTHER SAFETY LEGISLATION

Although the HSAWA is intended as a piece of umbrella legislation that eventually will incorporate all other health and safety statutes it does not replace existing health and safety laws, which currently operate in parallel with the 1974 Act. The major statutes that you are likely to encounter in your managerial work are outlined below.

## The Offices, Shops and Railway Premises Act 1963

This Act applies to offices everywhere, even those on premises normally used for other purposes (factories, for example) although temporary offices or those operated for less than 21 hours a week are excluded. Among the Act's major provisions are the requirements that:

(a) premises, furniture and fittings should be kept clean, and floors should be washed weekly;

(b) each person should have at least 40 square foot of space;

(c) rooms should be properly ventilated, lit and heated (ie to at least 16°C after the first hour);

(d) washing facilities with hot water, soap and towels should be provided, and lavatories should be accessible and properly maintained;

(e) no worker should be expected to lift dangerously heavy weights;

(f) floors, passages and stairs should be kept clear and safe, and all machinery and equipment should be guarded;

(g) first-aid boxes should be provided, the contents of which conform to the requirements of the Health and Safety (First Aid) Regulations 1981;

(h) seating must be available, and staff must be given facilities for keeping clothing not worn at work.

## The Fire Precautions Act 1971

The essential requirement of this Act is that certain classes of premises (including those covered by the Offices, Shops and Railway Premises Act, factories, and buildings to which the public has access) should possess a 'fire certificate' issued by the local fire authority, which must be satisfied that the means of escape from the building and other fire precautions are adequate. Your firm should register its premises with the local fire authority, await an inspection, and then adhere to the fire authority's advice. Over and above this, however, you should encourage your subordinates to be fire conscious and to remove fire risks. Ensure that all your staff know how to use fire appliances, the location of fire exits, and how to operate the alarm system. Under the Act, staff must be given training in evacuation procedures and the use of fire-fighting equipment kept on the premises. Moreover, written records of all training sessions must be kept, stating the topics covered during the session, who supervised the session, and who attended.

## The Factories Act 1961

This contains similar provisions to the Offices, Shops and Railway Premises Act, but for factories. However, additional regulations are included on the maintenance of hoists and lifts and, importantly, it specifies maximum working hours for young persons (restrictions on women's working hours were abolished in 1986), and that all young persons (ie people between 16 and 18 years of age) working in factories must be medically examined within two weeks of starting work. A firm may request exemption from the Act's restrictions on working hours for young persons if it needs to meet exceptional demand for output, provided the firm can demonstrate that adequate welfare facilities will be provided. Exemptions are not issued for more than one year.

# CURRENT ISSUES

Three health and safety issues have attracted large amounts of attention in recent years: the protection of workers who operate computer visual display units (VDUs), the protection of night workers, and the protection of pregnant employees.

## Visual display units

Critics allege that heavy VDU users (especially those who operate word processors) suffer eye strain, headaches, muscular dysfunctions, and absorb excessive amounts of radiation. It may be that the heat and static electricity generated by VDUs engender lethargy and general feelings of ill health among long-term users, and this might cause persistent tiredness. Pregnant women — it is alleged — are especially vulnerable. Staring into a VDU hour after hour can make workers clumsy, drowsy, and unable to think clearly or concentrate.

Such accusations are denied by the manufacturers of computer equipment, and much research is being undertaken on the subject. The present legal position is that work involving VDUs must conform with the European Community Directive on work with display screen equipment, which is binding on all EC member countries. Under the Directive, employers must:

(a) analyse display screen workstations to identify potential hazards and take measures to remedy any health and safety problem discovered;

(b) train employees in the proper use of display screen equipment, inform workers of relevant facts, and consult employee representatives about VDU matters;

(c) plan VDU operators' daily schedules in order to interrupt long periods of screen work and to create changes of activity;

(d) ensure that workstations satisfy the technical requirements of the Directive in relation to screen sizes and luminosity, keyboard design, working environment, etc;

(e) provide employees with eye and eyesight tests before they commence VDU work and at regular intervals thereafter. Firms must supply special spectacles if employees' normal spectacles are not suitable for display screen jobs.

## Shift work

The introduction of 'lean' production methods, just-in-time systems, intensive capacity working, etc has led to an increase in the incidence of shift work in Britain and with it a corresponding increase in the health, safety and welfare problems that shift work entails. These include:

(a) disruption of biological rhythms (adrenalin secretions, sleep/waking patterns, body temperature, etc);

(b) reduction in the quantity and quality of sleep, accompanied by constant tiredness;

(c) digestion problems and possible loss of appetite;

(d) disruptions to family life, anxieties about childcare, social isolation and worsening social relationships.

Shift workers, on average, have more severe accidents than others, and the quality of their output is often lower. There are perhaps two explanations for this. First, there is less continuity of supervision on shift-work systems. If you manage each of (say) three shifts for a few weeks or months at a time you will regularly have to supervise a completely new set of people. You establish satisfactory working relationships with one group, and then move on to another. Night-shift supervision is especially onerous because no administrative support (personnel staff, wages clerks, specialist engineers, etc, who are at home in bed) is available. Either you must refer problems to day-shift managers or take decisions unilaterally, without discussing them with colleagues. Second, shift workers are often unable to relax properly, causing fatigue, inattentiveness and accidents. Several weeks are required to adapt fully to a new time system; but then days off and weekends — when the worker reverts to a normal lifestyle — disrupt the newly established pattern.

If you are in charge of a night-shift operation, ensure that as much preparatory, non-essential and administrative work as possible is done during the daytime. Senior management may arrange special transport for workers coming or going at odd hours (when public transport is irregular or unavailable), and provide proper canteen facilities throughout the night. Check that all first-aid facilities are available on late shifts and that fire precautions and other safety arrangements are not ignored following dayworkers' departures.

At the time of writing there is an EC Draft Directive (ie one that has been proposed but not yet agreed by all Community member nations) on night and night-shift working that is likely to be adopted in the near future. Under the proposal, night workers would not normally be able to work more than eight hours in any 24-hour period, and overtime would not be permitted without special permission (if permission is granted, the overtime working must not last more than six months).

Nightworkers would be entitled to free medical examinations before starting night shifts, and periodically thereafter. Also, they should be given additional time off to compensate for their unsocial hours, must have a daily rest period of at least 11 consecutive hours, and at least one day off work each week.

## Protection of pregnant employees

Maternity rights are discussed in Chapter 11. An EC Directive on the protection of pregnant workers requires employers to adapt — without loss of pay — a pregnant woman's hours, duties and working conditions to ensure her health and safety. Pregnant employees normally engaged on night work have to be given alternative day jobs for a 16-week period, of which eight weeks must be immediately before the expected date of birth of the child. Fourteen weeks' paid maternity leave are available, with no loss of employment rights (including the right to reinstatement). Two of the weeks have to be taken immediately before the expected date of birth of the child. Pregnant employees are protected against dismissal on the grounds of pregnancy, regardless of their length of service. The Directive also requires the protection of pregnant women from specific harmful processes or substances.

## SAFETY TRAINING

Two types of safety training are needed: basic training in rules and procedures, and policy training for managers. Basic training can be done via lectures on induction courses. These should include information on hazards in specific jobs, the safety policies of the firm, use of protective clothing and equipment, location and use of fire appliances, first-aid facilities, procedures for reporting accidents, and evacuation procedures. Further basic training could include first-aid courses and regular films/talks on topics such as how to lift weights, identify dangerous situations, attend to injured persons, etc. Training sessions should be held regularly and not just when serious accidents have occurred.

### Policy training

This should cover the law on health and safety — both generally and specifically in relation to the regulations and codes of practice relevant to the industry — plus training on the organisation of safety committees, dealing with safety representatives, inspection requirements, the analysis of statistical data, etc. Note that since the Health and Safety at Work Act explicitly requires an employer to provide such 'information, training, instruction and supervision' as is necessary to ensure the health and safety of employees, you need from your superiors full details of the legal minimum health and safety requirements applicable to your department's work. Then you can conduct a 'safety audit' to examine checking procedures for equipment and hazardous materials, provisions for storing and handling materials, evacuation systems, etc.

# Part 3

# COMMUNICATING

# 13

# MOTIVATING EMPLOYEES

## INTRODUCTION

People management is far more than hiring, firing and controlling workers. It concerns everything to do with putting together and organising teams of employees for the purpose of helping the business to achieve its objectives. Accordingly, it involves:

- designing jobs to make them as interesting as possible;
- matching the personal aspirations of employees to the needs of the organisation;
- developing and motivating workers.

If the firm's recruitment, training, appraisal and employee support systems are working satisfactorily then the people it employs will:

- want to work hard;
- be able to think for themselves;
- initiate activities rather than waiting to be told what to do;
- seek responsibility.

Firms with sound personnel policies and procedures will, in general, have better motivated workforces than others. The following are examples of well constructed personnel policies:

- wherever practicable, giving workers security of employment;
- establishing fair procedures for dealing with inevitable redundancies and complaints against management by staff;

- providing employees with opportunities for retraining and the acquisition of new skills;

- avoiding discrimination in recruitment and/or in promotion on the grounds of sex, ethnic origin, religion, marital status, age or physical disability;

- offering promotion to suitably qualified staff;

- consultation and negotiation with employees' representatives on issues affecting terms and conditions of employment and working environments.

Employees are motivated in part by the fact that they have to earn a living, and partly by human needs — for job satisfaction, security of tenure, the respect of colleagues, and so on. The organisation's reward system (pay, fringe benefits, job security, promotion opportunities, etc) may be applied to the first motive, and job design to the latter. The role of wages in motivating employees is considered in Chapter 11.

## JOB DESIGN

Certain types of work provide employees with opportunities for creativity and the exercise of initiative (managerial work, for example), and those who undertake such work typically derive great satisfaction from its completion. For others, however, work can be drudgery; neither enjoyable nor satisfying — just something that has to be done. The latter situation is particularly unfortunate in situations where individuals are in jobs which are clearly unsuited to their abilities and aptitudes.

### Boredom at work

Boredom can be a particularly serious problem for some workers. It may result from continuous repetition of a simple task, or from the social environment in which tasks are undertaken. A task might be interesting, but the worker could still feel bored if he or she must complete it in isolation. Equally, jobs can be trivial and repetitious, but do not create boredom because workers are able to communicate pleasurably with others. Workers who perform complex tasks typically become absorbed by them and are not bored.

Further problems with repetitive jobs are feelings of lack of control over working methods or the speed of production, having to do work perceived as meaningless, and not being involved in workplace decision making. Reactions against repetitive work can include aggression (quarrels with colleagues, hostility towards management), apathy (manifest in high rates of lateness and absenteeism), unwillingness to assume responsibility, poor-quality work, high propensities to have accidents, and high levels of labour turnover.

## Nature of job design

Job design is the process of deciding which tasks and responsibilities will be undertaken by particular employees and the methods, systems and procedures for completing work. It concerns patterns of account-ability, authority, and interpersonal relations among colleagues. The purpose of job design is to stimulate the interest and involvement of the worker, thus motivating the worker to greater effort. Jobs may be 'enlarged' or 'enriched'. Job enlargement means increasing the scope of a job through extending the range of its duties and responsibilities. Instead of dividing work into small units, each of which is performed repetitively by an individual employee, you deliberately broaden the range of duties undertaken.

Job enrichment means the allocation of more interesting, challenging and perhaps difficult duties to workers in order to stimulate their sense of involvement with their work and concern for the achievement of objectives. Extra decision-making authority may be assigned to workers, or they might be given duties requiring higher skill levels or be required to have greater contact with customers and/or suppliers. Equally, exist-ing single tasks might be combined into a composite whole or workers might be made responsible for controlling the quality of their output, or be allowed greater discretion over how they achieve objectives.

The term 'job extension' is used to embrace both enlargement and enrichment. Its underlying philosophy is, quite simply, that the wider the variety of tasks undertaken the more the worker realises the signifi-cance of the job in the wider organisation and the happier and more productive he or she will become. Of course, some jobs are more easily extended than others. Assembly lines in automated factories offer few opportunities for interesting work. In this case, higher pay and/or greater worker participation could be primary motivators. Note also that not everybody wants to assume extra responsibility.

## How to design jobs

To initiate a job design exercise you must first analyse the work that needs to be done within the department, using existing job descrip-tions (see Chapter 5) and any other information available. You need to know which jobs are least interesting to the people who do them (and why) and what steps are necessary to make these jobs more interesting. So you should interview colleagues individually (performance appraisal discussions (see Chapter 6) offer convenient opportunities for this), confidentially and sympathetically in order to get the feel of their jobs. Unfortunately, people often exaggerate the difficulties and problems associated with their work, so you must pin interviewees down when describing their jobs; do not accept vague statements about tasks and responsibilities.

Having described the jobs of members of the department, list the interesting duties — those which carry responsibility and which involve planning and self-control — associated with each position. Then specify exactly the changes necessary to make particularly boring jobs more interesting, eg regrouping activities (taking some interesting work away from certain individuals for reallocation to others), allowing workers to alter the pace or methods of their work, or allocating broad rather than specific objectives. Participation in the setting of targets can also enrich employees' work, especially if the workers are encouraged to contribute completely new ideas.

Look critically at physical working conditions within the department. Can they be improved? And can you enhance the perceived status of employees, say by giving each of their jobs an impressive-sounding title? Possibly you can improve colleagues' sense of job security through frequently complimenting their standards of work, and you might perhaps reduce the amount of supervision you apply by removing various controls (time sheets, rigid directives on working methods, standard layouts for equipment and materials, etc). Can the staff be brought into contact with final customers, or even other departments which utilise their work — much satisfaction can be gained from observing the pleasure of a customer when he or she is presented with a high-quality finished product. Try to make your people feel important; praise them, and be seen to take a personal interest in their work.

## Job satisfaction surveys

Job satisfaction in employees is not easy to measure because no standard measurement criteria exist. Tasks which bore some people can interest others, and people might work hard even though greatly dissatisfied with their jobs (in pursuit of high wages, for example). Some firms issue questionnaires to employees asking them to list in rank order the tasks they find particularly tedious and/or unpleasant.

Equally, employees might be invited to comment on the working conditions they regard as most attractive (security, good interpersonal relations, responsibility, control over work, etc). Results from such surveys may help in designing jobs, although many of the workers' suggestions will in practice be unattainable, and again the problem arises that individuals will be subjective in their response, so that jobs designed according to the suggestions of one set of incumbents might not be suitable for the next.

It seems reasonable to assume that if employees are dissatisfied in their work they will take the maximum permissible time off. Perhaps, therefore, the best indicators of job satisfaction are punctuality among employees and low rates of absenteeism and labour turnover. Other important symptoms of unhappiness are the incidence of invocation of grievance procedures, and the frequency of arguments among staff.

## INTERNAL PROMOTION

Apart from improvements in pay and conditions of work, the most immediate incentive available to an employee is the possibility of promotion. If the firm has trained its staff adequately and ensured that their work experiences are sufficiently wide, internal promotion should present no problem. External recruitment should be necessary only for specialist positions or when no one within the organisation possesses appropriate qualifications for a post. Promotion prospects offer significant motivation to employees.

### Who to promote

The criteria used in selecting individuals for promotion can be based on ability or seniority. Ability-related systems accelerate the careers of exceptionally competent staff, whereas seniority-based procedures ensure steady progression for all employees. And knowledge that promotion is reasonably assured can improve morale throughout the entire organisation.

Promotion follows logically from training, performance appraisal, management development and management by objectives programmes. People can be selected for promotion directly — management simply appointing chosen employees to higher posts — or vacancies can be advertised within the firm. Direct selection is quick, inexpensive, and suitable where management knows the abilities of all its workers. Internal advertisement is appropriate in large firms where several candidates of about the same level of ability might apply.

A fair internal promotion system has numerous benefits: internal personal relationships between managers and the people who work for them improve, labour turnover falls (since able staff do not need to leave the firm to do higher-level work), while efficiency should increase through utilisation in senior positions of the accumulated experience of long-serving employees. Additionally, there is little risk of the individuals who are promoted possessing unknown deficiencies, as occurs with externally recruited senior staff. On the other hand, outsiders can inject fresh ideas and apply new perspectives to existing problems, and external recruits might be of much higher calibre than internal candidates.

If you are called on to recommend colleagues for promotion you should adhere to certain principles in making your selection. Do not overlook a suitable candidate simply because that person is performing excellently in his or her present job. It is unfair to block an individual's prospects simply because — through hard work and personal competence — he or she has become indispensable in the current position.

In general, avoid promoting people who have only recently joined the firm. And always stand ready to justify your recommendations to colleagues, including those you feel are not yet ready for promotion.

## The EOC Code of Practice

Unfair discrimination in promotion upsets and demotivates staff, and should always be avoided. Promotion should never be denied on grounds of race or sex. Indeed, discrimination in selection for promotion on these grounds is illegal under existing sex and race discrimination legislation. The Equal Opportunities Commission Code of Practice on avoidance of sex discrimination recommends that promotion procedures are thoroughly examined to ensure that 'traditional' qualifications are actually relevant to the promotion opportunity under consideration. It suggests, moreover, that promotion based on length of service could amount to unlawful indirect discrimination since women typically have shorter lengths of service through time out of the labour force taken for child-raising responsibilities. Where 'general ability and personal qualities' are the main requirements for promotion, the Code insists that care should be taken 'to consider favourably candidates of both sexes with differing career patterns and general experience'.

## Monitoring the promotion system

Organisations that operate in sensitive multi-cultural or multi-ethnic environments sometimes monitor the consequences of their promotion policies by checking whether certain groups are overrepresented among those who do not achieve promotion. So if it is found that females or members of ethnic minorities are prominent in the non-promoted category, the reasons for this are isolated and remedial measures applied. Specifically, the following questions can be asked of the promotion system:

(a) What are the characteristics of non-promoted groups, and are there valid reasons explaining why individuals in these groups are not promoted?

(b) What contributions have non-promoted groups made to the work the firm? Have they been adequately rewarded for their contributions?

(c) Why do non-promoted individuals remain with the firm?

(d) What help can be given to non-promoted groups in order to help them qualify for promotion? What are the obstacles confronting non-promoted categories, and how can they be rewarded?

(e) What can management itself do to improve its knowledge of the backgrounds and difficulties experienced by non-promoted groups? How does management feel about these people?

## PARTICIPATION

Participation in taking decisions that affect individuals' working lives greatly motivates them to increase effort. At the organisational level, participation may occur via works committees, advisory groups and other formal joint consultation procedures.

### Joint consultation

Essentially joint consultation is a communication exercise; management retains control over the decision-making process, but seeks to utilise the expertise, energy and initiative of the workforce in decision-making activities. Management informs employees of its plans and opinions on various issues, and invites comment. The advantage to management is that expert advice is obtained from employees — who possess detailed knowledge of workplace procedures and conditions. Also, workers who exert even limited control over their environments are likely to cooperate with management and be receptive to change.

Note, however, that workers will not be happy with consultative procedures if they are invoked only when difficulties arise, especially if financial economies are needed. Joint management/worker decision taking should extend to all aspects of the firm's work, not just the areas it finds convenient.

## Suggestion schemes

Suggestion schemes might be useful for motivating staff, although problems occur in deciding who is to receive the financial benefits that result from profitable recommendations.

In general, the patent rights of a new invention belong to the firm that employs the inventor, not the individual worker. Also, once a suggestion has been submitted it becomes known to the firm, and it might be impossible subsequently to prove the true identity of the inventor. Indeed, a firm might initially reject a worker's suggestion only to take it up after the worker has left the organisation, without rewarding that person. Nevertheless, suggestion schemes are popular with both management and workers, and firms introducing them often experience significant benefits.

## Advantages and disadvantages of participation

Participation, in whatever form, has advantages and drawbacks. The principal argument in its favour relates to its mobilisation of the talent, resources, experiences and expertise of employees, who are positively encouraged to develop their decision-making capacities. People can influence the events that determine their working lives; they feel involved, useful, valued and secure. Management is forced to think hard about the implications of its actions for the staff, and analytical approaches to decision taking are encouraged. Further benefits could be greater willingness by workers to abide by decisions they helped to make, and the fact that bad, unworkable decisions are less likely because those who would have to implement them receive opportunities to point out potential difficulties.

On the other hand, participation interferes with managerial prerogative, it delays decisions and possibly leads to inefficient working methods. Workers, moreover, rarely possess the administrative and problem-solving skills needed for effective management. Other criticisms of participation include the following:

(a) Much managerial information is confidential — often involving personal matters relating to individuals — and should not be disclosed to employees.

(b) Conflicts of interest between management and labour are inevitable, and are best resolved through collective bargaining.

Workers cannot simultaneously represent their colleagues and be part of management.

(c) Participation does not alter fundamental financial realities. Businesses sometimes fail despite extensive prior consultation.

(d) Workers sometimes adopt short-term and mercenary approaches to complex issues which really require long-term consideration.

If participation is to succeed, both management and workers must want it to succeed. Hostility from either side guarantees failure. At the departmental level, participation involves seeking advice from employees, exchanging information, joint determination of targets, and joint planning and control of activities. For participation to work you need to be *seen* to be willing to share your decision-making powers; yet formally established procedures are not necessarily the most appropriate for achieving this objective — indeed they can be counterproductive if management representatives only grudgingly and reluctantly join a formal participation system. *Ad hoc* joint decision making together with regular briefing sessions might be more effective in generating feelings of involvement.

Note that some of your colleagues might not want to participate in decision taking, and that others may not possess the skills and experience necessary to be able to do so. Do not force people to become involved in a participation scheme, and recognise that even if they are willing to offer suggestions their contributions might not have much value in the early stages of the process. Joint decision taking implies shared responsibility for jointly determined decisions, and some employees (especially those who represent others) may not be happy about this.

## PROBLEM PEOPLE

A major task of a departmental manager is to ensure that everyone in the department is kept busy. Problems arise when employees lack effort and/or deliberately avoid work. The latter situation can arise from:

- malingering — persistent unpunctuality, taking unnecessary breaks, doing 'walkabouts' around the firm, appearing to be absorbed in a task while actually doing nothing, shifting files from one location to another, going somewhere half an hour before lunch and not returning until the lunchbreak has ended, etc;

- exchanging easier or more enjoyable duties for work that actually needs to be done;

- spending large amounts of time on marginally relevant tasks;

- detailed examination of colleagues' contributions to activities, together with careful perusal of associated documents and correspondence, double-checking, and complaining about minor errors (the time spent querying an insignificant mistake can exceed the time needed to perform a task).

Often the root causes of such behaviour relate to employees' desires for status within a department and/or employing organisation. The desire to be seen to be important can exert great influence — high-status work is normally associated with taking decisions and it need not matter which particular decisions are taken, only that a certain individual is observed taking them. The problem, therefore, is to ascertain who should take various classes of decision, and how delegation (see Chapter 1) should be organised.

Another possible problem is that the people who work for you will probably have their own ideas about what constitutes a fair distribution of authority and responsibility within the department. And they may hold definite opinions regarding how much of their working day 'belongs' to the firm (quite independent of official working hours specified in contracts of employment). Ideally, formal divisions of working time and of authority and responsibility structures should correspond to divisions regarded as fair by employees. In practice, however, individual roles might be unclear; people may feel 'put on' by others — that they are being asked to do things beneath their dignity and/or which are not an integral part of their official duties. Petty resentments then arise. There are arguments about who should do what. Much energy is spent on uncoordinated activity. Nothing gets done; individuals either assume that someone else will complete difficult or disagreeable tasks, or they lack the resources or personal authority (perhaps even the inclination) to execute them.

## Solutions

These are debilitating problems, and there are no easy solutions. Note in particular that drafting job specifications, organisation charts and manuals more precisely will not necessarily improve the situation. The more detailed the job description the more quickly it will become out of date. Cries of 'That's not my responsibility, it's not in my job specification', or 'I can't do this without permission' resound through organisations attempting to tighten their job and responsibility description procedures.

The more precisely defined the tasks which an employee ought to do, the greater the scope for declining to undertake work not strictly covered by a job specification. And no organisation chart or job description can comprehensively define all possible tasks that an employee might reasonably be expected to perform. Ultimately, individuals must interpret their own roles and organisational status. Yet this very process of analysing and interpreting the wording of a job description, of expounding to others the organisational implications of the chain of command in a complicated line and staff system, is itself time consuming and diverts attention from more pressing issues!

Opportunities for elaboration of individual roles and responsibilities abound. A devastating technique for work avoidance in such circumstances is for employees to remain silent about the fact that tasks allocated to them are beyond their job specifications, and then use this fact — belatedly — as the justification for not having done the work.

There are a number of things you might do in order to deal with this situation, as follows:

1. Allocate important and/or complicated duties to two (or even three) people to complete together. Each partner will complement and motivate the other, and their joint experience can be brought to bear on a problem. Working in pairs or threesomes builds in employees a sense of interdependence and an awareness of the benefits of cooperation. The people involved will probably stimulate one another to greater effort, and useful new ideas might emerge. Unconscious work avoidance is less likely when two individuals must jointly accomplish a task. Personal incompetence or malingering in one of the partners will soon be exposed. And if partners are changed periodically then even if one or two colleagues of a malingerer have been persuaded to remain silent, the offending party must eventually be discovered.

2. Introduce a system of task rotation so that different people are responsible for particular duties for set periods of (say) three, six or twelve months. Then the performance of the person currently responsible for those duties may be evaluated against successes achieved by predecessors in that same role.

3. Issue to all members of your team a preprinted questionnaire asking them to specify what they feel they need from you in order to be able to work more productively. The form should begin with the words 'In order to do my job more effectively I need:', and then be followed by sections headed 'more of' and 'less of' in respect of various facilities and resources.

4. When distributing work to people or sections, allocate tasks to categories created around types of work rather than level of responsibility. So someone who, for example, is good at negotiating can be given all work that embodies a major negotiating component. An expert communicator can be put in charge of all the external communications of the group — no matter how important or trivial. In consequence, all employees will have at least some higher-status work to do, and thus will want to structure their working time efficiently.

If none of these measures succeeds you need to consider more drastic (and disagreeable) measures, including:

- strict supervision in the immediate short term;
- putting staff on to a payments-by-results basis (or at least making future pay rises contingent on the achievement of targets if existing contracts of employment prohibit payment by results);
- allocation to indolent workers of lots of extra jobs;
- short sharp shocks, disciplinary interviews, formal warnings and the dismissal of staff whose work does not improve.

## Criticising employees

If you have to criticise a colleague, criticise an action rather than the individual, and always precede the criticism with a compliment regarding some other aspect of that person's work. You may find the following a useful procedure for presenting a criticism:

(a) Choose a private place for the conversation, do not dramatise, and never cause the person to feel that you will publicise the criticism to others.

(b) Show that a problem has been caused by the employee's substandard performance. Ask for a comment on the situation.

(c) Suggest a means of overcoming the problem, and together examine the implications of the actions you jointly need to take.

(d) Sympathise with the cause of the colleague's inadequacy, and offer practical help.

# 14

# LEADING AND
# COUNSELLING

## INTRODUCTION

How you behave as a manager will result from your personal inclina-
tions, your training, and from environmental factors. It should depend
also on a conscious decision about your management style and, in
particular, how you lead others. You choose the clothes you wear, you
choose the food you eat there is no reason at all why you should not
equally choose how you manage!

The style of management a person adopts affects his or her relations
with colleagues and (importantly) the patterns of interaction among
members of the department. It will also affect departmental productivity, line and staff relationships, whether the firm uses project terms, the
frequency and character of committee meetings, and so on.

## LEADING A DEPARTMENT

Staff will expect you to lead the department. You are, after all, the
appointed manager, and leadership is an integral component of the
departmental manager's role. So you need to choose a leadership style.

Between the extremes of complete autocracy on the one hand and a
totally democratic mode of leadership on the other, there is a contin-
uum of possible approaches. You might, for example, consult your staff
when considering problems, while reserving all final decisions for yourself; or you could impose your decisions without comment or discussion; or you may resolve issues in a totally democratic way. Basically
you have to decide whether to supervise the people who work for you
extremely closely, issuing precise and detailed instructions covering

every task, or to specify overall objectives and leave employees to achieve them as they think fit.

*Effective management*

The question, 'What makes a good leader?' has no simple answer. Personal qualities, the leader's behaviour and the situation confronted might, it seems, affect performance. Thus you need to experiment with a variety of styles and select whichever works best for you.

Recognise that there need not be any 'best' style — some people prefer being told what to do rather than being consulted and expected to participate in taking decisions. 'Task' centred leadership, properly applied, can be extremely effective. You take the initiative in developing activities, in defining problems and suggesting solutions — you propose new ways of doing things rather than reacting to events. You consciously seek out information and ideas, and issue instructions based on the facts you discover — seeking always to help your colleagues in their work. You clarify issues, put things together, and generally become the centre of the team.

Democratic leadership, on the other hand, also has advantages. You specify broadly defined overall objectives and leave people to attain these in whatever ways they believe to be best. There is much communication with colleagues, and extensive employee participation in management decisions. Workers' job satisfaction, skills and capacities to undertake more demanding duties should increase. At its best, 'people' centred rather than task centred behaviour brings employees together through involving them closely in all the work of the team. Here, you concentrate on encouraging staff to initiate activity and suggest new ideas. You listen, empathise, explore differences of opinion, inspire friendliness, and encourage the acceptance of other people's views. You suggest rather than impose solutions to problems, and accept compromises when colleagues disagree with your opinions. Problems with people centred leadership include slow decision making, possible lack of positive direction, and the fact that certain people are not capable of contributing to decision taking or working without close supervision.

# BEING ASSERTIVE

Assertive behaviour has unpleasant connotations for some people because of its apparent association with aggression. But there is in fact a difference between aggression and personal assertion. Aggression is intended to hurt, injure, frighten or destroy. It is hostile and harmful, resulting from base motives — deprivation, greed, fear, extreme frustration — rarely encountered in normal business situations. Assertion, on the other hand, helps individuals to exercise initiative, translate ideas into action and maximise their creative potential. Positive and decisive attitudes — 'attacking' problems, 'defeating' obstructions, 'mastering' situations — generate states of mind that alleviate feelings of inadequacy, overdependence on others, and lack of self-confidence and self-determination. Personal assertiveness enables individuals to seize initiatives and translate ideas into action — with no implication of aggressive intent.

## Stating your position

Someone who believes not only in the correctness of a position, but also in his or her fundamental right to state that position, should not experience too many inhibitions when putting forward a case — if you feel you possess the right to express yourself forcefully, you expect others to take seriously what you have to say. Importantly, mistakes and minor failures, passing anxieties and petty personal inadequacies, do not assume momentous significance in your mind. So you will not worry too much if on occasion you perform inadequately; and if you fail you will want to try again. A further benefit is greater empathy, respect and genuine concern for others — inward strength is usually accompanied by heightened awareness of the feelings of fellow human beings, since assertive attitudes equip individuals not only with the internal sense of security necessary for assertive action, but also with an unselfish outlook and greater consideration for colleagues.

## The right to manage

As a manager, you have the right to issue instructions and have them carried out, you have the right to express forcefully your own point of view and have it taken seriously. And other people should listen carefully to what you say (although you must recognise that they are entitled to disagree). You have the right to initiate activity, to achieve and — importantly — to make reasonable mistakes, occasionally fail, but nevertheless try again. Why shouldn't you feel uncomfortable from time to time? Anxiety indicates your genuine concern to complete the task — you are fully entitled not to know everything about the job when you first begin, and need to learn by experience.

Try to adopt an identifiable position on all important issues, but be ready to change your mind if circumstances alter or new facts emerge.

Having a definite position provides an anchor for the expression of your opinions — it helps to prevent your thoughts meandering and the enunciation of ambivalent views. Criticism by others then assumes a positive, constructive purpose since it helps you to evaluate the validity of your views. Personal assertion is not emotionally selfish; you are not demanding anything you are not prepared to repay, you simply recognise an emotional self-interest in the social interactions that affect *you*.

Some individuals do not stand up for themselves for fear of causing anger, resentment or depression in colleagues. If you feel this way ask yourself whether such thoughts are really the consequence of your behaviour, or that of the other side. Does the other person have the 'right' to react to you in a hostile fashion? If he or she possesses such a right, then rethink your position — look for an alternative course of action or a better way of explaining why you need to take the action you propose. Otherwise, why worry?

## Saying no

Managers must sometimes refuse requests from colleagues. It is not always easy to say no firmly and clearly, without creating offence. We all know how to say no, when we ought to say no, and why certain requests cannot be accepted, but too often we end up agreeing to an unreasonable request instead of rejecting the proposition. If you believe you should should refuse a particular request, ask yourself the following questions:

- What consequences will result from the refusal?

- How will the other person feel about the rejection, are those feelings justified, and do they matter?

- What are the costs and benefits of the refusal, to you, and to the other person?

- What are your real motives for refusing the request? Are they selfish, or in the best interests of the work of your department?

Saying yes when you should say no may lead to a quiet life in the short term, but can eventually result in disruption. Your apparent friendliness and willingness to cooperate might encourage unreasonable demands from others.

## Strategies for refusing requests

You are, of course, at a disadvantage because the person making a request has time to prepare his or her approach and devise a strategy for asking the question. Identify the purpose of the request as well as the required action, and try to empathise with the feelings of the other party. If you have to refuse, preface your refusal with a remark such as, 'I know you feel strongly about . . ., but I'm afraid I'm really not in a position to be able to . . . because . . .' (give reasons). And if possible, offer a compromise. Do not allow yourself to be side-tracked; if the conversation begins to meander then restate your initial refusal but with a different choice of words. Aim to be pleasant, and recognise that saying no does not necessarily imply dislike of the other person or necessarily earn the animosity of that individual. It is not a crime to refuse a request, and you have every right to reject unreasonable demands.

### Avoid being a bully

Some managers become bullies. They get so used to having their own way that they interpret queries as insubordination, and the exercise of independent initiative as the deliberate sabotage of their work. Because they are never answered back, they become pompous, conceited and insensitive to the feelings of other people.

### Anger and self-control

Anger is caused by, and arises within, the individual. Unfortunate external events do not necessarily make a person angry, only the way in which they are perceived. Everyone feels angry occasionally. Managers, unfortunately, sometimes vent their anger on people who cannot answer back, and so never realise the extent of their anger. The absence of fair, constructive criticism can cause individuals to believe that they are always right and that their feelings and demands are always justified. Anger results when a desire is converted into a 'demand', and the demand is rejected by another person. You do not become angry just because a wish is not satisfied (otherwise you would be angry all the time); yet you might be furious if an 'entitlement' is not realised. Hence a good way to begin to overcome anger is to ask yourself whether it is reasonable for you to demand that the thing causing your anger is completed, since if you demand nothing you will never be disappointed.

Paradoxically, people who lose their temper most often are frequently those who most lack the skills of personal assertion. Try consciously to discover alternative ways of dealing with anger-inducing situations without resorting to sarcasm or verbal abuse.

### Examine your anger

Analyse your own aggressive feelings — what is your aggressive behaviour intended to achieve? Do you consider yourself to possess a reputation that needs defending; are you seeking to impose on others standards they are reluctant to adopt; do you feel unable to cope and hence occasionally explode when faced with unresolvable issues?

If you are prone to aggressive outbursts then you need to learn how to relax, converse, and listen. It is up to *you* to control your behaviour. You choose the clothes you put on every morning — you must similarly learn how to choose appropriate emotional reactions to various stressful and anger-inducing situations.

# COUNSELLING

The need to counsel others arises in many areas of a manager's work: appraisal (see Chapter 6), handling employee grievances, disciplinary procedures (see Chapter 9), one-to-one training, and so on. Counselling is the process of helping people to recognise their feelings about problems, to define those problems accurately, find solutions, or learn to live with a situation. A counselling session could involve giving advice, encouraging a change in behaviour, helping an employee to accept an inevitable situation, or assisting someone to take a difficult decision.

Counselling should occur in private, and without interruption from telephones, secretaries with messages, etc. The aim is not to impose but rather to induce people independently to learn how to overcome difficulties and take appropriate decisions.

## Directive and non-directive counselling

There are two approaches to counselling: directive and non-directive. With non-directive counselling, the counselling manager assumes that only the counsellee is capable of defining accurately his or her problems and that the most effective way of getting to the heart of a difficulty is to encourage the other party to discuss the issue at length. It presupposes that solutions to problems will not be implemented unless counsellees wholeheartedly accept their implications.

Directive counselling, conversely, involves taking the initiative and actually suggesting solutions. The possible consequences of various courses of action are outlined, and a range of actions is considered. Here the counsellor charts a path towards the correct decision.

## The counselling interview

A major problem with counselling is that you never know at the outset of an interview how long it will last. It could be ten minutes, three hours, or all day — and extra sessions may be required. Nor do you know at the outset just what it is the counsellee will want and expect. An open-door policy on counselling might lead to people coming to see you just because they want to chat or, insidiously, because they want to run down colleagues who have incurred their displeasure. Non-directive counsellors will never specify in advance how long an interview is to last, whereas a directive approach might begin with a statement of how much time you have. In either case, however, you should never appear restless, hurried, bored, or to be 'watching the clock'. Rather, you need to project a quiet confidence in your ability to help.

During the interview, you will have to give 100 per cent attention to the counsellee. There is no respite, and counselling interviews lasting more than an hour or thereabouts are emotionally and physically exhausting. So never begin a counselling session when you are already tired; you will not be able to stand the pace. First thing in the morning or immediately after lunch are probably the best times. Counselling is very tiring, so do not take on too many counselling interviews in any one day. And give yourself plenty of time to recuperate, relax, think and reflect between each session.

## Starting the interview

Begin the conversation by establishing some common ground. Make a non-controversial remark about something with which your colleague is sure to agree. Then proceed to some straightforward questions requiring only short, non-analytical answers. Do not ask any critical or personal questions at this stage. And check with yourself to ensure you have not stereotyped the person before the conversation. Have you already categorised the counsellee as neurotic, overambitious, greedy, unreliable, dishonest, or in some equally unflattering way?

At first, be less concerned with seeking factual explanations than with rooting out how the employee feels about the issue.

## Listening

As the tempo of the conversation increases you will need to create pauses — breathing spaces — during which you can gather your thoughts and think ahead. This is an important element in the skill of listening; it is essential that the other party believe that you are listening attentively to what he or she has to say.

Listening is not as easy as it may first appear. In counselling you spend a lot of time listening, and the things you hear may bore you, irritate, offend and annoy. But you must not show that this is the case. Look at the person while he or she is speaking, do not yawn, do not look at documents (although you should of course have briefed yourself fully on the facts of the situation before the interview; you should *never* have to ask the counsellee to remind you of the circumstances of the interview), do not look at your wristwatch or otherwise appear disinterested.

## Empathy

Concentrate on determining the facts. A good way to test the extent of your empathy with the other party is for you occasionally to interrupt the conversation (when there is a natural break in the flow of the counsellee's remarks) and make the comment 'You feel . . . (now fill in your interpretation of his or her perceptions and emotions; anger, for example) because . . . (insert here your interpretation of the person's reasons for feeling that way)'. This simple device will convey to your subordinate the fact that you understand his or her view of the issue; and is preferable to gratuitously sentimental statements.

It is important that you seek to empathise with the subordinate's actual feelings rather than what you believe he or she ought to feel. Perhaps, in your opinion, the person ought to experience remorse for having neglected some particular employment duties — he or she might have messed up a major contract, mislaid important documents, offended a valuable client, or whatever — but the counsellee may see things in a totally different way. Try to share the other person's entire world, without making ethical or moral judgements about his or her behaviour. Do not ask impertinent or leading questions (which imply a particular response — for example, 'Well Mary, your production figures last quarter were pretty appalling weren't they?') — and never create the impression that you want to 'interrogate' or dominate the counsellee. Rather, you hope that he or she will volunteer additional information.

## Structuring the conversation

You need to create a structure for the conversation, break it up into component parts that can be easily digested and which have meaning to you both. Interrupt occasionally and repeat something your colleague has said or intimated, but rephrase the point in your own words. This acts as a check on your understanding of what he or she is saying and will stimulate the person to expand the point.

As the interview develops, use open-ended questions (ie which cannot be answered with simple statements or yes/no answers). Such questions are prefaced by the words 'who', 'what', 'how', or 'why'. For example:

● How did you feel at that time?

- What made you decide to do that?

- I can see that the incident deeply worried you, why was that?

Open-ended questions are good for eliciting feelings and attitudes, and for encouraging the employee to reveal his or her true feelings.

If you are nervous about the interview, if you lack self-discipline, or if you do not take your counselling duties seriously you will find that you, and not the colleague, do most of the talking. You will discuss your own feelings and problems, not those of the person who needs to be helped! The problem is that in the rest of your managerial work you are accustomed to exercising leadership, giving orders, and generally behaving in personally assertive ways. Passive listening may be alien to you, since all your training and past experience makes you want to respond. Instead of listening creatively via the conscious identification of points needing expansion or of wide generalisations that require more detailed explanation, you might either dominate a conversation or, realising this to be inappropriate, sit in complete silence waiting for the counsellee to speak.

## Is counselling really worthwhile?

Instead of counselling, why not assess the situation yourself, decide what is to be done, and issue directives? After all, counselling is a draining activity, requiring much preparation, self-discipline and intense concentration. It absorbs time (often the hours that otherwise would be the most productive of the day), exhausts the counsellor and can be extremely depressing. You have to absorb and be seen to absorb large amounts of information, you have to learn how to recognise symptoms of tension and distress, you are immersed in other people's problems and complaints.

You need patience, alertness and the capacity to offer sound advice to people with whom initially you might not have had a close relationship. The fundamental problem is that you are trying to do a highly personal job in an impersonal way. Your perceptions of events inevitably depend on your own experiences. It is impossible to remove personal value judgements entirely from a counselling interview — particularly when sensitive issues arise and during moments of stress.

Other questionable aspects of the value of executive managers counselling (rather than merely directing) employees include the following:

(a) 'Parkinson's law' applies to counselling. Problems can expand to fill the time that is made available for dealing with them. Yet, at the end of the day, intractable problems remain unresolved.

(b) Arguably, counselling approaches to personal problems encourage the malingerer, and incite the inefficient to look for excuses rather than confront directly the sources of a problem. More commonly, the emotional overprotection you provide to counsellees causes them to become dependent on you and to lack initiative; they become incapable of 'standing on their own two feet'.

(c) Open-door counselling may encourage individuals to complain about colleagues, terms and conditions of employment, etc.

Despite these problems, genuine attempts at counselling employees are usually worthwhile. Note that you will necessarily be required to counsel occasionally as a normal part of your management work. Confronted with a problem, individuals want to talk, to discuss the matter with someone who will not condemn their feelings or actions out of hand. People develop their own peer group counselling networks to lend comfort and support to individuals when things go wrong. Employees with problems will go to someone for help and advice. How much better it is if the person they turn to is you. You will know everything that happens in your department, and your personal influence will increase. Counselling will develop your overall interpersonal management skills. You will become more perceptive, cognisant of the problems of others, and better equipped to define precisely the substance of your managerial role.

# 15

# TEAMWORK

Work is a social activity; few people work entirely alone. Groups emerge within work organisations through the specialisation of functions, through the creation of teams to handle projects, or naturally in order to satisfy a social need. Groups may be formally established by management, or they might arise informally and spontaneously among employees.

## WORKING IN GROUPS

Formal groups are set up to perform specific tasks: decision taking, project completion, problem solving, communication, and so on. The key issue with formal groups is how best to direct, control and coordinate their activities. Should management impose highly structured group processes, with explicit and rigid roles and conventions; or should the group itself be made responsible for its internal organisation? Informal groups result simply from people intermingling in working situations. Workers establish customs and social relations among themselves; patterns of behaviour are constituted, informal rules, relations and working methods not shown in organisation charts or official staff manuals become entrenched.

Consider your own department for a moment. How many formal groups can you identify? Are there any informal groups? If so, do the informal groups conflict in any way with the work of the department?

## ROLES

To be good at handling group work you need to understand the idea of a 'role', because people's self-perceptions of their roles affect how they feel about their occupational status and the value of the job they do in comparison with others. Perceptions of role also influence how individuals behave, how they feel they ought to behave, and how they believe other people should respond to their actions. People occupy many roles during the course of their lives — as husbands or wives, mother or father figures, as office juniors, supervisors, senior managers, etc. Individual interpretations of roles within a group define the pattern of group interrelations — perhaps even the group's entire structure and organisation.

Associated with each role is a set of standards and norms of conduct that the role occupant (and others) expect from holders of the position. A supervisor, for example, might be expected to behave — perhaps even to dress and speak — in a certain manner. Role expectations are important because they guide individual actions. For example, colleagues who have worked together for several years usually possess efficient, smoothly functioning relationships because they know exactly how their workmates are likely to behave — each person anticipates the other's reactions to various situations, and then adapts his or her own behaviour in appropriate ways. Manifestations of a role (such as a certain mode of dress) provide information to others about how they should act towards the role occupant. Such external signals provoke definite attitudes concerning how others inwardly feel they ought to behave in interactions with that person.

Role strain arises when the individual does not behave in accordance with expectations attached to a role because to do so would place too great a strain on that person. The role occupant may experience difficulties in meeting its expectations, or might encounter expectations which conflict. The person who cannot live up to role expectations may experience feelings of inadequacy, embarrassment and guilt. Interactions with others become difficult and could eventually collapse.

## Defining role boundaries

Another problem is that an individual might be unclear about the exact nature of his or her role. The more explicit and specific the expectations attached to a role, the easier it is to conform to role requirements. Ambiguity in a role can cause stress, insecurity and loss of self-confidence. When an individual cannot possibly fulfil all the obligations associated with a role, he or she might seek to redefine the role's boundaries.

Serious problems can occur when role occupants and others disagree fundamentally about the expectations of a role, ie about what is included in the role, the range of acceptable behaviour, whether a certain behaviour pattern is voluntary or mandatory and (importantly) which role obligations should assume priority. In setting role priorities, the individual may adopt any one of several means of approach. He or she might select for priority those role behaviours which:

(a) are expedient;

(b) correspond to that person's perceptions of moral worth;

(c) bring the greatest personal reward and/or avoid personal cost;

(d) avoid controversy or unpleasant relationships with people the individual particularly respects.

## HOW GROUPS FORM

Whereas formal groups are deliberately constituted by management, informal groups develop without assistance or support. In a formal group, management selects group members, leaders, and methods of doing work. The group may be defined with respect to a task, function, status within the managerial hierarchy (such as members of the board of directors), or length of service with the firm (long-serving employees might receive privileges not available to others and hence constitute an identifiable group). Formal groups are characterised by a high degree of managerial involvement in coordinating, controlling and defining the nature of the activities they undertake. Informal groups can form without management support. They are established by people who feel they possess a common interest. Members organise themselves and develop a sense of affinity to each other and a common cause. Often it is an informal group that actually determines working methods and the quantity of work done. The aims of the informal groups that spring up within an organisation may correspond to the organisation's objectives, but they might not. Indeed, informal groups could form to oppose the wishes of management. A sensible management will thus recognise the importance of informal groups for organisational efficiency, and their potential for disrupting organisational plans.

*Primary and secondary groups*

A further important distinction is between primary groups and secondary groups. A primary group consists of members who come into direct, face-to-face contact with each other. Secondary groups are larger, less personal, and lack immediate direct contact between members. Examples of primary groups are small departments within a firm, project teams, families, sports teams or other direct contact recreational associations. Membership of such a group often provides social and psychological support during times of stress. Secondary groups might be factories, communities, long assembly lines where workers do not come into contact with each other, or geographical divisions of a company. These groups will be less solid and cohesive than primary groups, although interactions between members will still occur. Within primary groups, communications are rapid and direct.

## Importance of group norms

Membership of a group helps a person to interpret everyday events, identify his or her role in an organisation, and satisfy social needs for involvement with others. The group supports and reinforces the individual's view of the outside world, and this greatly encourages conformity to 'group norms'. A group norm is a shared perception of how things should be done, or a common attitude, feeling or belief.

Norms will exist about working methods, about how much work should be done (and how enthusiastically), about the quality of output, relations with management (and trade unions), how various people should be addressed and treated, etc. Norms are particularly important in determining workers' attitudes towards change, since norms can create or overcome resistance to new ideas and working methods.

As norms emerge, individuals start to behave according to how they feel other group members expect them to behave. Initially, entrants to an existing group feel isolated and insecure and hence will actively seek out established norms to guide them on how they ought to behave. Norms facilitate the integration of an individual within the group and thus will be eagerly accepted by new members. They are soon internalised into entrants' personal value systems, and help bind individuals to groups. In consequence, groups are often resistant to change. Members become set in their ways and attitudes; they come to believe that the group norm is always correct — no matter what the circumstances. Any deviation from a norm has to be explained and justified by the individual to other members. And if the deviation is not accepted by the group the deviant member is socially isolated.

## Conflicts within groups

Membership of a group provides individuals with companionship, social experience, opportunities for self-expression and social intercourse. Against these benefits, however, individuals must be prepared to modify their behaviour to fit in with group norms. The greater the value the individual places on group membership, the more he or she will want to conform. Feelings of attachment increase, and the power of the group to compel obedience to established norms is enhanced. Eventually group behaviour settles down to a fixed routine. New entrants are expected to conform and to demonstrate their willingness to abide by group norms. The group can then continue to function despite changes of personnel.

Conflicts and contradictions within the group now begin to emerge, caused (for example) by:

- new technology which demands new working methods and/or new divisions of labour among group members;

- members perceiving group objectives differently;

- breakdowns in communications between group members;

- personal disputes;

- changing expectations of what might reasonably be demanded from membership of the group.

Such conflicts create the need for readjustments in internal group relations, including perhaps the introduction of new group norms.

## Need for cohesion

Group cohesiveness is the degree to which members are prepared to cooperate, content to work together, and share common goals. High cohesion results in high productivity and morale. A cohesive group will support, in thought and action, the continuing existence of the group and its current activities.

Several factors contribute to the creation of group cohesion, including how often its members come into contact with each other, members' enthusiasm for group objectives, and the exclusivity and/or homogeneity of members of the group. The more frequently and intimately the members interact the more they will perceive themselves as a distinct group. If membership is selective, members feel a sense of achievement in being admitted; and to the extent that members share a common background, education, age, outlook, ethnic or social origin, they will be like-minded and share common perspectives.

External environments can also affect group cohesion. An environment consists of a multitude of physical, technological and social circumstances. If individuals see their environment as hostile they will feel great affinity to any group offering protection from external threats. Other factors conducive to cohesion are as follows:

(a) *How easily members can communicate within the group*. Poor interpersonal communications will inhibit the emergence of a collective sense of purpose. Note that a group is more likely to be internally cohesive the less contact it has with other groups.

(b) *The nature of the task to be completed*. Individuals engaged on identical or very similar work are more likely to see themselves as a group than others. Incentive schemes can encourage cohesion; a group that is able to reward or punish its own members can exert great pressure on individuals to conform.

Cohesion is a most attractive feature in a working group, causing high morale, strong interpersonal relations, and reinforcement of individual perceptions. The activities of a cohesive group are easy to coordinate since the group itself will monitor the efficiency of its operations. Members are encouraged to work hard in support of the group, and may derive great satisfaction, even excitement, in so doing. Unfortunately such enthusiasm might be directed against management, since powerful informal groups can arise to oppose management's wishes. Moreover, high group cohesion need not be associated with high productivity, low absenteeism and labour turnover, enthusiasm for work and other desirable characteristics, but rather the reverse. Cohesive groups might conspire to restrict output, perhaps even to disrupt the organisation's work.

## POWER AND AUTHORITY

Formal groups have appointed leaders. Informal groups have leaders who emerge naturally from the ranks of the group. Within a formal group, an unofficial leader might arise and function in parallel with the appointed leader. Unofficial leaders are important, and their influence is sometimes formally recognised (for instance through the unofficial leader becoming a departmental shop steward). They exercise authority, albeit intermittently, but have no formal 'power' as such. Formal leaders offer stability (appointed leaders are permanent, they remain despite changes in the structure of the group) and a focus for group identity. Usually they can impose formal rules on individual members. Official leaders are responsible for communicating with other groups and for expressing the collective opinions of the group. In practice, however, unofficial leaders are frequently the people who actually direct and motivate others.

There are important differences between authority, influence and effective power. Influence is the effect of one person on the behaviour of others. It may be exercised by either formal or informal leaders and can operate through suggestion, persuasion, example or threat of sanctions. Authority is the right to control. In a supervisory context this might involve the determination of subordinates' workloads, taking decisions on behalf of the group, giving orders, possibly recommending pay rises, or initiating disciplinary action. Formal authority is often accompanied by outward displays of status: different clothing (such as managers wearing suits while operatives wear overalls), separate canteens, different modes of speech and behaviour. These may even differ for each of several levels of authority within the managerial hierarchy. Lower ranks are expected to treat superiors with deference and respect. There is a clear system of command, coordination and control.

Power, in contrast, is a quality that other people perceive an individual to possess, giving that person the ability to influence the actions of others. An employee might have low occupational status and occupy no formal leadership role, yet still exert enormous power within the organisation. Appointed leaders may or may not be powerful, depending on the following factors:

(a) their ability to coerce others into obedience through threats of punitive action;

(b) personal charisma;

(c) group members' willingness to accept the directions of appointed leaders;

(d) the extent to which group members identify with the values of appointed leaders;

(e) appointed leaders' abilities to satisfy group members' needs;

(f) whether group members perceive appointed leaders to possess expert knowledge about the activities on which groups are engaged;

(g) the extent to which members feel that a formal leadership position is legitimate, say because of seniority within the group;

(h) control over information, resources, and access to higher levels of formal authority.

Group activities inevitably change over time. It follows that those members who are able to understand, interpret and accommodate change will become powerful in the eyes of the rest of the group. Note how it is possible for powerful people, because of their ability to affect the behaviour of others, to act in innovative ways and initiate change.

Group members who possess much power but little formal authority are fortunate in that they do not have to take the blame when things go wrong. Appointed leaders, however, have to accept the consequences of their actions. If they make bad decisions they are expected to pay. In consequence, official group leaders are often reluctant to take crucial decisions, either passing difficult problems upwards to higher management or ignoring them in the hope that other group members (those with power) will quietly sort them out. Responsibility, then, is a constraint on the exercise of authority, and might restrain the exercise of power.

## STRUCTURING A WORKING GROUP

Well constructed groups can greatly enhance employee commitment, job satisfaction and sense of purpose. Specialised skills develop within groups; members collaborate, liaise, offer help and advice to others, and generally interact through their work. Note, however, that working in groups is not always more efficient than working alone. Frequent disturbances from colleagues and the need to consult before taking action can retard progress and constantly irritate the individual worker. You need therefore to seek ways of making group work enjoyable and able to fulfil individual members' social needs. In particular, you must prevent informal groups from taking over the functions that official (management-created) groups should undertake.

*Rules to follow*

When creating groups (eg through establishing project teams to achieve particular objectives) observe the following rules:

1. Try to keep group sizes reasonably small. Groups of more than a dozen people require extensive supervision, and internal communications become difficult. Much time is spent coordinating group activities, and decision taking is slow. Large groups encourage the emergence of subgroups and factions differentiated in terms of status, length of service, opinions on social and work issues, etc.

2. Encourage joint decision taking within groups. Participation improves morale and stimulates cooperation; it facilitates the flow of information through the group and the emergence of new ideas. Reassure group members that their contributions will be taken seri-

ously and that they are free to express opinions. Of course, complex problems require careful and detailed analysis and not all the group members will be capable of understanding the issues involved. In this case you (or the group leader to whom you have delegated official command of a subunit) should inform all the group members of the nature of the difficulties and how those members selected to handle these complex problems intend tackling them.

3. Define group objectives clearly and precisely. Members should see the point of what they are doing and how it fits in with wider organisational goals.

Sound leadership is essential. As an appointed group leader you have to motivate, direct, set standards and monitor subordinates' performances. You allocate work to members, clarify issues and explain what needs to be done, settle disputes among members, resolve grievances, and generally keep the peace. A particularly important leadership role is that of introducing new members to the norms of the group. Newcomers initially feel anxious about their status and look to whomever they perceive as the group leader for cues regarding how they should behave. At first, formal rules will be followed to the letter, even if personal identities are sacrificed in the process. Then as newcomers are gradually absorbed into the group they learn to manipulate its conventions. They come to terms with other members and begin to assert their independence.

Groups function more efficiently if their leadership can be easily transferred. Critical dependence on a single person leads to the total collapse of the group when its leader resigns. Ensure, therefore, that someone is trained and ready to take over your group should you be transferred, promoted, temporarily absent, or leave the firm.

## GROUPS AND TEAMS

Working groups can adopt one of three organisational structures: the hierarchy, the network, or the team. Hierarchies typically exhibit a pyramid form of authority and decision making, with a distinct chain of command from the apex of the organisation to its base. There is a single group leader whose immediate subordinates lead their own immediate subordinates through clearly defined spans of control. Each person is accountable only to his or her immediate superior in the hierarchy.

A 'network', in contrast, consists of a number of workers (or collections of workers, each with its own leader) who operate autonomously but nevertheless consciously seek to coordinate their activities. Members are jointly responsible for achieving the network's objectives, although each person takes independent decisions and there is no coherent chain of command. Rather, members are (usually) of equal rank and are accountable to a single central control. Networking is an increasingly popular form of business organisation, particularly when people prefer to work from home (computer software experts, for example) and/or when highly specialised professional skills are involved.

A team is a special sort of group. All teams are groups, but groups do not necessarily behave as teams.\The defining characteristic of a team is that its members cooperate and voluntarily coordinate their work in order to achieve group objectives./

## Team dynamics

\Team members are highly interdependent, and each individual must to some extent interpret the nature of his or her particular role/Members feel especially upset, therefore, when they consider that a colleague has let them down, say by not doing a fair share of the work of the team. In a team, each person feels responsible for promoting the interests of the working group and personally accountable for its actions.

Teams have leaders who may or may not be appointed by an outside body (higher management, for example), but the authority of the leader of a team — as distinct from any working group — is fully accepted by all its members. The team leader represents the group to the outside world and is formally answerable for its behaviour. Within a team there will be a high degree of group cohesion, much interaction, mutual support and shared perceptions of issues. Team members will be willing to interchange roles, share workloads and generally help each other out. Typically, each team member will hold other members in high regard, and will experience much satisfaction from belonging to the team.

A working group can develop into a team, and vice versa — a team can lose its coherence and begin to operate as if it were a network (with each member working independently and in emotional isolation from other participants), or as a hierarchy within which individuals will not initiate activity unless they are instructed to do so by a direct superior.

## Team spirit

Team spirit is obviously desirable in a working group. To foster team spirit you need consciously to implement a participative management style. Try to adopt the following rules:

(a) Praise and encourage members' suggestions for altering working methods: never be sarcastic about new ideas, no matter how impracticable they might appear. If, in your view, a suggestion stands no chance of success then simply point out its prohibitive cost or another reason for its unacceptability. You could be wrong — so invite discussion on your objections.

(b) Clarify 'territorial divisions' among team members. Ensure that all members are fully aware of the extent of their individual and collective responsibilities. Much conflict can arise from petty 'who does what' ambiguities. See to it that formal job specifications correspond to the duties that team members actually undertake.

(c) Represent and defend the team in the outside world. Do not criticise members in front of outsiders. As far as possible, back up team members' decisions even when you believe them to be wrong.

(d) Fight for resources for staff development and extra training for individuals within your team. Even if you do not succeed, your efforts will be appreciated by team members.

If people have to work well together in order to carry out their individual duties they are more likely to want to cooperate with others, and will soon develop a common bond. This is true even if team members are of unequal rank — mutual dependence of higher and lower levels of authority quickly creates a unity of purpose. Other causes of good team spirit are a fair distribution of work and responsibility within the group, especially of unpleasant or exceptionally demanding tasks; well designed work programmes with realistic completion dates; and compatibility of the personal characteristics of participants.

## Dealing with problems

If the team's workload is unacceptably demanding (as happens when some members simultaneously fall ill or resign without being immediately replaced) then you must determine priorities and consciously reduce the volume of tasks undertaken. Exclude first those duties that absorb the greatest time and create the least benefit, but take care not to cut out essential tasks simply because they are disliked by members of the team. If you are completely overwhelmed with work, try to isolate a distinct subgroup of activities that can be put together and allocated to another team.

In situations where team morale suffers through the behaviour of one of the team's members, you need to try to alter the behaviour of the person concerned. Recognise, however, that sometimes an individual's conduct and demeanour are so embedded in his or her personality that they will never change. Here you must either accept that person as he or she is, or hope that he or she will grow out of the behaviour which is causing difficulties, or make arrangements for that person to be transferred to another team. Bad conduct is rarely perceived as such by the person concerned.

You need, therefore, not only to draw the deviant member's attention to the undesirable consequences of the bad behaviour, but also to break it down into component parts and analyse the causes and effects of each element against the background in which it occurs. Whether behaviour is 'good' or 'bad' often depends on the context of the incident — it is 'bad' to ignore paperwork that is essential for the efficient functioning of the team, but good to discard superfluous paperwork that would interfere with more important work. Thus you ought not to criticise a member for failing to respond to letters and memoranda until you know the full circumstances of the events.

Define precisely the behaviour you believe needs to be altered, and how exactly you would like it to change. List the things the person is currently doing that you would like him or her to stop, and all the things the person is not doing that you wish he or she would do. Arrange an interview with the person concerned, and during the interview approach the issue circumspectly, focusing your conversation on the effects of the undesirable behaviour on the efficiency of the team.

## Leading a team

Morale within your team will be enhanced if you know each of its members personally. You should know their names, something about their backgrounds and what they expect to achieve through involvement with the group. Make it known that you welcome initiative, new ideas and independent attempts to solve problems. Consult regularly with individual members, and be ready to alter working structures and arrangements following the consultations. Treat subordinates as individuals, be aware of their strengths, weaknesses and potential. Keep everyone informed of the progress of the team, and ensure that each member's contribution is fully recognised.

Participative decision taking is good for encouraging team spirit. In certain circumstances, however, participation in decisions is not feasible — highly technical and/or specialised matters might be involved, or decisions may need to be taken so quickly that consultation with subordinates cannot occur. Having taken a decision in such circumstances, do not merely impose it on the group, but try instead to persuade the group that you have made the correct choice. Otherwise, try to suggest (rather than impose) solutions to problems. Invite comment and alternative views on issues, and seek consensus on a common approach. Make sure that everyone understands the team's decision-making procedures, and whether responsibility for decisions will rest with you as the appointed leader or, in the case of democratic decisions (based ultimately on votes), with the entire team.

Symptoms of poor teamwork are easily recognised: absenteeism, lateness, high staff turnover, bad temper, deprecatory remarks about other team members, and so on. Staff lose confidence in the team's ability to achieve its objectives; comment is interpreted as criticism, the quality of work declines, staff lack effort, and petty grievances arise. When this happens, undertake a complete review of the objectives and activities of the team. Look at physical working conditions, wage levels and relativities, terms and conditions of employment (whether the staff feel secure in their jobs, for example) and interpersonal relations within the group. Examine also the status of the group in the hierarchy of the total organisation. Has it sufficient resources? Does senior management appreciate the work the team performs, and does management understand the problems it faces? Consider introducing job enrichment programmes, and reassess the adequacy of your own leadership style, especially the extent to which you allow subordinates to participate in decisions and act independently.

# 16

# PRESENTATIONS AND WRITTEN COMMUNICATION

As a manager you need to be able to write reports, make presentations, handle meetings, and counsel the people for whom you are responsible. Counselling is discussed in Chapter 14. This chapter considers the more routine elements of management communications.

## MAKING A PRESENTATION

Most managers are required at least occasionally to address groups of people. Common examples are team briefings, giving instructions to several people at a time, training employees, making a formal presentation of a new proposal to senior management, making short speeches when colleagues retire, or inducting groups of recently recruited workers. Effective presentation skills are not about innate abilities to perform well in front of an audience; rather they result from training, observation and practice The ability to present information to an audience clearly, concisely and convincingly is something you will use time and time again throughout your career, so the sooner you master the basics the better (assuming you have not already done so) and, once you have acquired elementary competence in making presentations, you need to develop your presentational abilities to their maximum extent.

Many managers dread having to make presentations. They have no experience of public speaking, and are fearful of how the audience might respond. This is unfortunate, because the ability to speak confidently before an audience is an extremely valuable interpersonal management skill.

## Speaking

Of all the ways you communicate with others, the manner of your speech conveys most directly how you think and feel. Body language, posture, dress and gesture contribute to the impression you create, but your speaking voice is, above all, the means whereby you project your true identity. You must learn, therefore, to use your voice — to intonate, respond to the cues of others, pause at appropriate moments, and so on.

When addressing a group, speak slowly. A pace that you regard as slow will in fact be perceived as normal by an audience, which has both to assimilate what you say and interpret your emotions. So, intentionally pace your speed of delivery, and consciously articulate each word. It seems strange at first, but it will result in clear and unhesitant delivery, since you will emphasise the words most relevant to your meaning.

## Coping with nerves

Fear is a natural physiological response to threatening situations. It tells you to get away from a potentially harmful environment. Unfortunately, the voice is extremely sensitive to feelings of unease and will emit distress signals — quivering, a high-pitched tone, loss of inflexion, etc in moments of stress. The neck, throat and tongue become tense; you dry up, physically as well as emotionally.

To overcome anxiety you must relax, and rationalise the situation. When fear overcomes you, pause, breathe slowly, deliberately loosen your head, neck and shoulder muscles, starting from the top of your head and working down. The audience will not notice the interruption; to them it is simply a natural pause in the flow of the presentation. Look directly at the friendliest face in the audience. If you begin to tremble, increase your use of body language in order to dissipate the surplus energy. Then smile. This will help you to relax and generally connect with the audience.

Remember always that the people you are addressing want to hear what you have to say. And bear in mind that you have the right to express an opinion. You are fully entitled to be taken seriously! If you honestly believe in what you are saying and in your fundamental right to state a firm position, then mistakes and minor inadequacies in your presentation will not become too important in your own mind. It is vital, however, that you prepare your talk diligently and in great detail.

## Preparation

The first task is to crystallise your objectives in making the presentation in the first place. What do you want to achieve? Are you asking for money (an increase in the departmental budget, for example), seeking to induce colleagues to accept the implementation of change, transmitting information, or what? Techniques that are effective for achieving one set of presentation objectives are unlikely to succeed in other situations. Do not attempt to make a presentation if you do not know what you are talking about. Listeners will soon recognise your ignorance and your integrity will be questioned. At the end of the presentation you normally have to take questions, and if you cannot handle these your credibility is destroyed. Analyse your potential audience. Are they likely to be well informed on the subject? What are their values, opinions, and perspectives? How easily will they absorb the material you need to present? Are they capable of concentrating for long periods? To which arguments, examples, etc are they most likely to respond? Who will be present, and what will be their likely state of mind? Thinking about these matters should help you determine the style and depth of your presentation; whether it will be necessary to explain technical terms, whether to include humorous anecdotes in your talk, etc.

Plan the talk. Draft an outline with sections for the introduction, a statement of your proposition, supporting arguments, and recommendations. Then fill out each section as fully as you can. Predetermine a central theme that will run through the entire presentation and to which all comments will relate. Organise your points into a logical sequence and write each one on a separate card or small piece of paper, which can then be rearranged as the body of the material you intend presenting expands and develops.

Normally you speak at the rate of about 150 words per minute, so your introductory remarks should be no more than one or two minutes long. The introduction could be an anecdote, a rhetorical question, or a controversial remark. Begin your notes with a precise definition of the topic you wish to discuss, and then write a formal declaration (without justification at this point) of your feelings or position on the subject. You should then explain why you are giving the talk, leading on to detailed consideration of issues.

Make your points one by one, with examples, evidence, and justifications of previous assertions. All your points should relate to the central theme, and lead you towards a clearly defined conclusion which should be firmly stated and take no more than a couple of minutes (about 300 words) to present. Then summarise the major elements of your argument. It is always wise to prepare more material than you think you will need; and be sure to segment it into a visibly logical progression.

## Convincing the audience

Emphasise the fundamental points you want to drive home. You may repeat these (perhaps using different words) several times during the talk. Speak to the whole of the audience, and consciously modulate your voice.

If you use a whiteboard or flipchart, be sure you continue to address the audience and not the visual aid. Otherwise you become inaudible while (discourteously) presenting your back to the audience. Stand in front of rather than behind a desk, since the presence of a desk creates a psychological barrier between you and your listeners. Avoid lazy speech — especially phrases such as 'you know' and 'errs' and 'ums' during the presentation. Try to appear friendly and pleasant, since these emotions induce positive responses from other people.

Timing is important. Stick to the schedule laid down in your written notes, and remember that the span of attention of the average person is quite short (concentration wanders usually after about 15 minutes). Do not be afraid, therefore, to insert the occasional controversial statement to surprise the audience or otherwise stimulate their attention. Intersperse short sentences with long ones.

Aim to project an image of relaxed competence. Do not fidget. Be aware of what you are doing with your hands, bearing in mind that excessive arm and hand waving can be extremely disconcerting to others. Body language may overwhelm verbal messages.

## Persuasion

On occasion, you will have to convince a group of the correctness of a position, or that its members should willingly accept a change. In these cases, you cannot simply allow the facts to speak for themselves; you must also express opinions. The following principles should be applied when trying to persuade other people:

(a) Use plenty of illustrations to support your case. Quote several different examples to reinforce the same point.

(b) Begin the body of the talk with subject matter that the audience will agree with. Once people have started to agree with you — no matter how trivial your initial comments — they are likely to continue agreeing with you when more controversial topics are introduced. Proceed from the known and agreed to the unknown and controversial.

(c) Explain rather than argue your case. Do not draw attention to the existence of alternative interpretations of the issue.

(d) Motivate the group into acceptance of the proposition by pointing out how it will benefit group members.

Persuasive talks are more difficult than others because you have to ask the audience to give you something, even if it is only their emotional support. And the audience could turn hostile! Allow for this possibility in your initial planning. Predict likely objections, and have an alternative set of less controversial points available for discussion. You might not solve the problem there and then, but through withdrawing a controversial, unpopular proposition you may be able to retain the sympathy of the group.

## Visual aids

Visual aids serve two functions. They clarify issues and hence reduce the number of words that need to be spoken, and they help the speaker to segment a talk into natural divisions. Although visual aids can greatly impress an audience, there is a danger that the aids themselves might become the focus of the audience's attention instead of the speaker, and they can actually distract an audience. Used properly, visual aids:

(a) add variety to the presentation;

(b) create interest and enthusiasm among the audience;

(c) create an impression of competence on your part;

(d) reinforce key concepts;

(e) stimulate audience involvement with the discussion;

(f) increase the audience's rate of retention of information;

(g) help you complete the talk faster and in a logical manner.

They are particularly useful where complex diagrams or technical details are essential to the presentation. Aids should be large enough to be clearly visible to all parts of the audience; and each diagram, heading or statement should be self-contained, clear, and relevant to the discussion.

## Timing the use of visual aids

Do not introduce visual aids too early in the talk. Try first to create verbally a general context to which each aid can be related. Tell the audience what the aid is intended to demonstrate, and explain its significance to the point being discussed. If you can introduce a new visual (say) once every seven or eight minutes, your talk will be well segmented. But do not use aids merely for their own sake. Each should have a definite and identifiable purpose.

*The overhead projector*

Overhead transparencies are by far the commonest visual aid used during presentations. They focus the audience's attention and reinforce verbal messages. The following rules should be applied when using an overhead projector (OHP):

(a) Do not use an OHP to present a simple point that could be put across better by a verbal statement.

(b) Restrict the amount of information on any one transparency. Complex tables are best put into handouts (see below). If tables are necessary they need to be short, and the numbers within them kept to just three or four digits.

(c) Look at the audience while the transparency is being shown, not at the screen. Maintain eye contact with the audience.

(d) Turn off the OHP as soon as you have finished discussing the information on the transparency. Only switch on again when you need to present a further transparency.

(e) Do not use more than five or six lines of text per transparency, and use large letters: text that is too small to read is totally useless.

(f) Do not merely read out the words on the transparency; discuss generally the point to which they refer.

(g) Position the OHP slightly to the side of the centre of the room, while you retain the central position. In this way you remain the focal point of the presentation.

## Handouts

If you need to present detailed information to an audience this is frequently best achieved via a handout distributed before, during or after your talk. Use of handouts leaves you free to concentrate on major points, which are then reinforced by the materials handed out. One problem with handouts is how to ensure they are read. Handouts distributed at the close of a presentation are likely to be taken home and forgotten. Everyone intends reading a handout at the first convenient moment, but relatively few people actually get around to doing it! If conversely the material is given out during or at the start of the presentation the recipients are likely to read it while you are talking and not listen to what is actually being said. Also the process of distributing material during a presentation can itself be highly disruptive.

## Awkward questions

Always assume that someone in the group you are addressing will ask the question you least want to answer. Before the presentation, write out a list of likely questions and prepare model answers. When a hostile question is asked, try if possible to agree with at least one aspect of the speaker's comments. Never be discourteous to the questioner; the audience is far more likely to side with that person than with you. If you can, emphathise with the questioner. Ask yourself why the questioner feels that way. It is better to take questions at the end of, rather than during, a presentation. Questions asked during the talk will interrupt the continuity of your statements. Give as much additional information as you possibly can in each of your answers. Divide a complicated  question into its constituent parts, and give a separate answer to each component.

## Briefing sessions

Team briefings seek to transmit information about decisions that have already been taken or events that have already occurred. In a briefing, you aim not only to impart news, but also to instil in employees a sense of participation in the organisation's affairs. Sessions should be short (about ten minutes, plus perhaps five more for questions) and cover such topics as:

- changes in working arrangements;

- news of staff transfers and promotions;

- results of implementation of new working methods;

- details of new recreational/welfare facilities;

- examples of how efficiency has been improved in other departments;

- news about how the organisation is progressing generally, including plans for the future.

Briefing sessions are not suitable, however, for collective bargaining or for the discussion of fundamental issues about terms and conditions of employment.

Briefings should occur at predetermined intervals, say once every two months, rather than irregularly — assuming of course that on each occasion you have some significant information to communicate. A common mistake is for managers to brief employees only at times of crisis, so that briefing sessions transmit only negative information and views. Sessions should be relatively informal, but structured, preplanned and systematic.

### Advantages of team briefings

Team briefings are better than staff circulars, magazines or other written material because of the personal, face-to-face contact they involve. Circulars rarely include everything that needs to be said about an issue. They cannot emphasise all the significant points, and they might not be read by affected parties. Also, colleagues will probably want to ask questions about important matters. Note that a briefing session is an 'event' to the people who work for you. The fact that you have announced and organised the session implies that you have substantial news to transmit, and colleagues will feel let down if the information turns out to be trivial.

### Conducting the session

Tell the team where and when the briefing will take place, what it will be about and why you have called the session. The best time for a briefing session is perhaps just before lunch. People are relatively fresh, and no extra time is involved in restarting work at the end of the briefing. In order to create a sense of occasion, hold the session (if possible) in a room away from the workplace. The room should be comfortable — and have enough chairs; otherwise you will waste time collecting chairs from other rooms and in so doing you will diminish the dignity of the meeting. Arrange the chairs in a semicircular U-shaped pattern (assuming you are dealing with about 12–15 people) and sit (rather than stand) facing them at approximately the same distance from them as they are from each other. You will then be seen as an integral part of the group rather than as someone giving instructions. Copies of relevant documents should be available at the session.

Begin by saying why you called the meeting, give the facts, quote examples, and highlight the major features of the issue. Your aim is to transmit information clearly and quickly, so pre-empt as many questions as possible by providing the answers to likely questions in the main body of your presentation.

## A PRESENTATION TO A RETIRING COLLEAGUE

Sooner or later, someone in your department will reach retirement age and, naturally, you will be expected as section leader to make a short speech at the retirement presentation. Nowadays, we tend to speak in simpler and more direct terms at such functions than previously has been the case — without an elaborate introduction and without flowery language. Never alter your accent, your manner of speaking, or use long words you would not normally employ. You will come across as silly and 'affected' if you do. The following points should be included in the presentation:

- An expression of how much the colleague will be missed.

- The person's contributions over the years and his or her special characteristics (courtesy, kindness, willingness to help others, etc).

- A brief outline of the colleague's career.

- A mention of the person's outside interests and what he or she will be doing when retired.

- Best wishes for the future.

## WRITTEN COMMUNICATION

Reports are a widely used method of collecting and transmitting information for management control. They can be widely circulated and studied at convenient times. A report is a presentation of facts, opinions and recommendations for action. Information contained in a report should be concise, accurate and logically organised. The precise structure of a report will depend on its purpose, but all reports should contain statements of their terms of reference and brief summaries of major conclusions. All report writing involves the following tasks.

### Collection of material

Obtain information, conduct research, check the accuracy of facts, distinguish facts from opinions.

### Selection of material to be included in the report

Isolate important material, decide which facts to use in support of your arguments.

### Ordering sections

Classify material, placing sections in a logical order and decide on headings and subheadings.

## Writing the report

Choose a style appropriate to the audience for which the report is intended, choice of illustrations, tables, graphs and diagrams.

## Presentation

There is no single correct way in which to structure a report. Here is one possible layout:

- title page;
- summary;
- table of contents;
- introduction;
- text of main body of the report;
- conclusions;
- recommendations;
- appendices containing tables, technical calculations, references, etc.

The first thing to consider is for whom the report is intended, and what you hope it will achieve. Unfortunately some managers have split personalities where report writing is concerned. They write in pompous language they would never otherwise use. The style of a report should aim to inform rather than impress. It should be clear, concise and comprehensive. Here are some guidelines for writing reports:

(a) Put the title (which should fully describe the contents of the report), together with your name, departmental address, date of submission and circulation list on a separate covering page.

(b) Begin the report with one or two paragraphs summarising its major findings. For long reports, have a contents page with page references to sections.

(c) Start the introduction with a clear statement of why the report is necessary and its terms of reference. Outline previous investigations undertaken on the same subject, then state the objectives of the current report. Terms of reference are extremely important — a 'report on office stationery', for example, might involve a listing of stationery currently in use, a report on stationery theft, waste or improper utilisation, a review of procedures for stationery issue, investigation of stationery procurement methods, and so on. Thus your report should begin with a precise definition of its contents sufficiently detailed to inform readers whether the information is relevant to their particular needs.

(d) In writing the body of the report, put yourself in the position of the eventual reader, asking what he or she needs to know, what sorts of illustrations, examples and supplementary data will help the reader to understand the discussion, and what background knowledge the reader already possesses.

(e) Keep within your terms of reference. Check the relevance of each paragraph against your central thesis, and arrange the material in order of importance from the reader's point of view. State the fundamental points first, the detail later — readers find assimilation of detail easier if they have been given a general framework into which it can be fitted.

## Writing instructions

When writing instructions you have to describe, explain, and/or specify quantities or relations. You do not normally have to evaluate, justify, persuade or recommend (as you would in some other forms of written communication, reports for instance). It is essential that employees understand your instructions, but they do not have to remember them, because in implementing the instructions they can refer to the document you have prepared. So you do not have to repeat points to ensure they are memorised; but you must provide foolproof procedures for getting things done. Clarity of exposition and logical ordering of material are thus fundamentally important.

The introduction to your document should describe the equipment or system to be operated, explaining its purpose, why it is needed, and providing an overall context for its use. Specific instructions are normally prefaced by an action: 'Unscrew the top from the bottle', 'Take a piece of metal four inches long', 'Carefully remove the contents', etc. Ask yourself the following questions:

- *Who will use the instructions?* Never assume that people reading your instructions are as competent and motivated as yourself. There is nothing wrong in 'talking down' to the reader (within reason) if by so doing you clarify the exposition. Instructions must be clear, complete, concise and simple. But an instruction that is clear to one person might confuse someone else. Try therefore to predict every conceivable question that a reader might ask, and incorporate the answers into your text. The more varied the readership the greater the detail with which you need to describe each aspect of the instructions.

- *How knowledgeable is the reader?* In choosing an appropriate style of presentation and vocabulary, consider the backgrounds, knowledge and experience of potential users of the instructions. Do not use technical terms that will not be familiar to the typical reader and always choose the lowest common denominator for your model. An expert reader will find much of the material presented to be superfluous, but the expert will forgive you and no harm is done. Conversely, an inexperienced novice may find brief instructions — which assume prior knowledge or experience — to be incomprehensible. If potential readers are drawn from diverse backgrounds then you might need to draft several different sets of instructions, explaining the same thing in different ways depending on the likely knowledgeability of the intended reader.

- *What do you want the reader to be able to do?* Define precisely a successful outcome to the operation. List all the materials and other resources needed, and list all the things that could go wrong. How quickly should the reader be able to complete the operation? Is it necessary for the reader to understand the thing before operating it? For instance, you do not need to understand how a petrol engine works in order to change a spark plug; but you cannot fine-tune an engine without knowing something about how engines work.

### Rules for writing instructions

There are certain rules for writing instructions:

(a) Arrange the instructions in the exact order in which operations should be completed.

(b) Write each instruction in the simplest language possible.

(c) Be comprehensive. Ensure that all necessary steps are included. Do not assume that readers will themselves be able to fill in missing sections. Readers will not be annoyed if you write too much — they will simply skip through what to them is superfluous information. Spell out every detail that could cause doubt.

(d) Write in the imperative (as in this list) and in the second person. Imagine you are 'bouncing' the thoughts in your head into the head of the reader — rather like a tennis ball being served from one side of the court to the other — using the written page of instructions as the medium of delivery. Avoid abbreviations, and use complete sentences rather than instructions written in note form.

(e) Set out the information in the form of a list, like this one, with each instruction numbered or lettered. Use plenty of headings. Key words may be typed in capital letters.

(f) Avoid ambiguous words. Ambiguity might arise through words having meaning relative to a position (for example, the 'left' of this page could mean the left as you look at it, or its own left as it lies on the table); or through words having double meanings (the word 'replace', for example, could mean either 'refit the existing' or 'fit a new part'). And avoid using unfamiliar words that some readers might not understand. Few readers will bother looking up the correct meaning in a dictionary, so some readers might misinterpret words.

(g) At the end of the list of instructions, insert a checklist of things to look for if the operation has gone wrong. A brief summary of the major steps might also be useful.

Finally, get someone who has not previously performed the task to work through the instructions, without help from anyone. Then get a second person to do the same. Revise your instructions in the light of what goes wrong. Once the final version has been circulated, check periodically to ensure the instructions are actually understood.

### Letters and memoranda

Most people in business would claim to be able to write a letter. Yet when one reads many of the business letters one receives — often from high-ranking executives — it is soon obvious that this is not so. The problem, perhaps, is that letter writers unconsciously create two categories of letter: those regarded as 'important' and which in consequence they consider carefully and redraft several times; and those classified as 'routine', which are drafted just once — typically towards the end of a tiring day — without much thought and which, stylistically, leave much to be desired.

To improve the quality of your routine letter writing you should adopt certain predetermined rules. Start by jotting down — in the order they occur to you — the points you want to make. Think of the reader. How do you want and expect the reader to react to the letter? Much of the impression you create will depend on the organisation of the letter — the ordering, layout and tone of its presentation. So arrange your list of points in a new and more logical order. Have a centred subject heading at the top, and go straight to the point of the letter in the first paragraph.

The current convention when replying to a letter from someone else is to begin with the words, 'Thank you for your letter of . . . (date) concerning . . . (details of subject)', followed by further information on the matters discussed. Four sections are needed, information, starting with the most important point; supporting details, evidence and views; a summary, stating your conclusions and the actions that need to follow; and the closure, thanking the reader for his or her attention and looking forward to a reply. If there are enclosures to accompany the letter, list them after your signature. If you are initiating correspondence, state at the outset the information you need to transmit or require from the other party.

Aim for a simple and direct style. Be as clear and concise as you can. Avoid pompous phrases or anything hinting of intimidation. You need to connect with the reader and invoke in that person an empathetic response. When you conduct a verbal conversation, you supplement your spoken words with gestures, facial expressions and body movements that indicate the emotional context of your remarks. In a letter, however, you have none of these supplementary means of communication. The tone of the letter is the sole indication of your state of mind during its composition. So you must choose your words carefully, and constantly check to ensure they will not cause offence. Write in the first person, and keep your letters brief; if a letter is more than two pages long it is possibly better to rewrite it as a report (see above), to be sent accompanied by a short covering letter.

*Memoranda*

Memoranda are used instead of letters for interdepartmental communication within organisations. They are usually shorter and more direct than letters. There is no need for a salutation ('Dear Sir') at the start or 'Yours faithfully' at the end. Otherwise, memos should be structured in the same order as letters. Avoid long sentences, use plenty of headings and subheadings, and number the points so that recipients can refer to relevant details in their replies. A memorandum is better than a telephone call in that it provides a permanent record of the communication (memos should always be signed, or at least initialled). The disadvantage of their use, however, lies in the tendency of many managers to write too many memoranda and to distribute copies of each one to people with only marginal interest in the content.

# 17

# MEETINGS

Meetings are a primary medium of communication within organisations. Most involve 'committees', which are groups of people to which issues are referred for consideration, investigation or resolution.

## ADVANTAGES AND DISADVANTAGES OF COMMITTEE MEETINGS

Meetings are the most popular vehicle for taking important decisions in industry and commerce. They have several advantages:

(a) Increased communication between people and departments leading to easier coordination and management control.

(b) Utilisation of the talents, experience and creative abilities of several people. An individual might not recognise some key element in a problem, or be aware of all potential solutions.

(c) Shared responsibility for decisions. No one person has to bear sole liability for mistakes.

(d) Extensive discussion of issues and the generation of fresh ideas. Problems can be examined in depth. Opposing views will emerge, consideration of which should improve the quality of final decisions.

(e) Compromises between conflicting positions will have to be reached. Arbitrary or extreme decisions can be avoided.

(f) Representatives from many interest groups can take part in organisational decision making. In principle, this should encourage acceptance of joint decisions by all who are involved in the decision-taking process. Participation should raise enthusiasm for the implementation of the decisions.

(g) Avoidance of the concentration of power in small numbers of hands. Individuals are required to justify their intentions before colleagues, who may challenge the views expressed.

Although widely used, committees need not be the best medium for taking decisions. Indeed, cynics describe committees as comprising 'the unfit, selected by the unwilling, to do the unnecessary'; and without doubt, procedures that rely solely on individual authority can be extremely effective. Problems faced by committees include the following.

## High operating costs

Typically, committee members are highly paid managers whose time could be profitably spent elsewhere. The wage cost of a committee of, say, ten people meeting for half a day is substantial. Decisions taken by individuals require only one person's time.

## Discussion of trivial issues

Each committee member has a right to express opinions and to question and challenge the views of other participants. Sometimes members reiterate sentiments that have already been expressed in slightly different forms. Personal conflicts can develop; arguments might be tedious, long winded and add little to the quality of the discussion.

## Indecision

Unanimity of opinion within a committee is rare. Were participants to agree on all issues there would be little need for the committee; decisions reflecting members' views could be taken by a single representative. Committee decisions, therefore, are usually compromises which do not fully satisfy any interested party. More positive courses of action may be preferable. The problem is acute in committees which require unanimous agreement for decisions rather than a simple majority vote. Here, minority groups hold great power. They can hold up a committee's work through withholding their consent to particular proposals.

This tendency to indecision can lead to one or a few members assuming disproportionately influential roles. Anyone who repeatedly offers definite middle-of-the-road solutions may quickly assume a position of leadership. Other members follow dominant participants not because they agree with their views, but merely to avoid stalemate and interminable discussion.

## Abrogation of individual responsibility

Collective decisions do not require individuals to assume personal responsibility for mistakes. Thus it is hard to identify blameworthy staff. Guilty parties can hide behind the ambiguities created by joint decision making; it is difficult to investigate how a bad decision came to be taken within a particular committee.

## Slow decision making

The larger the committee and the more it discusses issues, the longer it takes to reach decisions. Some important items on meeting agendas might not be dealt with in the time allowed, and so may be held over until the next scheduled meeting. Exceptionally difficult problems are often referred to subcommittees, so increasing the delay in reaching final decisions.

## Conditions for success

Committees operate within normal line and staff organisation structures. Ideally, they should complement — not replace — individual executive power. In some cases, line executives initiate committees to examine problems which are beyond the limits of their personal knowledge. Otherwise committees exist permanently, their members being either appointed (by higher management), elected (by colleagues), or holding *ex officio* positions. To avoid subsequent disagreements about what is actually decided, all committee decisions should be minuted. Usually the minutes of a meeting are circulated to committee members who, at the next meeting, will accept or reject them as a fair and accurate record of actual discussions.

If committees are to operate successfully, a number of basic requirements should be met. Committees must:

(a) have definite, identifiable purposes with explicit terms of reference. The end result of a committee's work should be a clear decision, accompanied by a statement of how the decision is to be implemented, or a written report addressed to a higher level of authority. The people or departments responsible for carrying out a committee decision should be specified in the minutes of the meeting;

(b) be of reasonable size. What constitutes a reasonable size varies depending on circumstances; precise judgements are impossible. Committees should be large enough to incorporate all relevant specialisations and people with appropriate experience, but not so large that decisions cannot be taken with speed and efficiency. A meeting of three or four people is more of a discussion between colleagues than a committee as such; there would be little point in adopting formal committee procedures (agendas, minutes, chairperson, secretary, etc) in such circumstances. Numbers exceeding 15 (approximately) create problems of control and it is unlikely that all members could make significant contributions to the work of such a large group;

(c) consist of competent people who are interested in committee work. Often *ex officio* committee members care little about items under consideration and attend only for the sake of being seen. Participants with insufficient technical knowledge, or who cannot put across their ideas, are burdensome to the group.

Apart from possessing these positive characteristics, it is important that committees should not:

(a) consider issues beyond their terms of reference or authority. What is the point of wasting time deliberating over matters which the committee cannot control?

(b) be established to deal with unimportant matters. Trivial decisions can be taken by a single executive without incurring the costs and inconvenience of committees.

## Inequality of status

A fundamental but essentially insoluble difficulty with committee work is the inequality of status of participants. For instance, a board of directors typically contains a managing director, who is the chief executive of the firm, and other full-time directors who are heads of functional departments. Outside the boardroom, executive directors are subordinates of the managing director. Within the board of a public company, all directors are equal in that their primary duty is to protect the interests of the shareholders who elected them. Issues will be discussed and votes taken, but disagreement with and, ultimately, voting against the managing director is a serious matter indeed for an individual director, since after the meeting a dissenting director reverts to the role of subordinate.

Note here that ability is not necessarily related to status. The contributions of junior committee members might outweigh those of participants possessing greater status and authority within the firm.

# CONTRIBUTING TO A COMMITTEE MEETING

You attend a management committee meeting, the agenda of which contains an item you particularly want to discuss. The item is introduced from the chair, other people comment; the point approaches where you feel you ought to interject. Your heart pounds, your mouth is dry, you blush, breathe quickly, your throat is tight, your hands tremble slightly. You try to speak, but your voice quivers. Your mind is blank, you cannot even remember the points you intended raising. Instead of contributing to the discussion, you make a single inane remark before hurriedly withdrawing to the anonymity of silence. You conform totally to the views of others, although after the meeting you feel deeply unhappy about the decision finally taken.

Most managers have experienced this situation at least once in their careers — for some it is a common occurrence. To overcome such emotional reactions you need to understand why you lose control. Usually these feelings are triggered by one of two categories of anxiety: fear of humiliation, or of adverse consequences that might result from your intervention. People who are friends, who converse and interact socially outside a meeting, will typically behave differently towards each other once a meeting has started. You need therefore to shift your consciousness during meetings.

Accept that once you begin to address the meeting you become separated from the group. Temporarily, you and not the chairperson are its leader. As a silent member you are anonymous and unthreatened. You cannot be embarrassed or overwhelmed by the situation. But as a speaker, you are exposed and vulnerable — your (self-created) image of yourself is put to the test and becomes subject to external attack. So you have to switch (consciously) from one mode of behaviour — the informal conversational approach which you adopt in your normal day-to-day activities — to a formal communications role. You can only do this effectively if you prepare meticulously for the meeting. If you feel that preparation is not worthwhile, then you should seriously consider whether it is worth attending the meeting. There are three steps involved in preparation: analysis of the 'audience', analysis of the agenda, and drafting your intended comments.

## Analysis of participants

First, analyse the context in which the meeting is to occur. What purpose is the meeting intended to serve? Why are the other members attending? What benefits might accrue to other members from their attendance?

Often people attend a meeting with little intention of contributing to its business, but simply to gather information and to be seen to attend. The mood of a meeting convened to take important decisions is usually quite different to that of a meeting which gathers merely to review matters of general interest. Write out a list of who will be present, and alongside each name write a sentence describing what in your opinion that person wants from the meeting. Try to find out what happened during and after previous meetings.

It may be that the primary purpose of a meeting is not so much to take decisions as to act as a focal point for organisational loyalty. Attendance at non-executive meetings might create a bond between the individual and the institution. In these cases your contributions will be best appreciated if they are uncontroversial, flatter those present, and reinforce favourable images of the organisation. If the meeting has firmer and more ambitious aims then ask yourself how and to what extent these aims were realised following previous meetings. Who initiated activities, and who followed them up? What mistakes has the committee made in the past; what successes has it achieved?

## Agenda analysis

Distinguish between items which simply present information, and items requiring a decision. Identify the items that are likely to be boring and/or absorb large amounts of time. When you receive the agenda, write alongside each item a brief statement of its purpose and, if appropriate, its implications for your own work. For 'information-giving' items, list the points that you or someone else will be expected to transmit.

If the item is intended to stimulate discussion without taking a decision, list the advantages and disadvantages to you of adopting a particular position on the issue. Predict the reactions of other members to the points you might raise. For decision-taking items, write out the various possible outcomes to alternative courses of action and briefly list their implications for each committee member.

## The unfair agenda

Unfortunately, some unscrupulous chairpeople know that committee members are liable to analyse an agenda carefully and so they fiddle the agenda by incorporating controversial matters into a blanket item such as 'chairperson's report' or 'matters arising', since this prevents committee members knowing that a controversial issue is to be raised

— thus preventing them from preparing an adequate response. In consequence, opposition to the chair's (carefully prepared) position on the issue is muted. Those who disagree with the chair do not have sufficient time to put together a convincing argument.

If you suspect this has happened then, following receipt of the agenda, send a politely worded note to the committee secretary asking for confirmation that the issue in question will not be discussed at the meeting, and suggest that it be included as an agenda item in the next meeting but one. A fair chairperson will not allow decisions (rather than general discussion) to ensue from important items raised by other committee members under 'Any other business'.

## Addressing the meeting

The major advantage of addressing a meeting compared to other types of audience is that you do not have to say anything until the proceedings are well under way. You can judge the mood of the participants just before you speak, and thus can make last-minute adjustments to your (written) contributions. Against this benefit, however, is the fact that yours is just one of several contributions. The audience might not listen properly to your remarks, and may misunderstand your position. Participants may become tired, restless and overly critical towards the end of the meeting. Remember that you have to continue to work with your colleagues after the meeting, and their future behaviour may be affected by what you say. Note also that since your colleagues already know you, they might not show the same respect they would give to a stranger. Indeed, disagreements in meetings can lead to criticism of a highly personal nature. Anticipate this, and try not to respond aggressively.

When someone criticises you, look for some point of agreement with the other person's position. For example, you might state that the alternative view is correct in principle, but that your point raises an exception to the general rule — for reasons that you then proceed to explain. Or you might admit that the other party's case is a very good one, soundly constructed and presented, but go on to point out objections to, or contradictions within the other person's argument.

Whenever you go into a meeting, assume that you will make a contribution. Be prepared; anticipate all the difficulties that might arise, and predetermine your position on issues. If you take these points seriously, if you prepare for a meeting as diligently as you would prepare a speech to an external audience, you are not likely to encounter significant difficulties. Also, your assertiveness will increase naturally the more knowledgeable you are about the issues to be discussed and the more strongly you feel about them.

# CHAIRING A MEETING

The fact that committee members might not interact socially outside committee meetings, and the need to get things done quickly and efficiently, create the requirement for a group leader in the form of a committee chairperson. This individual is the 'custodian' of the committee's rules of procedure. The ideal chairperson will:

- recognise significant issues;
- encourage minorities to air their views;
- ensure that all aspects of a problem and its possible solutions are considered;
- systematically structure the debate.

Chairing a committee is not easy. An effective meeting will:

- start and finish on time;
- be as short as reasonably possible;
- have clear objectives and go at least some way towards achieving them;
- involve only the people whose presence is really necessary;
- take concrete decisions that are acceptable to all participants;
- allow everyone in attendance to express a view;
- determine the actions required to implement decisions and specify who is to be responsible for particular actions, plus a timetable for events.

A chairperson needs to be competent, experienced in committee work, and have his or her authority accepted by all the sectional interests involved. If you have to chair a meeting, you need to do three things: plan, prepare, and perform.

## Planning a meeting

Planning involves having the committee secretary issue the notice of the meeting's occurrence, ensuring that administrative details (room booking, etc) are dealt with, and drafting an agenda with the secretary.

Routine matters should appear first, more substantial matters later. Note that each significant issue should be listed as a separate agenda item. As previously mentioned, it is bad practice to conceal major and contentious matters under the blanket heading 'chairperson's report' or similar catch-all item, since members with views on these issues will be caught unawares, not having been given sufficient time to prepare their positions. A typical order for an agenda is as follows:

- apologies for absence;

- agreement of the minutes of the last meeting;

- matters arising from the minutes;

- chairperson's report;

- other items;

- major items for discussion and resolution;

- any other business;

- arrangements for the next meeting.

Usually the chair has discretion to alter the order in which agenda items are discussed, provided the changes are announced at the beginning of the meeting.

## Minutes

The secretary will take minutes, recording briefly what was said and noting the decisions reached. It is essential that all decisions are recorded; not just some of them. Minutes should be written up immediately after the meeting (while the memory is still fresh) and circulated to participants. They must be confirmed at the next meeting as a fair and accurate record of those proceedings. Accurate minute taking is essential. It prevents subsequent 'who said what' arguments and facilitates the implementation of decisions. Minutes provide a permanent record of matters discussed, highlight individual contributions and outline the analytical processes applied when taking decisions. The problem, of course, is that minutes are historical, typically appearing some considerable time after a meeting has taken place. Hence it might be useful to maintain a 'running record' of the major points that arise as the meeting proceeds. This can be achieved by having a flipchart on which problem statements, ideas or decisions can be written. The sheets then provide a means for focusing the attention of participants, and can be kept as a permanent record of events.

## Getting organised

The following matters must be determined:

(a) Who should attend the meeting?

(b) Who will attend the meeting if there are limits on the number of participants? The people invited should be knowledgeable about the subject matter of the meeting, interested in contributing to the solution of relevant problems, and reliably expected to turn up.

(c) What decisions must be taken, if any? (Some meetings are convened simply to convey information.)

(d) The meeting's time and location.

Then you must familiarise yourself with all agenda items — if necessary by approaching informally the members who asked for their inclusion. You should identify the contentious items, predict who will want to speak about them, and how long each item will take.

Write out a list of new members (if any) who will need to be introduced to the meeting, and if possible approach newcomers beforehand to brief them about how the business of the meeting will proceed. Make sure they know how to put items on the agenda and the rules of debate. Circulate background papers to members, indicating aspects of particular interest to each person and warning them if they will be expected to make presentations or special reports on specific issues.

## Performing

In the performance of your duties try always to facilitate rather than lead discussion. Recognise, however, that you are ultimately responsible for conducting the meeting properly in accordance with standing orders or other predetermined rules. So participants should address the chair, not each other, and should speak only when invited to do so by the chair. Your aims are to utilise to the best advantage all the talents and experiences of participants, ensure that all interested parties have opportunities to express their views, and avoid unnecessary conflicts and animosities among participants. Your specific duties include the following.

## Controlling debate

As a chairperson you must ensure fair play during meetings. You must get through the agenda in good time, while enabling all participants to air their views. You call on people to speak, and hurry them up when the usefulness of their contributions has been exhausted. If votes must be taken you decide when these should occur. A good chairperson is neutral between the parties but, nevertheless, always in control. Occasionally you might have to tell speakers to finish their points quickly or not to digress into irrelevant areas. Aim for the maximum involvement of members. If members' contributions are not treated with respect then they will quickly stop contributing. Refer to members by name (nameplates are useful for large meetings), and always be courteous.

## Dealing with arguments

Conflicts among committee members sometimes arise and it is important not to allow them to get out of control. Intense debate is to be welcomed; it arouses the interest of participants, increases the flow of information and stimulates creative thinking. Insults and sarcasm, on the other hand, can wreck a meeting and cause irreparable damage to interpersonal relationships. Conflicts can result from differing attitudes and perceptions of issues, breakdowns in communications between committee members, or through aggression and bad manners. You can use the following devices to settle unruly arguments within the meeting you are chairing:

- Insist that each of the protagonists states his or her position openly, forbid any interruptions while either party is speaking, and allow each person the right of reply to the other's assertions. Emotions are released, the air is cleared and everyone should feel better after the confrontation.

- Suggest a compromise solution and make anyone who rejects the compromise give their reasons.

- Assert your personal authority and impose a solution. This is the managerial equivalent of 'knocking the protagonists' heads together'.

- Restate the objectives of the meeting and clarify the issue that is causing disagreement, looking at the matter from as many points of view as possible.

- Postpone further discussion of the contentious issue until tempers have cooled.

Sometimes disagreements occur not through fundamental hostilities but because issues are unclear. Try to clarify problems, independently or by drawing other people into a discussion. One method is to ask everyone in attendance (assuming of course the number of participants is reasonably small) to state an opinion on an issue. Dangers arise in that the aggression between participants might turn against you, creating further potential for conflict.

The chair must balance conflicting demands, offer new ideas for compromise, and cajole participants into accepting outcomes less favourable than originally desired. A chairperson should be capable therefore of perceiving issues from various points of view, and explaining the benefits of particular proposals. Equally, you may need to suggest caution and identify disadvantages to advocates of certain actions. Periodically, you should summarise the essential points of recent discussions, and clarify the implications of decisions reached.

### Implementing decisions

Often, the chair assumes responsibility for ensuring that decisions taken within a meeting are actually carried out. Accordingly, you might have to write letters and memoranda to appropriate executives and monitor the progress of implementation of decisions.

### Leadership style

Various styles of leadership are relevant for various situations. Problem-solving meetings, for example, can be run in comparatively unstructured ways to encourage free interchange of ideas. Meetings where large amounts of information have to be transmitted, and where agendas contain very many items, need structured, relatively authoritarian procedures. Democratic leadership styles are appropriate for meetings where grievances are aired or where compromise outcomes are necessary. A relaxed style can sometimes defuse potential flashpoints.

Note that a chairperson can cause problems by dominating conversation, imposing arbitrary solutions, or not giving meetings sufficient time to reach conclusions. Democratic chairing can lead to loss of effective control; subgroups, each with a dominant participant, may arise to challenge your authority.

### Encouraging open discussion

To stimulate the participation of quieter committee members in a meeting's discussions you can ask questions directed either to the group as a whole or to specific individuals. Examples of general questions are:

- How does the committee feel about . . . ?

- I'm not sure I understand the group's position, is it . . . ?

- Are there any other ways in which we could . . . ?

Examples of questions that might usefully be directed to individuals include:

- Mary looks rather unhappy about this, can I ask her to state her position?

- John, what is your interpretation of this point?

- What prompted you to take that particular action?

- David, how do you think we should proceed?

Avoid questions that require one-word answers, and do not ask a question if it is obvious that no answer exists.

Questions can be asked at the start of the meeting or during the meeting to maintain its continuity. In consequence, the chair will draw out the knowledge, skills and experience of relevant parties; assuming of course that participants are willing to express opinions on the questions asked. In this way weaknesses in stated positions can be probed and all the implications of suggested actions examined. The problem, of course, is that replies to questions frequently raise yet more questions, and the replies themselves might be phrased as questions. Confusion then ensues, issues are clouded, and the participants have differing perceptions of the purpose of the discussion.

Explain to members the purpose of the agenda, and begin with the informational aspects of each item — moving then to ideas and discussion, and finishing with a proper decision. Periodically, summarise what has been said and decided, and make sure that everyone has been able to contribute, that all members are perfectly clear about what the decision means (particularly if it involves technical jargon), and what each person will have to do to achieve its implementation.

# INDEX

# Also available from Kogan Page:

# The Effective Supervisory Management Series

The *Effective Supervisory Management Series* provides a step-by-step guide to every aspect of the modern supervisory manager's role. Comprising three books, all of which have been completely revised and up-dated in their second editions, the series gives comprehensive coverage of the following syllabuses:

- **National Examining Board for Supervisory Management (NEBSM) — formerly NEBSS — Supervisory Management Certificate**
- **The Institute of Supervisory Management (ISM) Certificate in Supervisory Management Studies**
- **The Institute of Bankers (IOB) Banking Certificate — "Supervisory Skills" and Diploma — "Nature of Management".**

Specially designed for use by supervisors at all levels of responsibility, these three books can be used individually or as a reference pack to be consulted time and time again. Each chapter commences with a set of objectives which, by the end of the chapter, the reader will have achieved. Focusing on state-of-the-art management methods, particularly those involving information technology and the crucially important Codes of Practice which affect managerial issues, each chapter then concludes with a succint summary of the key points.

The three books in the series are:

*Managing People*
*Managing Activities and Resources*
*Personal Effectiveness*